The View from the Ground

NEW DIRECTIONS IN SOUTHERN HISTORY

SERIES EDITORS

Peter S. Carmichael, *University of North Carolina at Greensboro*
Michele Gillespie, *Wake Forest University*
William A. Link, *University of Florida*

*Becoming Bourgeois: Merchant Culture
in the South, 1820–1865*
Frank J. Byrne

*Southern Farmers and Their Stories:
Memory and Meaning in Oral History*
Melissa Walker

THE VIEW FROM THE GROUND

EXPERIENCES OF CIVIL WAR SOLDIERS

EDITED BY AARON SHEEHAN-DEAN

WITH AN AFTERWORD BY JOSEPH T. GLATTHAAR

THE UNIVERSITY PRESS OF KENTUCKY

Publication of this volume was made possible in part by a grant
from the National Endowment for the Humanities.

Scholarly publisher for the Commonwealth,
serving Bellarmine University, Berea College, Centre
College of Kentucky, Eastern Kentucky University,
The Filson Historical Society, Georgetown College,
Kentucky Historical Society, Kentucky State University,
Morehead State University, Murray State University,
Northern Kentucky University, Transylvania University,
University of Kentucky, University of Louisville,
and Western Kentucky University.
All rights reserved.

Editorial and Sales Offices: The University Press of Kentucky
663 South Limestone Street, Lexington, Kentucky 40508-4008
www.kentuckypress.com

10 09 08 07 06   5 4 3 2 1

Library of Congress Cataloging-in-Publication Data

The view from the ground : experiences of Civil War soldiers /
edited by Aaron Sheehan-Dean.
     p. cm. — (New directions in Southern history)
     Includes bibliographical references and index.
     ISBN-13: 978-0-8131-2413-1 (hardcover : alk. paper)
     ISBN-10: 0-8131-2413-1 (hardcover : alk. paper)
     1. Soldiers—United States—History—19th century. 2. Soldiers—Confederate States of America—
History. 3. Soldiers—United States—Social conditions—19th century. 4. Soldiers—Confederate
States of America—Social conditions. 5. United States. Army—History—Civil War, 1861-1865.
6. Confederate States of America. Army—History. 7. United States. Army—Military life—History—
19th century. 8. Confederate States of America. Army—Military life—History.
9. United States—History—Civil War, 1861-1865—Social aspects.
I. Sheehan-Dean, Aaron Charles.
     E607.V54 2006
     973.7'4--dc22
                                    2006029964

This book is printed on acid-free recycled paper meeting
the requirements of the American National Standard
for Permanence in Paper for Printed Library Materials.

Manufactured in the United States of America.

Member of the Association of
American University Presses

Contents

INTRODUCTION

Confederate soldier George Washington Miley spent the first months of 1864 exchanging letters with his future wife, Tirzah Amelia Baker. Confined to the south bank of Virginia's Rapidan River and facing Union soldiers across the water, Miley lamented his continued presence in the army and his absence from loved ones, especially during the just-passed Christmas season. Baker recounted activities in their community and anticipated Miley's return on furlough. However, after reenlisting for the duration of the war and recognizing that a furlough was unlikely, Miley paused to consider what record might be left of his service. "Three years, I can scarcely reconcile myself to the truth—think of happy schoolday hours—they appear as but yesterday," he wrote. "Think of the scenes, the trials we have all witnessed and experienced, it appears to be an age since they began. Three long years . . . lost and even forgotten by many."[1] Miley's lament—that civilians had forgotten the rigors and sacrifices of soldiers' experiences—was a common refrain among veterans on both sides of the conflict. Equally troubling was the suspicion that history itself would ignore their contributions to the war effort. Despite soldiers' meticulous recording of their actions, preserved in hundreds of thousands of letters and diaries, most believed that a true record of their service would never be written.

Miley's concern was well founded. For many years, scholars of the Civil War paid little attention to soldiers as individuals. Historians mined diaries and letters, but that material was rarely used to frame explanations of the war that soldiers would have recognized. Over the last twenty years, however, scholars have rediscovered the trials of soldiers. They have sought to understand both the "deeds" and the "passions" (to quote Walt Whitman) of the men who fought the war. What did they believe about the conflict? Did those beliefs change over the course of the war? What actions did they take as a result of those beliefs? How did prewar attitudes shape wartime behavior? And, conversely, did wartime experiences fundamentally alter soldiers' views of the world?

Miley might be surprised to find that there is a whole subfield of scholarship in soldier studies today, but he would surely appreciate those scholars' efforts to comprehend the all-too-human nature of most soldiers. Historians of soldiers begin from the assumption that soldiers are real historical actors who have the potential to shape, not simply respond to, their environment. This is an important point in a field that frequently mobilizes abstract ideas—liberty and slavery, federalism and states' rights, or simply the force of war—to explain historical change. Scholars of soldiers share a methodology that builds from the experiences of common people to explain larger patterns of historical change. They typically share a common body of sources as well: the tens of thousands of diaries and letters written by soldiers and their families during the war. The scholars who contributed to this collection rely heavily on those traditional bodies of evidence but also demonstrate the usefulness of new or underutilized sources. Chandra Manning's essay, for example, relies on evidence gathered from regimental newspapers produced on both sides during the war. Although more common among Northern units than Southern ones (owing to the high cost and scarcity of printing resources in the Confederacy), these papers provide an important window into how soldiers explained the conflict as it occurred. Likewise, both Timothy Orr and Charles Brooks draw new insights based on regimental resolutions. They use these sources to ask new questions about the political orientation and behavior of Civil War soldiers. Some of the essays that follow focus exclusively on one side or the other, while others are explicitly comparative. The result is an opportunity to identify the values and practices that Northerners and Southerners shared, as well as those that drove them apart. Last, these essays share an outlook that emphasizes the value of soldiers as subjects for broad and meaningful histories. As the essays in this collection reveal, these historians are as interested in the larger questions of American history—the nature and practice of democracy, the character and influence of religious belief, and the shifting attitudes toward race—as they are in questions about the war itself.

All the essays in this collection show that soldiers on both sides were autonomous historical actors. They did not necessarily control every aspect of their worlds, and they did not always fully understand the situations they found themselves in or the effects of their actions, but they willfully shaped the course of the war. The men that we call soldiers thought and acted as citizens. Miley made this explicit in his correspondence. Despite his lament about the lack of recognition of soldiers' sacrifices, he remained committed to the war for reasons that he identified as explicitly political. "Our lives are staked for that which naught but life can obtain—Liberty and Independence," Miley wrote.[2] Soldiers like Miley did not choose only one aspect of their lives to fulfill—soldier or citizen—but lived them simultaneously. Volunteers faced a difficult struggle to balance their competing obligations, just as civilians did in their multiple roles. A recognition of this reality makes the war experience both more complex and more interesting, and this holistic perspective, increasingly common among scholars of the war in general, promises even more fruitful studies that link the experiences of the home front and the battlefront.

Equally important are the ways that soldiers identified themselves as Christians, as men, and in racial terms. In some cases, religious identity strengthened volunteers' commitment to their national cause; in others, it created tensions between their competing duties. The evidence on this topic demonstrates that questions of faith were inextricably tied to questions of state. Likewise, questions of gender permeated every aspect of military life. Husbands and wives argued about where a man could best serve his family and his nation, Northerners criticized the enervating effects of slavery on Southern men, and Southerners responded by condemning Northern invaders as barbaric. Even as black men enlisted in Northern armies and used their new position to claim American manhood, whites in both sections articulated competing visions of race and citizenship. Southerners labored under the stress of war to hold slavery intact and drew sustenance from their position as defenders of the racial order. Northerners responded more ambivalently, with some decrying the shift toward emancipation and others leading the charge. The prospect of abolishing slavery imbued many soldiers with a sense of righteousness and emboldened them in their fight against the South. Last, the panoply of competing forces that created soldiers' understandings of the war shaped how veterans memorialized the conflict in later years. The essays that follow explore all these themes and reveal how fully historicized the study of Civil War soldiers has become. They also reveal the promise of future scholarship that begins from the premises outlined above and leads to new conclusions about and new insights into America's greatest conflict.

The volume opens with a survey of the literature on soldiers. Early writers on the war relied on soldiers' accounts principally to fashion broad military and political narratives. Since the early 1980s, studies of Civil War soldiers have grown increasingly sophisticated in their scope and interpretation. The emergence of this perspective in the literature begs the question: why then? What can explain the explosion in research on soldiers in the 1980s and 1990s? The first essay proposes an answer that stems from both disciplinary innovations, such as the rise of social history, and historic events, such as the Vietnam War and the civil rights movement. The analysis of the literature provides an important background for understanding the rest of the essays in this collection.

The next three essays investigate the problems soldiers faced because of the war. Chandra Manning, Jason Phillips, and Lisa Laskin reveal the fundamentally historical nature of the current scholarship on soldiers; all three authors show soldiers responding to the changing context of war by revising their beliefs and actions. In 1861 and much of 1862, most Northern soldiers preferred not to think about slavery and emancipation, but the problem—in the form of runaway slaves—was forced upon them. Contrary to the standard perception that emancipation generated anger and resentment among Northern soldiers, Manning shows that white Union soldiers increasingly supported emancipation, and they did so before many civilians or political leaders in the North came around to that point of view. As Ohioan George Landrum explained to his sister, writing from Alabama in early 1862, "We are all becoming Abolitionists here. I detest the institution of slavery." These soldiers saw emancipation as a way to end the war more quickly and punish the South; unfortunately, few could make the transition from opposing slavery to supporting racial equality. Phillips's essay investigates a similar intellectual transformation among Confederates. Refuting previous interpretations that stressed the common Americanness of Civil War soldiers, Phillips demonstrates the depth of antipathy engendered by four years of brutal warfare and shows how Confederate soldiers demonized their Union adversaries. Condemning the invasion of Northern "Vandals," "Hessians," and "ruffian hordes" energized Confederates while distancing them from their former fellow citizens. If we recognize that the experiences of soldiers become the memories of veterans, Phillips's research offers another explanation for the deep divisions of the Reconstruction era and beyond.

Whereas Manning and Phillips discuss elements that might bind soldiers of either the North or the South together, much recent literature has demonstrated the power of experience to divide each section internally. In her essay, Lisa Laskin explores the tensions and strife that existed within the South. She shows us the breach that opened between Confederate soldiers and civilians, especially when the former saw the latter as being insufficiently invested in the cause. South Carolinian Peter McDavid, for instance, lectured his sister on the lack of support soldiers received from civilians, even when "you who are at home [live] as well as ever you did in the halcyon days of peace." McDavid's lack of sympathy for the hardships experienced on the home front reveal the tensions between the two communities. Laskin's careful sequencing of morale and events opens a new window on Confederate culture, showing that the war warped soldiers' ability to perceive the world from other perspectives and enforced a deadly solipsism.

Of the various attitudes and beliefs that soldiers brought with them into the armies, perhaps none was as important as Christianity. Nonetheless, previous scholars have been divided over the extent to which soldiers remained obedient to their faith and the effect of religious beliefs in sustaining or depressing morale.[3] As the essays of David Rolfs and Kent Dollar demonstrate, none of these questions has a straightforward answer. Rolfs's essay plumbs the Northern experience to understand how soldiers reconciled the act of wartime killing with Christian precepts of charity and peacefulness. He summarizes the dilemma by noting that soldiers worried "that the same Bible . . . used to justify their holy crusade against the South also seemed to condemn the violence of war." Rolfs attributes soldiers' ability to find satisfactory solutions to these dilemmas to the flexibility of nineteenth-century Christianity and the moral and intellectual demands placed on the men who became soldiers. Dollar explores the isolation that many men of faith felt in the early months of the war. On both sides of the conflict, soldiers perceived themselves as living in a world that was hostile to religion. In response, Christian soldiers labored to retain a sense of faith and spirituality. Traditional accounts emphasize the revivals of late 1862 and 1863 as the moments when soldiers reconfirmed their faith, but Dollar shows that these revivals were successful partly because they were built on a foundation of religiosity established by Christian soldiers in the war's early months. Whether in private prayer or in one of the many ad hoc communal worship services he describes, soldiers from both sides took time to practice their faith. Like Rolfs, Dollar shows that soldiers' crises of faith were often the most significant religious events in their lives, thus demonstrating that the records of Civil War soldiers contain a wealth of material for historians of religion.

If religion was crucial to how soldiers conceptualized the war, politics was a competing faith for many men. The essays by Timothy Orr, Charles Brooks, and Kevin Levin all demonstrate the continuing relevance of politics in the lives of soldiers. Historians often use Clausewitz's aphorism that war "is a continuation of political will carried out by other means" as an epigram for the Civil War.[4] These three authors illustrate another aspect of this idea: the process of war, and of soldiering, is political as well. Orr's analysis of Pennsylvania soldiers reveals their insistence on retaining the political identities they possessed as civilians. Vigorous in their battles with Rebels, they were equally vigorous in their battles with Democrats at home. Members of the 100th Pennsylvania passed a resolution asserting that Democrats who opposed the war were an "integral part of the Rebellion . . . and as such, should suffer the traitor's doom." In his suggestion that Union soldiers were prepared to do physical battle with those they perceived as their enemies at home, Orr also reveals how the context of war changed the acceptable means of protest and disagreement. Brooks describes the importance of officers' respect for the autonomy of each enlisted man. Those who failed to show such respect faced the fate of Colonel R. T. P. Allen, who, within days of his appointment, was hoisted onto his horse and driven "out of the regimental grounds amid the hoots and jeers of the boys," never to be seen again. In his analysis, Brooks proves why the Civil War should truly be considered a "popular" struggle. The summary dismissal of haughty officers by Texas soldiers demonstrated that they would demand the same political independence in the army that they were fighting to protect at home. Levin shows how postwar political disputes could be framed in terms of the war itself. In particular, he reconstructs the bitter and divisive conflicts between Virginia veterans and their fellow Confederates from other states over who deserved credit for repulsing the Union attack at the battle of the Crater in 1864. His essay is part of an emerging literature on veterans that emphasizes how soldiers' wartime experiences shaped their postwar lives. As Levin's research reveals, the same soldiers who defended their rights as political men during the war defended their memories of the conflict as a way to enact the politics of the 1880s and 1890s.

All these essays convey two important lessons about the history of the Civil War. They show that the war as a subject of study holds real promise for new and insightful research. Even more important, by exploring the connections between the experience of the war and the larger world of nineteenth-century America, they demonstrate how rewarding that research can be.

I would like to take this opportunity to thank a number of people who helped make this volume possible. First are the contributors, who responded cheerfully and efficiently to every deadline and request. Editors often tell horror stories of having to chase down recalcitrant contributors or of projects that take decades to complete, so I thank the writers for ensuring that I have no such stories of my own. Peter Carmichael, Bill Link, and Michele Gillespie were supportive series editors throughout the project. Pete encouraged me when the volume was just an idea, Bill drew on his deep experience to explain the process to a novice, and Michele offered insightful comments. At the University Press of Kentucky, Joyce Harrison was delightful to work with; her enthusiasm and professionalism helped carry the project along. On behalf of all the contributors, I would like to thank the anonymous reviewers, who gave us detailed and serious suggestions that strengthened the volume considerably. Finally, I would like to thank several people who supported me during this project. Dale Clifford at the University of North Florida offered a careful critique of my contribution and has been a consistent supporter of my scholarly efforts. Gary Gallagher provided a worthy model of professional achievement in editing and, as always, was generous with his encouragement. Last, my wife Megan offered the support and love that sustain me. Thanks to them all.

NOTES

1. George Washington Miley to Tirzah Amelia Baker, April 12, 1864, George Washington Miley Papers, Virginia Historical Society, Richmond.

2. Ibid.

3. For the argument that religious faith stabilized Confederate morale, see Drew Gilpin Faust, "Christian Soldiers: The Meaning of Revivalism in the Confederate Army" *Journal of Southern History* 53 (February 1987): 63–90.

For the opposite argument, see Richard E. Beringer, Herman Hattaway, Archer Jones, and William N. Still Jr., *Why the South Lost the Civil War* (Athens: University of Georgia Press, 1986).

4. Carl von Clausewitz, *On Strategy: Inspirations and Insight from a Master Strategist* (New York: Wiley and Sons, 2001), 184–85.

THE BLUE AND THE GRAY IN BLACK AND WHITE

Assessing the Scholarship
on Civil War Soldiers

Aaron Sheehan-Dean

One of the persistent frustrations of historians of antebellum America is the paucity of primary sources from common people, black or white. The prohibitions on teaching slaves to read and write and the conditions of slavery partially explain the absence of extensive firsthand evidence from slaves themselves, but no such explanation exists with regard to middle- and lower-class whites. Thus, historians of slavery have to fall back on a method of triangulating their subjects through a variety of secondhand documents: court records, wills, census reports, newspaper accounts, and travelers' observations. The difficulty this poses for historians of the antebellum South is fairly evident in most writings on the topic. Historians of the Civil War face the opposite problem. They have not too few sources from common people but too many. The mass of diary and letter collections, which has grown steadily over the past 140 years and continues to do so with each publishing season, threatens to overwhelm even the most dedicated reader.

Despite the plethora of evidence from the war years, however, only in the last two decades have scholars begun using it in a systematic way to understand the experiences of common people during the Civil War. Soldiers' accounts, in particular, have proved to be invaluable sources on questions ranging from emancipation and race to nationalism and reunion to gender and the family. The records created by soldiers on both sides of the conflict, the vast majority of whom can be classified as common people, have long been mined by historians to tell traditional stories regarding battles and elections. Anecdotes and records of individual movements are often crucial for scholars seeking to piece together a sequence of events during the typically chaotic Civil War battles. What was missing until the mid-1980s was an exploration of soldiers' accounts that treated them as autonomous and important historical actors. How did soldiers understand the purpose of the war? How did they perceive the shift to emancipation and hard war? How did they conceptualize victory or defeat? The subfield of soldier studies within Civil War history developed rapidly in the 1980s and 1990s. Historians effectively addressed the questions just posed, and others, by turning their attention to the people who actually fought the war. Researchers also discovered that the utility of soldiers' records goes well beyond questions regarding the war itself and its outcome. In the last few years, historians have also begun reading the accounts of soldiers to address larger questions about the American past. As the essays in this collection demonstrate, the correspondence of soldiers and their families reveals the beliefs and practices of ordinary men and women on a range of topics.

The study of soldiers, along with the study of battles, defined the earliest attempts to gain historical perspective on the Civil War. In the decades after the conflict, veterans, their relatives, and their admirers began this effort by composing thousands of regimental histories.[1] This writing reflected all the strengths and weaknesses of history as it was practiced in the mid-nineteenth century. Simultaneously antiquarian and heroic, these accounts served more a memorial purpose than a historical one. The authors of regimental histories usually described the process of enlistment, tracked the movement of the unit, and explained the military engagements in which the soldiers were involved. Regimental histories often included extensive detail regarding soldiers' lives, but they tended to be mostly institutional in their focus. The units were treated as representative of the communities within which they were organized, and their performance, usually on the battlefield, was analyzed as a means of assessing the virtue of those citizens. This tradition of writing continues today, with regimental histories that often include substantial information about soldiers but rarely analyze that material in historically useful ways.[2] Although this approach to the study of soldiers is the chronological antecedent of current writing, the narrow focus and celebratory tone of most regimental histories ensured their isolation from the more analytical studies of soldiers that have emerged in the last two decades.

Alongside regimental histories, the narratives written for several decades after the conflict focused mostly on the actions of generals and politicians. Description trumped explanation, and authors spent much of their energy showing how particular battles or campaigns unfolded. Ascertaining the correct sequence of events in a war is certainly essential to understanding how the final outcome was reached, but a fascination with Lee and Lincoln often replaced a deeper explanation of the meaning of the events under review. For writers operating in this mode, the diaries and letters of soldiers helped explain particular decisions or events. Little consideration was given to thinking about the war from the perspective of those who fought it; instead, their testimony was used to corroborate or explain the story of the war written from the headquarters tent or the White House.

With little scholarship focusing on soldiers in the generations after the war, most historiographers have identified the origins of this field of research in the work of Bell Irvin Wiley.[3] Wiley's work was seminal, and the questions he posed have influenced several decades of scholarship. The study of Civil War soldiers, however, also developed as a response to larger changes in the discipline of history, such as the growth of social history and the use of quantitative methods. Over the last two decades, the field has moved toward increasingly analytical and historical studies that allow scholars to answer questions about the experience and outcome of the war as well as the course of American history in the nineteenth century. Contrary to the conventional wisdom that the Civil War has been exhausted as a field of productive research, the growth and continuing development of soldier studies reveal historians' ability to enrich well-established topics with new questions and new modes of analysis.

Albert Burton Moore, with his study of Confederate conscription, and Ella Lonn, with her study of desertion, should be credited as the first scholars to treat soldiers on their own terms.[4] Both crafted stories of the war that identified soldiers as the central agents of change and demonstrated the range of influences that inspired soldiers to act. Moore and Lonn provided a useful model for later scholars by using soldiers' experiences to revise the standard accounts of the war. It was Wiley in the 1940s, however, who wrote the first holistic accounts of soldier life and helped inspire future scholars to see the range of topics that could be addressed by making soldiers the main objects of study. Wiley wrote at nearly the same time that Frank Owsley was working to put common whites back into the center of narratives on the antebellum South.[5] Like Owsley, Wiley clearly liked his subjects. He saw most Civil War soldiers as good men who were earnestly committed to the causes they fought for, even if those causes did not factor too much into his explanation of their world. Wiley painted a comprehensive picture of the experiences of both Northern and Southern soldiers, emphasizing description instead of analysis. With the exception of a handful of articles in the 1960s and 1970s, Wiley's work remained the main source and standard for histories of soldiers. Among the studies that did appear, many assumed a simplicity of calculation that later histories have rejected. David Donald's 1959 article "The Confederate Man as Fighting Man" explained the loss of the Confederacy partly as a result of Southerners' inability to overcome their democratic and localistic nature.[6] Similarly, a 1969 article by Harry Scheiber assumed unalterable Southern opposition to centralized government and then worked backward to locate one source of the collapse of Confederate morale in tardy pay for Southern soldiers.[7] Although these pieces improved on Wiley in their attention to argument, they retained the static quality that hampered much of the early writing on the topic.

Calls to rejuvenate the study of soldiers emerged in the 1980s and were answered by a host of rigorous studies. Marvin Cain initiated the new movement with his request for American historians to produce something similar to John Keegan's work on European warfare in his groundbreaking *The Face of Battle*.[8] Keegan's sympathetic and intimate evaluation of how soldiers acted and felt provided a lofty example for scholars, but it also emphasized soldiers' military experiences at the expense of all else. Pursuit of Keegan's model yielded dozens of important insights regarding why the war happened as it did and how people experienced it at the time, but this approach did not exhaust the ways that the writings of Civil War soldiers could be used. In particular, scholars have recognized that soldiering was only one part of most men's identity. Nearly all Civil War soldiers volunteered, and it is fair to say that all of them retained their sense of being both soldier and civilian through the conflict. Alongside his historiographical analysis, Cain reminded scholars to treat soldiers as a part of their societies and to consider the moral implications of war and fighting.[9] Cain's primary focus on Union soldiers reflected an existing bias in the field, a trend that has been reversed only in the last several years. Most usefully, Cain raised a series of questions that future scholars could use as the starting points for their research: What was the relationship of officers to enlisted men? How did they understand each other? Why did soldiers follow orders? Cain also issued one of the earliest appeals for a study of Union soldiers' reactions to emancipation, an issue that continues to interest and challenge historians.

Maris Vinovskis issued the next plea for new research with his article "Have Social Historians Lost the Civil War? Some Preliminary Demographic Speculations."[10] Although the article appeared in the middle of the wave of soldier scholarship produced between the early 1980s and the late 1990s, it influenced the direction of research in important ways. Vinovskis called on scholars to undertake another sort of investigation into the material left by soldiers, different from that recommended by Cain and other historians. Rather than asking traditional questions regarding battles, campaigns, and politics, he urged scholars to consider more general topics from U.S. history. Vinovskis bemoaned the lack of attention to what he called "the effects of the war on everyday life in the United States." He encouraged social historians in particular to incorporate the war into their studies of people and places in the nineteenth century. Questions regarding birth, marriage, and death rates; class conflict; ethnic identity; race relations; and national memory all require a careful analysis of the war's impact. Vinovskis's article helped direct scholarly attention to soldiers as the place to begin addressing these topics.

Vinovskis's injunction came at the start of an outpouring of research into soldiers and their experiences. Beginning in the early 1980s and cresting in the late 1990s, historians produced dozens of studies on the nature of the Civil War as it was lived by participants. Some of the best writing on soldiers has focused on the issue of motivation. American historians largely agree that slavery caused the Civil War, in the elemental sense that conflicts over slavery drove people of the two regions apart and precipitated the political breakdown of secession. Although accurate at the grand level of causation, slavery, in the abstract, does not explain what motivated individual Southern men to enlist and remain in armies, just as emancipation does not provide a satisfactory explanation for what motivated individual Northern men to do the same. Historians have responded to this problem by crafting increasingly sophisticated analyses of how soldiers understood the crisis of secession, the initiation of the war, and the changing nature of the conflict. Alongside these explanations of why citizens chose to make themselves soldiers has been a pressing need to explain why some also unmade themselves as soldiers, deserting the ranks to either return home or join the ranks of their former enemy. In addition to motivation, scholars have explored how soldiers impacted the course of the war and how the experience of war impacted them. The best studies demonstrate the interconnections among all three issues—motivation, experience, and effect.

Joseph Glatthaar's seminal study, *The March to the Sea and Beyond: Sherman's Troops in the Savannah and Carolinas Campaign,* offers one of the clearest analyses of how soldiers had to rethink the nature of the war as they experienced it. Glatthaar's analysis begins with the army in 1864, but the early chapters include a demographic and intellectual portrait of Sherman's men that addresses the question of initial motivation. In a chapter entitled "The Army and the Cause," Glatthaar explains that most Northern men enlisted to defend the Union and remained in the army because of a continued commitment to that goal and faith in their commander, "Uncle Billy," and because of the accumulated investment made in blood over the previous three years.[11] Glatthaar's analysis paved the way for future scholarship by showing how the experience of the war forced soldiers to reconsider the elements that held them in service. For Sherman's troops in particular, fighting their way across the Lower South, the problems of race and slavery forced themselves into the soldiers' consciousness. Although few Northerners entered the war to emancipate slaves, the experience of fighting through Southern communities and of coming to know slaves and their masters firsthand shifted the opinion of many Union soldiers. By historicizing the opinions of soldiers, Glatthaar added a crucial temporal dimension to studies of soldiers that had previously been missing.

The recognition that soldiers could change their minds over time, although perhaps not revelatory to those outside the field, opened up a variety of possibilities for scholars of the war. Reid Mitchell, Gerald Linderman, and Mark Grimsley all crafted vigorously historical accounts of soldiers that demonstrated significant change over time. Mitchell's first book, *Civil War Soldiers: Their Expectations and Their Experiences,* characterized soldiers on both sides as retreating from the noble beliefs that spurred the conflict. Mitchell offered one of the first clear analyses of Confederate enlistment, arguing that it was motivated by defensive, fearful visions of the North imposing a new racial order. He captured this outlook with the insight that "the Civil War was a war to protect freedom before it was a war to extend freedom."[12] Northern soldiers, for their part, enlisted to protect liberty as well, but they identified the Union as the bulwark of that liberty. Family honor, the demands of masculinity, and patriotic loyalty to one's country factored significantly into the motivations of both Northern and Southern men. Whereas Glatthaar's narrative captured a sense of the partial redemption that Union soldiers experienced through the dual accomplishments of emancipation and military victory, Mitchell showed the dehumanizing effect of military service and the extent to which the war exacerbated sectional animosity on the individual level.

Gerald Linderman's *Embattled Courage: The Experience of Combat in the American Civil War* showed a similar arc of change, but one that was explained through a constellation of Victorian values that slowly eroded during the war.[13] Like Mitchell, Linderman saw soldiers as entering the war with refined and unrealistic notions of service. Courage, manhood, religion, honor, and knightliness all died in the mud alongside comrades at Shiloh, Antietam, and Gettysburg. The institutional qualities of discipline and obedience held the armies together after the disillusionment of modern warfare forced itself on the soldiers. Linderman's interpretation satisfied those who longed to see soldiers treated not as static objects but as thinking beings, but the obvious imprint of twentieth-century military experiences left others dissatisfied.[14]

Mark Grimsley's *The Hard Hand of War: Union Military Policy toward Southern Civilians, 1861–1865*, though not focused exclusively on soldiers, offered a still more nuanced account of the transformation of values.[15] Grimsley's account explained the shift in Union military policy, from the "rosewater" policy of the war's first year to the "hard" war of 1862 and beyond, as partly the product of a change in how Union soldiers understood the war. The anger and hostility of the mostly Confederate civilians of the white South contradicted early expectations of a grateful and largely Unionist Southern public. In response, Northern soldiers increasingly sanctioned direct reprisals against the property, both human and inanimate, of Southern citizens. Grimsley's work neatly joins a careful analysis of how the war reshaped soldiers with an equally insightful analysis of how soldiers, in turn, reshaped the terms of the war. The reciprocal nature of this historical relationship demonstrates the maturation of the field as a whole—Civil War soldiers are no longer objects to be pulled out of the war for dissection but are living parts of the whole experience that can be understood only in relation to the context within which they existed.

During the 1980s and 1990s, a blizzard of studies descended. Most of these were tightly argued and focused on wartime questions. All drew on the substantial base of archival material that was still relatively underutilized by Civil War scholars. One of the most obvious places for Civil War scholars to focus their energies was on the experience of fighting. Virtually every author who writes about soldiers also writes about combat, but several authors made it their exclusive focus. Joseph Frank and George Reaves used the battle of Shiloh to explore the effect of combat on novice soldiers, and their conclusion was that soldiers survived with generally the same worldview as they had before the battle.[16] This somewhat surprising summary reflects the emerging historiographical shift that defines soldiers as being shaped and influenced more by their civilian experiences than by their military ones. Current scholars do not deny the impact of service, but their research tends to reinforce factors such as political philosophy and family relations as being central to soldiers' conception of the conflict.

Earl Hess's analysis of Union soldiers and combat revealed a type of evolutionary growth, whereby volunteers processed their military experiences through outlooks formed as civilians. In a direct rejection of the chronology laid out by Linderman, Hess argued that most men became better soldiers over time. Hess addressed the questions of cowardice and suffering raised by Linderman but found that seasoned soldiers performed their jobs more efficiently rather than becoming disaffected. Hess characterized the effects of the transformation as follows: "becoming men of war did not necessarily destroy the soldier's commitment to the issues of the conflict or his willingness to temporarily embrace the deadly game of the warrior to achieve the war's goals."[17]

Alongside combat, desertion remains one of the key unresolved topics in Civil War literature. Interest in the subject stems partly from the inherent fascination of both scholars and readers in the question of loyalty and the nature of men who abandon a commitment to defend their nation. A broad set of community studies demonstrated the difficulty of generalizing about patterns of desertion.[18] These works opened questions that have yet to be fully answered. The old assumption, that desertion was a minor problem attributable to cowardice on the part of individual soldiers, proved to be incorrect. Confirming the conclusion reached by Lonn in her pioneering study, most of the recent scholarship has demonstrated that desertion had serious effects on both armies. Still, many of the studies, such as Judith Lee Halleck's on New York and David Smith's on Texas, situate the causes of desertion in the particular places where the units originated. Kevin Ruffner's study of one regiment in the much-lauded Stonewall Brigade revealed surprisingly high desertion rates, which he explained as a consequence of the officers' failure to secure proper supplies for a hard winter, as well as poor leadership in general. Thus, Ruffner's conclusion, like those of many other local studies, inhibits scholars' ability to offer desertion as evidence of mass disillusionment or as an explanation for Confederate defeat. Conversely, in the only book-length study of desertion, Mark Weitz argues that the invasion of Georgia by Union troops and the consequent hardships imposed, particularly on lower-class residents, spurred high rates of desertion after 1863 among north Georgia units.[19] The loss of these men weakened the ability of Confederate troops in the region to resist Sherman's advance and led to high numbers of people abandoning the Confederacy. Only more state studies and thorough study of the whole Confederacy and the whole Union can yield a definitive answer on the question of how desertion affected the war as a whole.

The issue of loyalty raised by studies of desertion has inspired historians to probe more deeply into nationalism as it relates to both the Union and the Confederacy. One of the defining elements of modern, popular wars is that soldiers fight partly, if not mostly, out of loyalty to the nation-state that sends them into battle. Beginning with the French Revolution and the successful effort to raise a mass army, democratic governments built militia systems to eliminate the need for standing professional armies. Although America's antebellum militia system did not necessarily produce effective soldiers, it was one of the many mechanisms that reinforced the notion that the rights of citizenship were balanced by the obligation to defend one's nation militarily. Civil War scholars have explored how both Northerners and Southerners conceptualized this obligation and how it changed over the course of the war. For most Northern soldiers, an ideological belief in a perpetual Union demanded a physical defense of that Union.[20] Because the North won the conflict, the distorting power of hindsight can obscure wartime challenges to Northern unity and assume as fact the failure of Confederate nationalism. Sectional hostility to the South made fighting easier, but the increasingly antislavery policies of the North required reluctant emancipators to confront the notion of fighting for a nation despite opposition to its policies. Although a belief in the Union remained a viable source of inspiration for many Northerners throughout the conflict, the length and nature of the war severely tested Northern soldiers' sense of nationalism.

Scholars of the Confederacy have had even greater difficulty with this issue. Finding Confederate soldiers who opposed the policies of their government is relatively easy—the draft, impressment, and the tax in kind generated intense controversy and a mountain of complaints. Determining whether that dissatisfaction indicated disloyalty to the nation has been more difficult. Some scholars have argued that soldiers' active engagement with the political issues of the day reveals a commitment to improving the nation, and hence their support; others have stressed the divisiveness of such debates.[21] The role played by white Southerners who retained their faith in the Union through the conflict and fought on behalf of the United States further complicates the issue.[22] Still, the fact that Southern communities mobilized roughly 80 percent of their eligible men to fight in the war must be regarded as evidence that many people supported the Confederacy. Regardless of the argument being advanced, changes in the study of Confederate nationalism in recent years reveal the strides that historians have made, as new investigations ground themselves in a serious consideration of the people who made nationalism at the ground level, as opposed to those who formulated it in Richmond.[23]

While historians of combat, desertion, or nationalism used soldiers' accounts and experiences to answer traditional questions about military and political affairs, other scholars adopted new strategies to investigate previously overlooked aspects of the war. In particular, studies of religion and gender allowed social and cultural historians entry into the Civil War arena. Gardiner Shattuck penned one of the first treatments of religion and Civil War armies.[24] Shattuck was writing against the hagiographical treatment of Confederates and religion favored by J. William Jones in *Christ in the Camp: Or, Religion in Lee's Army.*[25] Whereas Jones lionized the religiosity of Confederate leaders, Shattuck began by describing the differences between prewar Northern and Southern Protestantism. For example, Northern churches advocated a "social morality" that sponsored reform movements, but Southern churches focused on "individual morality" and left social and political issues to the state. The result, according to Shattuck, was that Southern soldiers did not derive the same kind of inspiration from religion that Northern soldiers did. Later scholars tended to disagree. Drew Gilpin Faust, in her study of Confederate revivals, argued that although religion could propagate social conflict, it sustained most individuals through a traumatic time and offered a language with which to conceptualize defeat.[26] Samuel Watson went even further, arguing that "religion pervaded the discourse of community at all levels; it played as important a part in sustaining individuals as it did in creating Confederate nationalism."[27] Religion continues to be one of the most fertile cross-fields, in part because it offers scholars the opportunity to comment on important pre- and postwar history while offering meaningful insights into wartime events.

In the same way, gender emerged in the 1990s as one of the subjects that allowed social historians to work on the Civil War. Although much of the work on gender and the war revolved around the home front and the experiences of women, important work was done linking the emerging study of masculinity to the war. Stephen Frank's study of fatherhood revealed the possibilities of blending cultural, social, and military history.[28] Frank read Civil War sources not for what they said about the war per se but for what they revealed about how men conceptualized their responsibilities as fathers. James Marten took this one step further in his study of Confederate fathers as soldiers. Building on Frank's argument that fatherhood constituted one of the most important aspects of soldiers' identities, Marten explored how this orientation affected the war. Rather than leading men to abandon the armies to protect their families, Marten found that, "in the minds of southern men, the war had made being a good and loyal soldier one of the duties of being a good father."[29] The fullest study of masculinity and soldiering came from Reid Mitchell, whose *The Vacant Chair: The Northern Soldier Leaves Home* offered new ways to understand the conflict and its impact on American society.[30] Mitchell identified the "ideology of domesticity" as the dominant mode within which most Northern soldiers were nurtured. As he explained, Union soldiers used the metaphors and values of domesticity to understand everything from how to interact with their officers and Southern women to the proper relations between races and classes.

The research on soldiers and masculinity distinguishes itself precisely because the majority of studies on gender and the Civil War focus on women and the home front. This work has demonstrated the necessity of keeping both "fronts" in view when writing a full history.[31] Women's historians have pushed their analyses even further, including studies of those women who served as soldiers.[32] This research, like the best of that on masculinity, has forced us to rethink how we explain motivation and other topics by showing that the traditional masculine imperatives of honor and aggression need to be recast or at least complemented by more universal notions of patriotism and civic duty. New perspectives on masculinity also help us rethink the larger narrative of American history. Although women served in small numbers—probably no more than several hundred on both sides during the war—their involvement reveals that women could become full participants in a public sphere from which they were actively excluded. As with other topics, war stories have the potential to upset long-standing notions about how Americans conceptualized their nation, their families, and themselves.

One of the most important components of the inquiry into Civil War soldiers has been the experience of black men who fought for the Union. The dominance of the Lost Cause interpretation of the war for much of the twentieth century meant that most historians excluded from their work the topics of slavery, emancipation, and the role of black people generally. The writings of black historians such as W. E. B. DuBois offered a counternarrative that put slavery and emancipation at the center of the war, but it was not until after the civil rights movement of the 1950s and 1960s that white scholars started paying serious attention to the role of black people in the war. It was an African American scholar, Benjamin Quarles, who first delineated the experiences of blacks, particularly those who served in the Union army. Quarles's 1953 *The Negro in the Civil War* accomplished for black soldiers what Wiley's work had done for whites.[33] Although subsequent scholarship on the black military experience has not kept pace with its white counterpart, a number of excellent monographs and important primary source collections have been published.[34] These works demonstrate the centrality of the issue of race to the causes and outcomes of the war and the importance of the contribution made by black soldiers to the Union war effort.

The studies of black troops in the Union army complicate the picture of a glorious army of liberation, revealing instead one fraught with institutional discrimination and deep conflicts over the purpose of the war. African Americans themselves, we now know, wrestled with the decision to support the Union. They were neither blind to Northern whites' reluctance to support emancipation nor sure that it would not be revoked later. Partly because of the unique nature of the issue, black soldiers are still generally treated as a topic separate from regular studies of soldiers. Joseph Glatthaar's *Forged in Battle: The Civil War Alliance of Black Soldiers and Their White Officers* is one of the few studies that focuses on the race relations that developed during the war.[35] Glatthaar's study of both races as they functioned in the segregated United States Colored Troops reveals the sympathy and support that even initially hostile white officers developed after leading black soldiers in battle. This shift of racial sentiment demonstrates the power of the war to reorder priorities and outlooks in important ways. Despite the progress made during the war, Glatthaar found that few officers became advocates for blacks in the postwar period; the disillusionment of battle and the strength of postwar racial ideologies overwhelmed the positive credit that black soldiers had earned. Yet Glatthaar's work and current research into the effect of the Civil War on racial outlooks—among soldiers and others—remind us that the outcomes of the war were neither foreordained nor predictable. Continued research into the black war experience and into the racial attitudes of white soldiers may reveal a history we have not yet seen.

The maturation of the field could be seen by the late 1980s, when a host of studies offered increasingly sophisticated interpretations of how and why soldiers acted as they did. Randall Jimerson and Earl Hess penned two of the most compelling treatments of motivation. Jimerson's study, which analyzed both Northern and Southern soldiers, provided the now standard explanation that Southerners seceded and fought to protect slavery, to preserve self-government, and to resist being conquered by Yankees. Northerners, in contrast, fought because the Union offered the best defense of both the institution of democracy and the freedom that democracy was designed to foster.[36] Hess's account, which focused on Northern soldiers, identified ideology as central to the war effort. In his telling, self-government, democracy, individualism, and egalitarianism were the key characteristics of the antebellum Republic and the values most threatened by a victory by the slaveholding South.[37] Writing a decade later, but in the same vein, James McPherson offered the fullest ideological explanation of the war yet. In McPherson's account, the soldiers of both sides were motivated primarily by a defense of liberty, defined according to regional tastes. Studies of World War II veterans had revealed that men valued their fellow soldiers and the camaraderie they shared above any abstract philosophical defenses of the war. Not so with Civil War soldiers, argued McPherson, who identified in their public and private writings a sincere commitment to abstractions that would have baffled modern soldiers.[38] These studies and others like them that singled out particular elements, such as religion, race, or masculinity, offered an intellectual history of the Civil War told through its participants. Although all three authors mentioned in this paragraph focused their analyses on explaining the war itself, they also pointed the way toward wider histories of the war that connected participants and events with the general trends of nineteenth-century America.

One more indication of the maturation of the field can be seen in how historians now integrate analyses of soldiers into their texts on all topics. In particular, studies of Confederate defeat, communities, and gender include thoughtful considerations of the role of soldiers. For the last decade, many historians have been preoccupied by the problem of how to explain the conclusion of the Civil War. Did the Union win, or the Confederacy lose? In particular, many scholars have argued that the Confederacy collapsed internally from an erosion of morale or lack of faith in its new federal government. In most accounts that make this argument, class conflict is offered as the central element eroding that faith.[39] Disaffection on the home front often plays a prominent role in these accounts, but a full and convincing argument must rest on evidence that a significant number of soldiers abandoned their willingness to fight for the Confederacy. So far, scholars have uncovered isolated instances of soldiers abandoning the army, but not the kind of uniform disaffection that the most ambitious texts argue for.[40]

Much of the best recent scholarship on the Civil War can be found in the community studies that explain the experience of the war across a wide range of perspectives,[41] including that of the soldier. Martin Crawford's recent history of Ashe County, North Carolina, provides a good example of how local histories are enriched when the soldiers who left a particular place are tied back into the story. Crawford's account alternates between the soldiers and the community they left, describing the shifts in belief and outlook as a product of the experiences of both places. The result is a much more nuanced picture of both soldiers and civilians than we could have expected two decades ago. G. Ward Hubbs's recent study of an Alabama community shows this phenomenon in even finer detail.[42] His subtitle, *A Confederate Company in the Making of a Southern Community,* indicates the extent to which battlefront and home front are intimately connected throughout the narrative. Hubbs fulfills this promise with a narrative that describes how the community of Greensboro, Alabama, was built by the sacrifices and hardship shared by white soldiers and civilians of the town. He shows that only by taking seriously the experiences of both home front and battlefront can we understand the racial and social order of the New South.

Gender is the last area where soldiers have emerged as a key source for scholars posing questions that transcend the Civil War. The earlier work done on masculinity by historians such as Frank, Marten, and Mitchell provided a foundation for scholars to build on and exceed the older and more narrow explanations of manhood, particularly among Confederates. Recent books by Paul Anderson, Stephen Berry, and Peter Carmichael demonstrate how a focus on soldiers can allow historians to craft rich and sophisticated stories.[43] Anderson's subject is Turner Ashby, an officer rather than an enlisted man, but his focus is the nature of masculine obligation and expression during the war. Anderson's portrait of Southern masculinity shares more with the work of Marten and Frank than it does with earlier treatments that dealt more exclusively with honor and anger.[44] Similarly, both Berry and Carmichael demonstrate that Confederate soldiers were motivated to fight as much by love as by fear or hatred. That conclusion brings us a fuller understanding of the nature of antebellum and wartime life for Confederates and generates important questions about the moral nature of love and war.

The high quality of much of the work done on soldiers in the 1980s and 1990s, and the success of that work in reshaping how we understand the Civil War, begs another question: how can an area of study that was dormant for so long suddenly explode into view and rise to prominence? Part of the explanation stems, as suggested at the beginning, from internal causes. The field of Civil War history in the 1970s was overburdened with narrow analyses of generals and presidents, battles and campaigns. Soldiers as a topic allowed historians to cut across military, political, social, and cultural lines rather than confining themselves to one area of study.

Changes within the history profession also played a role. The rise of social history, beginning in the 1960s in the United States, promised access to questions of pressing importance regarding class, race, gender, and region. Traditional as they usually are, Civil War historians resisted the opportunities promised by social history for longer than did researchers in most other fields. Historians of slavery, race, and emancipation led this disciplinary shift with careful studies of how and why the process of emancipation happened. Their studies of slavery focused on the experiences of the enslaved and demonstrated how social history could be used to answer political questions as well.[45] Scholars of Civil War soldiers followed, writing the history of the war and the nation based on the experiences of the men who fought it. Today, much of the best social history research being conducted on the war is concerned with soldiers and their families.

A consideration of the context within which historians matured is equally important. The civil rights movement and the Vietnam War, in particular, shaped the authors who redefined the field of soldier studies. Both events spurred scholars to rethink their understanding of the process of historical change. Because of the nature of the American experience in Vietnam, the public was able to sympathize with those who actually fought the war. The extensive media coverage of the war and the personal nature of war protests and rallies compelled an appreciation for the individual's experience of the conflict. As a result, historians developed a methodological impulse toward emphasizing people's capacity to shape their own histories or even the grand historical narratives in which personal histories are embedded. Recent histories of the civil rights movement also reflect this methodological outlook. Rather than emphasizing the nationally prominent leaders or legislative acts that traditionally defined the period, scholars refocused their attention on individuals and communities, showing us how their actions shaped the process in significant ways.[46] In addition, the Vietnam War and the civil rights movement revealed that the personal narratives of those who participated in large-scale events are not necessarily the same as the narratives that explain the nation-state. The similarities and differences between private and public memories have given scholars new insights into the past and into the process by which the stories of the past are constructed. The voluminous personal narratives of the Civil War have allowed historians of the period to apply the same approach to the mid-nineteenth century.

The broad and complex perspectives on the Civil War generated by scholars of soldiers suggest that perhaps the subject has been adequately covered. But like most important experiences in American history, new generations of Civil War scholars will find new questions to ask and previously overlooked areas on which to focus. The recent work on gender, for instance, reveals the potential for social and cultural historians to explore the relationship among masculinity, femininity, and war.[47] The shifting contours of racial attitudes during and after the war require further analysis.[48] The debates about Confederate nationalism and communities show no signs of flagging, and soldiers as subjects offer one of the best access points for this issue. In the future, the best work on soldiers may not even concern itself solely with the Civil War. Scholars of religion, politics, and intellectual and social life may all come to appreciate the value that firsthand accounts can add to their work. In short, historians will never stop fighting the Civil War, and we will continue to benefit from that struggle.

NOTES

1. Thousands of privately and professionally published regimental histories exist, both in wide circulation and in private collections. State historical societies or libraries are probably the main repository for the earliest sets of these writings. See, for example, Asa B. Isham, *An Historical Sketch of the Seventh Regiment Michigan Volunteer Cavalry* (New York: Town Topics, 1893), and George T. Williams, *Company A, 37th Battalion Virginia Cavalry, C.S.A.: A History of Its Organization and Service in the War between the States, 1861–1865* (Roanoke, VA: R. H. Fishburne, 1910).

2. The Virginia Regimental History Series, published by H. E. Howard in Lynchburg, is perhaps the best example of the modern genre. The series includes one volume for each of the more than 160 Virginia units organized during the war. Each volume contains a full roster for the regiment, which includes muster roll information on each soldier and often census information as well. The narrative sections of the volumes, however, are usually brief

descriptive accounts of where the units served and the engagements in which they participated.

3. Bell Irvin Wiley, *The Life of Johnny Reb: The Common Soldier of the Confederacy* (Indianapolis: Bobbs-Merrill, 1943), and *The Life of Billy Yank: The Common Soldier of the Union* (Indianapolis: Bobbs-Merrill, 1952).

4. Albert Burton Moore, *Conscription and Conflict in the Confederacy* (New York: Macmillan, 1924); Ella Lonn, *Desertion during the Civil War* (Gloucester, MA: American Historical Association, 1928; Lincoln: University of Nebraska Press, 1998).

5. Frank Lawrence Owsley, *Plain Folk of the Old South* (Baton Rouge: Louisiana State University Press, 1949); Frank L. Owsley and Harriet C. Owsley, "The Economic Basis of Society in the Late Ante-Bellum South," *Journal of Southern History* 6 (February 1940): 24–45.

6. David Donald, "The Confederate Man as Fighting Man," *Journal of Southern History* 25 (May 1959): 178–93.

7. Harry N. Scheiber, "The Pay of Confederate Troops and Problems of Demoralization," *Civil War History* 15 (September 1969): 226–36.

8. Marvin R. Cain, "A 'Face of Battle' Needed: An Assessment of Motives and Men in Civil War Historiography," *Civil War History* 28 (1982): 5–27; John Keegan, *The Face of Battle: A Study of Agincourt, Waterloo, and the Somme* (New York: Viking, 1976).

9. Civil War scholars also took inspiration from colleagues writing on the Revolutionary War and earlier conflicts. The work of John Shy and others showed Civil War scholars how to ask broad questions about military experiences that were connected to social and political issues in the field. See, for example, John Shy, *A People Numerous and Armed: Reflections on the Military Struggle for American Independence* (New York: Oxford University Press, 1990); Robert A. Gross, *The Minutemen and Their World* (New York: Hill and Wang, 1976); Charles Royster, *A Revolutionary People at War: The Continental Army and American Character, 1775–1783* (Chapel Hill: University of North Carolina Press, 1979); and Fred Anderson, *A People's Army: Massachusetts Soldiers and Society in the Seven Years War* (Chapel Hill: University of North Carolina Press, 1984).

10. Maris A. Vinovskis, "Have Social Historians Lost the Civil War? Some Preliminary Demographic Speculations," *Journal of American History* 76 (June 1989): 34–58.

11. Joseph T. Glatthaar, *The March to the Sea and Beyond: Sherman's Troops in the Savannah and Carolinas Campaign* (New York: New York University Press, 1985), 39–45.

12. Reid Mitchell, *Civil War Soldiers: Their Expectations and Their Experiences* (New York: Touchstone, 1988), 14.

13. Gerald Linderman, *Embattled Courage: The Experience of Combat in the American Civil War* (New York: Free Press, 1989).

14. Critics of Linderman raised another point that has troubled many studies—the extent to which he relied on memoirs composed after the war instead of on contemporary sources. Autobiographies and revised diaries published by soldiers present an attractive source for historians, but far too often the political and social changes wrought by the war color the material, making diaries and letters written during the war—which are also accessible in huge numbers—a more reliable source for historians seeking to capture wartime opinions.

15. Mark Grimsley, *The Hard Hand of War: Union Military Policy toward Southern Civilians, 1861–1865* (Cambridge: Cambridge University Press, 1995).

16. Joseph Allan Frank and George A. Reaves, *"Seeing the Elephant": Raw Recruits at the Battle of Shiloh* (New York: Greenwood Press, 1989).

17. Earl J. Hess, *The Union Soldier in Battle: Enduring the Ordeal of Combat* (Lawrence: University Press of Kansas, 1997), 157.

18. See, for example, Richard A. Reid, "A Test Case of the 'Crying Evil': Desertion among North Carolina Troops during the Civil War," *North Carolina Historical Review* 58 (1981): 234–62; Judith Lee Halleck, "The Role of the Community in Civil War Desertion," *Civil War History* 29 (June 1983): 123–34; David P. Smith, "Conscription and Conflict on the Texas Frontier, 1863–1865," *Civil War History* 36 (September 1990), 250–61; and Kevin C. Ruffner, "Civil War Desertion from a Black Belt Regiment: An Examination of the 44th Virginia Infantry," in *The Edge of the South: Life in Nineteenth-Century Virginia,* ed. Edward L. Ayers and John C. Willis (Charlottesville: University Press of Virginia, 1991), 79–108.

19. Mark Weitz, *A Higher Duty: Desertion among Georgia Troops during the Civil War* (Lincoln: University of Nebraska Press, 2000).

20. Melinda Lawson, *Patriot Fires: Forging a New American Nationalism in the Civil War North* (Lawrence: University Press of Kansas, 2002); Mary-Susan Grant, *North over South: Northern Nationalism and American Identity in the Antebellum Era* (Lawrence: University Press of Kansas, 2000).

21. For the former interpretation, see William A. Blair, *Virginia's Private War: Feeding Body and Soul in the Confederacy, 1861–1865* (New York: Oxford University Press, 1998). For the opposite interpretation, see David Williams, *Rich Man's War: Class, Caste, and Confederate Defeat in the Lower Chattahoochee Valley* (Athens: University of Georgia Press, 1998).

22. Richard Nelson Current, *Lincoln's Loyalists: Union Soldiers from the Confederacy* (Boston: Northeastern University Press, 1992). Several recent community studies highlight the role of Unionism in mostly civilian popula-

tions. See Thomas G. Dyer, *Secret Yankees: The Union Circle in Confederate Atlanta* (Baltimore: Johns Hopkins University Press, 1999), and Margaret Storey, *Loyalty and Loss: Alabama's Unionists in the Civil War and Reconstruction* (Baton Rouge: Louisiana State University Press, 2004).

23. Compare Faust's approach to the question of nationalism, which focuses on the production of nationalist symbols, to Rubin's account, which analyzes the changes in Confederates' understanding of their nation over time. See Drew Gilpin Faust, *Creation of Confederate Nationalism: Ideology and Identity in the Civil War South* (Baton Rouge: Louisiana State University Press, 1988), and Anne Sarah Rubin, *A Shattered Nation: The Rise and Fall of the Confederacy, 1861–1868* (Chapel Hill: University of North Carolina Press, 2005).

24. Gardiner H. Shattuck Jr., *A Shield and Hiding Place: The Religious Life of Civil War Armies* (Macon, GA: Mercer University Press, 1987).

25. J. William Jones, *Christ in the Camp: Or, Religion in Lee's Army* (Richmond, VA: B. F. Johnson, 1887).

26. Drew Gilpin Faust, "Christian Soldiers: The Meaning of Revivalism in the Confederate Army," *Journal of Southern History* 53 (February 1987): 63–90.

27. Samuel J. Watson, "Religion and Combat Motivation in the Confederate Armies," *Journal of Military History* 58 (January 1994): 52.

28. Stephen M. Frank, "'Rendering Aid and Comfort': Images of Fatherhood in the Letters of Civil War Soldiers from Massachusetts and Michigan," *Journal of Social History* 26 (fall 1992): 5–32.

29. James Marten, "Fatherhood in the Confederacy: Southern Soldiers and Their Children," *Journal of Southern History* 63 (May 1997): 279.

30. Reid Mitchell, *The Vacant Chair: The Northern Soldier Leaves Home* (New York: Oxford University Press, 1993).

31. See, for instance, LeeAnn Whites, *The Civil War as a Crisis in Gender: Augusta, Georgia, 1860–1890* (Athens: University of Georgia Press, 1995); Victoria Bynum, *The Free State of Jones: Mississippi's Longest Civil War* (Chapel Hill: University of North Carolina Press, 2001); and Jacqueline Glass Campbell, *When Sherman Marched North from the Sea: Resistance on the Confederate Home Front* (Chapel Hill: University of North Carolina Press, 2005).

32. Elizabeth D. Leonard, *All the Daring of a Soldier: Women of the Civil War Armies* (New York: Norton, 1999); DeAnne Blanton and Lauren M. Cook, *They Fought Like Demons: Women Soldiers in the American Civil War* (Baton Rouge: Louisiana State University Press, 2002).

33. Benjamin Quarles, *The Negro in the Civil War* (Boston: Little Brown, 1953).

34. Dudley Taylor Cornish, *The Sable Arm: Negro Troops in the Union*

Army, 1861–1865 (New York: Norton, 1966); John David Smith, *Black Soldiers in Blue: African American Troops in the Civil War Era* (Chapel Hill: University of North Carolina Press, 2002). For primary sources, see Ira Berlin, Joseph P. Reidy, and Leslie S. Rowland, *Freedom's Soldiers: The Black Military Experience in the Civil War* (New York: Cambridge University Press, 1998), and James M. McPherson, *The Negro's Civil War: How American Blacks Felt and Acted during the War for the Union* (New York: Ballantine, 1965, 1991). A much smaller literature on the role of African Americans in Confederate armies exists as well. See Ervin L. Jordan, *Black Confederates and Afro-Yankees in Civil War Virginia* (Charlottesville: University Press of Virginia, 1995).

35. Joseph T. Glatthaar, *Forged in Battle: The Civil War Alliance of Black Soldiers and Their White Officers* (New York: Free Press, 1989).

36. Randall C. Jimerson, *The Private Civil War: Popular Thought during the Sectional Conflict* (Baton Rouge: Louisiana State University Press, 1988).

37. Earl J. Hess, *Liberty, Virtue, and Progress: Northerners and Their War for the Union* (New York: New York University Press, 1988).

38. James M. McPherson, *For Cause and Comrades: Why Men Fought in the Civil War* (New York: Oxford University Press, 1997).

39. See, for example, Paul D. Escott, *After Secession: Jefferson Davis and the Failure of Confederate Nationalism* (Baton Rouge: Louisiana State University Press, 1978), and *Many Excellent People: Power and Privilege in North Carolina, 1850–1900* (Chapel Hill: University of North Carolina Press, 1985); David Williams, Teresa Crisp Williams, and David Carlson, *Plain Folk in a Rich Man's War: Class and Dissent in Confederate Georgia* (Gainesville: University Press of Florida, 2002).

40. See, for instance, Bynum, *The Free State of Jones;* Paul Horton, "Submitting to the 'Shadow of Slavery': The Secession Crisis and Civil War in Alabama's Lawrence County," *Civil War History* 44 (June 1998): 111–36; and Rand Dotson, "'The Grave and Scandalous Evil Infected to Your People': The Erosion of Confederate Loyalty in Floyd County, Virginia," *Virginia Magazine of History and Biography* 108, no. 4 (December 2000): 393–434. The last two articles show severe but geographically limited instances of class-based resistance.

41. See, for instance, Blair, *Virginia's Private War;* Daniel E. Sutherland, *Seasons of War: The Ordeal of a Confederate Community, 1861–1865* (Baton Rouge: Louisiana State University Press, 1995); and Martin Crawford, *Ashe County's Civil War: Community and Society in the Appalachian South* (Charlottesville: University Press of Virginia, 2001).

42. G. Ward Hubbs, *Guarding Greensboro: A Confederate Company in the Making of a Southern Community* (Athens: University of Georgia Press, 2003).

43. Paul Christopher Anderson, *Blood Image: Turner Ashby in the Civil War and the Southern Mind* (Baton Rouge: Louisiana State University Press, 2002); Stephen W. Berry III, *All That Makes a Man: Love and Ambition in the Civil War South* (New York: Oxford University Press, 2003); Peter S. Carmichael, *The Last Generation: Young Virginians in Peace, War, and Reunion* (Chapel Hill: University of North Carolina Press, 2005).

44. See, for example, Bertram Wyatt-Brown, *Southern Honor: Ethics and Behavior in the Old South* (New York: Oxford University Press, 1982), and Steven A. Channing, *Crisis of Fear: Secession in South Carolina* (New York: Norton, 1974).

45. See, for example, John Blassingame, *The Slave Community: Plantation Life in the Antebellum South* (New York: Oxford University Press, 1972); Herbert Gutman, *The Black Family in Slavery and Freedom, 1750–1925* (New York: Vintage, 1976); Sterling Stuckey, *Slave Culture: Nationalist Theory and the Foundations of Black America* (New York: Oxford University Press, 1987); and Lawrence W. Levine, *Black Culture and Black Consciousness: Afro-American Folk Thought from Slavery to Freedom* (New York: Oxford University Press, 1977).

46. See, for example, Robert Korstad, *Civil Rights Unionism: Tobacco Workers and the Struggle for Democracy in the Mid-Twentieth-Century South* (Chapel Hill: University of North Carolina Press, 2003); Timothy Tyson, *Radio Free Dixie: Robert F. Williams and the Roots of Black Power* (Chapel Hill: University of North Carolina Press, 1999).

47. Scholars who pursue this route can tap into a number of recent studies that explore gender and warfare in other periods. See Kristin L. Hoganson, *Fighting for American Manhood: How Gender Politics Provoked the Spanish-American and Philippine-American Wars* (New Haven, CT: Yale University Press, 1998), and Christina S. Jarvis, *The Male Body at War: American Masculinity during World War II* (De Kalb: University of Northern Illinois Press, 2004).

48. Chandra Manning's forthcoming work, based on her dissertation "'What This Cruel War Was Over': Why Union and Confederate Soldiers Thought They Were Fighting the Civil War" (Ph.D. diss., Harvard University, 2003), promises to advance the field considerably.

A "Vexed Question"

White Union Soldiers on Slavery and Race

Chandra Manning

If anyone had told E. C. Hubbard in January 1861 that he would fight to end slavery, he likely would have laughed or, if in a quarrelsome mood, thrown a punch. By his own admission, he "came into the service . . . thinking that a negro [was] a parallel case of a dog." Yet by December 1861, Sergeant Hubbard of the Thirteenth Illinois complained that the Union's failure to destroy slavery was prolonging the war, and he, like many of his fellow enlisted soldiers, demanded an end to the institution that they identified as the root of the conflict.[1] The first Americans to insist on a connection between emancipation and Union victory were black Americans; the first group of white Americans whose views they changed consisted of Union soldiers serving in the South, who in turn developed into advocates and agents of emancipation. Yet white soldiers' embrace of emancipation came with limits. Although blacks knew that slavery could not be separated from race, white Union troops initially ignored questions of racial equality or black rights. The fury of the war, God's apparent intervention in the July 4 victories at Gettysburg and Vicksburg, and the performance of black soldiers convinced many whites in the Union army that their racial attitudes made them complicit in the sin of slavery and even led some to demand black rights; however, support for the rights of African Americans varied with the course of the war. Together, the advances in and limitations of white Union soldiers' views on slavery and race help explain the achievements and disappointments of the war and its aftermath.

Although studies of Civil War soldiers abound, no methodical examination of white Union soldiers' changing views on slavery and race exists. Bell Irvin Wiley's seminal works, *The Life of Billy Yank* and

31

"Billy Yank and the Black Folk," conflated slavery and race and led to the long-standing assumption that Northern racism made soldiers oppose emancipation.[2] Later works, including Reid Mitchell's *Civil War Soldiers* and James McPherson's *For Cause and Comrades,* depict variations in Union views on slavery and race, but their thematic (rather than chronological) organization makes change over time difficult to track.[3] Joseph Glatthaar shows support for emancipation by the end of the war in *The March to the Sea and Beyond: Sherman's Troops in the Savannah and Carolinas Campaign,* but Glatthaar's subject precludes an examination of earlier developments and excludes men not in Sherman's army.[4] Still needed is a systematic examination of white soldiers' views on slavery and race, with particular attention to change over time and to the role of enlisted men as agents of change who expected to influence the progress of the war.

Drawing conclusions about white Union soldiers' views on slavery and race presents challenges, because the army consisted of millions of individuals who disagreed with one another on nearly everything. It is not difficult to find an example of a soldier to support virtually any point of view. The task here is not to make a case for harmony but to examine dominant patterns in white Union soldiers' positions on slavery and race as expressed in the letters and diaries of mainly enlisted men (along with some junior officers) from West and East, immigrant and native born, urban and rural—soldiers who came from every Union state and who fought in every theater of the war. In addition, this study draws on approximately 100 camp newspapers created by enlisted soldiers in the field.[5]

From the outset, black Americans knew that the war had to strike at slavery. A black New Yorker saw the war as "nothing more nor less than perpetual slavery against universal freedom," which meant that the Union would not win until it "put an everlasting end to negro slavery."[6] Slaves in the South demonstrated the links between Union victory and the end of slavery with their physical presence. Just weeks after Fort Sumter, so many slaves fled to Union lines at Fortress Monroe, Virginia, that General Benjamin Butler had to ask his superiors what to do about "entire families" of slaves. Their arrival in camp signaled that the Union army would have to pay attention to the status and future of African Americans.[7]

In contrast, white Union soldiers' views on slavery varied widely at first. Andrew Walker, the son of Irish immigrants, worked as a school-teacher in the spring of 1861. As soon as he heard about Fort Sumter, he predicted that the North would have the opportunity to "forever set aside Slavery," and before the year was out, he had enlisted in the Fifty-fifth Illinois to help.[8] Others denounced the very idea of a war to end slavery. The *Advance Guard*, a regimental newspaper written by soldiers of the Seventeenth Illinois, lambasted "the northern fanatic" who awaits "the probable abolition of slavery in the southern States, rubs his hands with delight and rejoices that the day of deliverance has arrived. All the horrors of civil war are of no consequence to him if his darling project is accomplished."[9]

For most Union troops, both Walker and the *Advance Guard* missed the point because the war's main purpose had less to do with either supporting or opposing abolition than with proving that republican government, established by the founders on the principles of liberty and equality and administered through free and fair elections, could work. A soldier stationed in Virginia maintained that the Union army aimed "to defend the Union of our Revolutionary sires, and protect and perpetuate a Government which the oppressed in every land have looked upon for half a century as the beacon of liberty."[10] The destruction of the Union would turn the idea of government based on liberty and equality into a worldwide laughingstock. As Private Leigh Webber of Kansas put it, "if we fail now, the hope of human rights is extinguished for ages."[11]

Despite early emphasis on the Union and republican government, it did not take long for much of the rank and file to echo the Wisconsin soldier who proclaimed, "the fact that slavery is the sole undeniable cause of this infamous rebellion, that it is a war of, by, and for Slavery, is as plain as the noon-day sun."[12] As men in the ranks saw it, Confederates had seceded to protect slavery from a president who opposed its extension: that made the war about slavery, whether an individual white Northerner liked it or not. If Southerners had not rebelled, a Pennsylvanian insisted, most Northerners would have continued "following their plow, minding their forge, or exerting their talents in the mercantile line," with thoughts of slavery and war far from their minds.[13]

At first, consensus on slavery's part in starting the war did not translate into agreement over what to do about it. Some men reasoned that if states seceded out of fear for the security of slavery within the Union, the quickest way to bring them back was to demonstrate that slavery was perfectly safe. As one regimental newspaper saw it, once white Southerners realized that the Union posed no threat to slavery, "they will certainly abandon their hopeless and hell-conceived undertaking."[14] Especially in the border states, which retained both slavery and tenuous ties to the Union, some soldiers considered a hands-off policy the best way to ensure loyalty. "The Secesh had represented that we were heare to free all their negroes," Private Edward Dwight remarked from Missouri, but when locals noticed that soldiers did not interfere with slavery, approval of the Union increased.[15] Others worried that the practical demands of fighting a war and ending slavery at the same time would be more than the Union could handle. When Lieutenant E. P. Kellogg read that the Wisconsin *State Journal*'s editor approved of freeing and arming slaves, Kellogg urged caution. The "question of the disposal of the negroes after their emancipation" would be complicated, he noted. Better to "have but one Gordian Knot at a time. If you give us more we shall have to cut them all, and perhaps cut our fingers if not our throats."[16] Other volunteers opposed emancipation simply because they disliked black people. A member of the First Kansas had his "*gorge* of contrabands" and wanted nothing to do with freeing them, lest former slaves move to Kansas. "Our prairies, rich in promised wealth, have already been converted from a living green, into a sickly ebony hue," he complained.[17]

Between August and December 1861 a striking pattern took shape, as soldier after soldier began to insist that because slavery had caused the war, only the destruction of slavery could end the war. "You have no idea of the changes that have taken place in the minds of the soldiers in the last two months," one enlisted man from the Midwest declared. Firsthand observations of the South forced men who had once ignored slavery "to face this sum of all evils, and cause of the war," with the result that "men of all parties seem unanimous in the belief that to permanently establish the Union, [we must] . . . first wipe [out] the institution of slavery." In short, "The rebellion is abolitionizing the whole army."[18] John Boucher agreed: because "it was slavery that caused the war," only "the eternal overthrow of slavery" could win the war.[19] Throughout the ranks, enlisted soldiers reasoned that eliminating the war's cause would end the rebellion and prevent its recurrence. As a result, they championed the destruction of slavery a full year ahead of the Emancipation Proclamation, well before most civilians or political leaders did.

As enlisted men's views on emancipation changed, they anticipated corresponding changes in policy. At first, many Union officers ordered strict respect for private property, including slaves, but by late 1861, the rank and file protested. As long as Confederates' "niggers [are] returned there is no chance to whip them," one sergeant grumbled. "The better course I think would be to confiscate . . . nigger and all."[20] E. C. Hubbard despised General Henry Halleck's practice of expelling fugitive slaves from camp on the grounds of strategy and humanity. For one thing, it made more sense to Hubbard to use the information that slaves provided than to restore laborers to disloyal owners, but beyond tactical concerns, most runaway slaves would rather risk the open road than return to their masters. "To expel them from camp is to expel them to starve," Hubbard shuddered. "Unless this policy is changed the Dept of the Missouri needs a new Commander."[21] In contrast, when General John C. Frémont's controversial proclamation of August 30, 1861, freed the slaves of secessionist owners, William Dunham reckoned that Frémont "has done more for to infuse energy into the Western Division of the service than all others together."[22] When Lincoln revoked Frémont's proclamation and removed Frémont from command, many soldiers, such as a Swiss immigrant in the First Minnesota, wondered angrily why the administration had "interfered" with an action that "would soon end this war by removing the cause of it."[23] The Confiscation Acts of 1861 and 1862, which permitted the confiscation of disloyal owners' slaves, struck men like Walter Reeder as signs "that Congress has, at length arrived at the conclusion *they* had arrived at long since."[24]

To be sure, measures such as Frémont's proclamation and the Confiscation Acts generated what E. P. Kellogg called a "diversity of opinion." Kellogg himself opposed Frémont's measure on the grounds of "practicability."[25] The timing of the Second Confiscation Act, soon after the Army of the Potomac's Peninsula Campaign failed to capture Richmond, angered numerous Union soldiers serving in Virginia. Roland Bowen wished the "damned set of Politicians who are everlastingly fighting about a Damned Nigger or some General" were "all in hell Rolling and Pitching upon the firey coals."[26]

Many others continued to oppose emancipation in general, especially as new rounds of recruits who had not yet witnessed the South or slavery enlisted. Massachusetts tinsmith Charles Knapp told his brother, "wee did not come here to fite for niggers and that is all that theay are fiting for now."[27] Henry Bandy made his position equally clear when he exclaimed, "hooraw for the union and not for the nigar."[28]

Although hostile attitudes never disappeared entirely, the desire to win the war transcended prejudice without erasing it, leading the bulk of the Union army to call for the destruction of slavery as the only way to win this war and avoid another one. Frustrated with Union heel-dragging, an Ohio soldier fumed, "there has got to be something done with the *niggah* for they are the root of the evil or else it will have to be fought over again."[29] Thomas Low agreed. "As long as we ignore the fact (practically) that Slavery is the basis of this struggle so long are we simply heading down a vigorously growing plant that will continually spring up and give new trouble at very short intervals. We must emancipate."[30]

Enlisted Union soldiers came to the conclusion that winning the war would require the destruction of slavery earlier than did most civilians partly because soldiers' personal observations of the South led many to decide that slavery blighted everything it touched. Private Leigh Webber marveled at the "reddish loam" soil of Tennessee, which, "if inhabited by Yankees would bloom like Eden." Instead, to Webber's eyes, "everything generally wears an aspect of neglect, *shiftlessness* and decay" thanks to "the blighting effect of slavery and secession."[31] Serving right next door to his own state, Illinoisan E. C. Hubbard determined that Missouri should have been "one of the richest states," instead of "the poorest." It was too close and climatically similar to the Midwest for distance or weather to account for the differences, so the cause, concluded Hubbard and others, had to be slavery. [32]

Soldiers who insisted that slavery impoverished Southern society did not simply mean that slavery reduced wealth; in 1860, the nation's twelve wealthiest counties were in the South, and one of the country's greatest sources of wealth—slaves—was located exclusively below the Mason-Dixon Line.[33] Soldiers also meant that slavery damaged the South's social health. William Gibson, a chaplain with the Forty-fifth Pennsylvania, wrote to his children about how the presence of chattel bondage doomed the South. For a start, slavery played havoc with proper gender roles. "Southern refinement does not pay much respect to the difference between male and female," reported Gibson. In Pennsylvania, Germans were sometimes viewed as lacking "due consideration for the female sex" when they "sen[t] their wives and especially their daughters in to the harvest field," but German immigrants' blurring of male and female roles paled compared with what Gibson saw on the plantations of coastal South Carolina. At least in Pennsylvania, female labor stayed within the family. "These Southerners work other men's wives and daughters," Gibson marveled. "Here we have the boasted refinement of America employing [slave] females in all kinds of plantation work, in common with the males." Slavery also interfered with class. "So far as I can see there has been no middle class," continued Gibson, who viewed the middle class as a repository of social virtue. Instead, "there was the Southern planter having nothing to do for the greater part of the year, but to devise means how he might best enjoy himself." Next came "the overseer," and finally, slaves "but little removed from a state of barbarism." Rather than civic equality, Gibson saw "the extremes of luxury and poverty, refinement and barbarism." Even among nonslaveholding whites, he found "nothing but a set of *toadies* for the rich planters: and what the South wanted to make the whole North—slave catchers."[34]

To some degree, Gibson's (widely shared) diagnosis that the South needed to be liberated from the grasp of an institution that violated middle-class values arose from Northern cultural attitudes that soldiers brought south with them.[35] Although there were variations between Northern and Southern states (for instance, staple-crop commercial agriculture in plantation districts versus diversified agriculture on Northern family farms), the attribution of those differences to slavery came partly from white middle-class Northerners' own assumptions and from popular travel literature. In *The Cotton Kingdom*, for example, Connecticut-born New Yorker Frederick Law Olmsted depicted a listless South that had been deprived by slavery of virtues admired by white middle-class Northerners, including thrift, self-discipline, and an ethic of civic improvement.[36] In short, many middle-class Northerners, especially those from New England and the upper Midwest, saw what they were prepared to see.

Even more influential than soldiers' preconceptions of the South as a place were their firsthand encounters with actual slaves, for which most white Northerners were completely unprepared. Many mentioned Harriet Beecher Stowe's antislavery novel *Uncle Tom's Cabin* as the closest approximation to the reality of slavery, but insisted that Stowe did not go far enough. George Landrum, for instance, told his sister, "*Uncle Tom's Cabin* should be enlarged upon. We are all becoming Abolitionists here. I detest the institution of slavery."[37] As soldiers confronted what

Leigh Webber scathingly called "the *beneficent* effects of slavery," they admitted their previous underestimation of slavery's cruelty and demanded an end to any institution that permitted such inhumanity. When Webber and two friends met a young boy whose "shoulders were all black and blue with red stripes, and was so sore that he could hardly raise his arm to his head," their "wrath was raised to the highest pitch." They stormed over to the home of the slave's owner, only to be told that the boy had received nothing more than a "*slight correction.*" Infuriated, the three men prevented the child's return to his owner and began seeking ways to undermine institutionalized bondage—one slave at a time, if necessary.[38] Not content with a one-slave-at-a-time approach, Luther Furst announced, "the more I see of slavery the more I think it should be abolished."[39]

Many white Union enlisted men grew especially hostile to slavery because their interactions with slaves convinced them that slavery violated female purity and destroyed families. Gunshots awoke the soldiers of the Seventh Wisconsin one November night. The following day, soldiers "learned, and saw the cause of the alarm in the form of two negro women—a mother and a daughter." The pair fled to Union lines to avoid the proposed sale of the "goodlooking" daughter into the "fancy trade," a form of concubinage that insulted soldiers' notions of female chastity. "Every private in the ranks" cursed "that system which tramples on the honor of man, and makes merchandise of the virtue of women," according to one member of the regiment.[40] They also vilified slavery because, by separating the mother and daughter, slavery violated family bonds. In the Upper South, where many Union soldiers were stationed in 1861, about one in three first marriages between slaves was broken by sale, and about half of all slave children were separated from at least one parent.[41] When an Iowan encountered a child about to be sold by her father, who was also her master, he vowed, "By G-d I'll *fight* till hell *freezes* over and then I'll cut the ice and fight on."[42] Any institution that traduced sacred ideals such as female purity and the family should be destroyed.

Other soldiers developed gratitude and admiration for slaves. In contrast to bitter white secessionists "plotting destruction for our Union," Sergeant Quincy Campbell noted that slaves provided Union troops with "any desired information they can" and with practical services, such as cooking in camp. "Is it anything but fair that our government should lend a helping hand to these Union men of Mississippi?" Campbell asked.[43] The daring lengths to which slaves went to reunite their families fostered new respect in a Pennsylvania soldier. In early 1862, a contraband working for artillerist David Nichol's regiment chanced his life and his freedom to make three trips "pass the Rebel Pickquets" to rescue "his wife & children (who are yet in slavery)." The determined man knew "the risk he was running" but "was bound to get them or die in the attempt." Surely men so steadfast and courageous in their love for family deserved freedom.[44]

Slaves themselves, in short, bore the primary responsibility for forcing emancipation onto the Union agenda, but one of the most important and earliest ways they did so was by influencing enlisted Union soldiers. In 1861 and 1862 white Union soldiers began developing into emancipation advocates who expected their views to influence the prosecution of the war.[45] Many soldiers wrote personal letters to sway the opinions of family members or friends. Private Jasper Barney was "sorry to heare" that his brother-in-law, John Dinsmore, opposed emancipation and aimed to change his relative's mind—a bold task, since Dinsmore, a Union army officer, outranked Barney. "I was of the same opinion of your self when I first came in service, but I have learned better," Barney admitted. "The ware never will come to a close while the negros is left wheaere they are. . . . Even if we could supress the rebellion and leave the main root wheare it was before, it wouldent be long before they would try the same game as before—but if we take way the main root of evil and confiscate all ther property they will have nothing to fight fore."[46] Other soldiers targeted wider audiences. A Wisconsin soldier who expressed his regiment's support for action against slavery in a letter to the *State Journal* wanted to make a difference. We "cannot dictate to law makers nor even to our officers," he admitted, "but I have every reason to believe that officers and government are looking more to the opinions of us poor soldiers than we know or they acknowledges."[47] Some men used camp newspapers to shape the views of folks at home. A December 1861 edition of the *Camp Kettle,* produced in Beaufort, South Carolina, repeatedly emphasized the theme that slavery ruined all it touched, inspired secession, and fomented war. The creators of the *Camp Kettle* wrote partly for their fellow members of the regiment, but they also boxed up 500 copies and sent them home to Pennsylvania.[48]

Anxious as many soldiers grew to stamp out slavery, most Union troops regarded slavery and race as distinct, separable topics. "I have a good degree of sympathy for the *slave*," one private admitted, "but I like the *Negro* the farther off the better."[49] Other soldiers used pejoratives such as "nigger" and "darky" and trotted out stereotypes such as "woolly-headed, good natured, with a tongue that never stops" to describe blacks.[50] Patronizing views toward African Americans demonstrated soldiers' prejudice, but they did not amount to tacit support for slavery; the same soldier who disparaged a slave as "woolly-headed" also raised money to help the youngster escape to freedom. Even if he and others took black inferiority for granted, they did not accept inferiority as license to enslave. Simply stated, many Union soldiers held antislavery and racist views at the same time. Pro-emancipation sentiment did not banish racism any more than continued racism invalidated support for emancipation.

White Union soldiers' distancing of slavery from race allowed many to call for an end to slavery regardless of their own ambivalent racial attitudes and therefore heightened support for emancipation within the Union army, but it also limited the rank and file's willingness to face complicated questions about racial justice. William Dunham noticed others' "concern" about "what disposition will be made with the Colored race" after emancipation, but he did not intend to be "troubled much about that question."[51] Ending slavery was one thing, but caring for or about freed black Americans was quite another; as Dunham put it, "*nigger* is a great *bugger boo* to the *delicate* and *refined American*," and most soldiers sidestepped the uncomfortable subject in the first two years of the war.[52]

The preliminary Emancipation Proclamation of September 1862 and the final Emancipation Proclamation of January 1, 1863, turned the destruction of slavery from a hypothetical slogan into a reality and a war aim, testing the sincerity of rank-and-file calls for emancipation and revealing the flimsiness of the partition between slavery and race. Despite its limited jurisdiction, the proclamation constituted nothing short of revolution, because it took direct aim at an institution that was even older than the nation itself, and it made the destruction of that institution a matter of war policy. As Connecticut Private Orra Bailey recognized, "this peculiar institution . . . has become so deeply rooted that [removing] it will shake the nation and our institutions to the very center."[53] To destroy slavery would be to create a new United

States unlike one that had ever existed. Given the immensity of that transformation, it comes as no surprise that the proclamation elicited a variety of strong reactions, but soldiers' responses were not nearly as negative or one-dimensional as has long been supposed. The idea that the Emancipation Proclamation stirred up fury and depressed morale among Union soldiers has been popular and tenacious, but it is based on assumptions about the effects of Northern racism rather than evidence of enlisted men's reactions to the proclamation.[54]

Chronology can make the Emancipation Proclamation seem like a morale crisis trigger, because Union morale did decline in the winter of 1862–1863, but soldiers' own words dismiss that explanation as simplistic and misguided. To many Union soldiers, emancipation and declining morale were distinct phenomena, not cause and effect. If soldiers' low spirits resulted from either the preliminary or the final Emancipation Proclamation, then morale should have dropped at the same time throughout the entire Union army, either in September, after the preliminary proclamation, or in January, after the final one. Instead, morale in the Army of the Potomac slid in November, prompted by the army's persistent failure to take Richmond and exacerbated by the November 7 removal of popular commander George McClellan. As one McClellan admirer commented, the loss of Little Mac cast a "gloom over [the] army."[55] The gloom deepened in December, after the disastrous assault on Fredericksburg, which a bitter Maryland sergeant described as the sacrifice of "ten thousand lives" for nothing.[56] Meanwhile, morale in the West did not drop until February, and most soldiers attributed their dreary spirits to idleness, soaring disease rates, and the futility of a plan to regain the Mississippi River by digging a new channel and moving it. The unhealthy conditions led to such rampant illness that Iowa soldier Charles Musser described duty along the Mississippi as "wholeSale murder" and warned, "if there is not some great movements made between this and spring, I believe one half of the army will throw down their arms and go home."[57] Demoralization struck eastern and western armies at different times in response to unique local circumstances, not as a result of emancipation, which soldiers everywhere had been expecting since September.

In fact, when the Emancipation Proclamation came, many soldiers regarded it as a sign that the poky federal government was finally catching up. Although the proclamation pleased Elijah Penny, the corporal muttered, "if the Presidents *proclamation* had been proclaimed one year sooner than it was I think the war would have been just so much nearer the end."[58] To soldiers who had been claiming that emancipation was the only way to end the war once and for all, the proclamation seemed like plain common sense. As one explained, "slavery is the primary cause, or the root of the matter," and the Emancipation Proclamation was simply a practical recognition that "to distroy the tree root & branch is the surest way to brake this rebellion."[59] Some troops praised emancipation's pragmatic benefits. "The white men of the South are in the Southern army, and their negroes are at home raising crops," an Illinois cavalryman pointed out. Free the slaves, and "the white men will be obliged to come home to look after the welfare of their families." Whatever else motivated soldiers, most of them wanted to go home, and they welcomed any developments that would get them there faster.[60] Other soldiers embraced emancipation because it moved the American Republic closer to its own ideals. Without emancipation, an Indiana private held, "this war has not done its work." Abolition constituted "a check to the tyrany of European monarchs" and a step in "the establishing of free government throughout the earth." If the existence of slavery had mocked the proposition of human equality, then eliminating slavery should strengthen American ideals and certify the success of the United States' republican experiment.[61]

Accounts of enraged soldiers stacking weapons rather than fighting for emancipation circulated then, as they do now, but in the main, the Union rank and file responded to those stories with outrage and wounded pride. Midwesterners were especially provoked, because numerous rumors specifically mentioned soldiers from Indiana, Illinois, and Ohio, and also because the state legislatures of Indiana and Illinois had denounced the Emancipation Proclamation. When James Dodds heard of letters in his hometown newspaper, allegedly from soldiers, "on the point of laying down their arms on account of the Proclamation," he furiously dismissed them as "all untrue," insisting instead that "the army was never more united than now." Dodds's claims about unity were exaggerated, but his disgust was sincere.[62] William Lewis insisted that officers must have been behind any antiproclamation demonstrations. "I no that the soldier had nothing to Doo with it it wer sholder straps and no one Elttze," he insisted. Enlisted men were too busy fighting the war to protest a measure that was likely to help win it.[63]

Without question, some soldiers opposed the Emancipation Proclamation. In July 1862 General George McClellan warned President Lincoln that "a declaration of radical views, especially upon slavery, will rapidly disintegrate our present armies."[64] Although McClellan consistently exaggerated the odds against any proposition he opposed, emancipation included, some soldiers shared his hostility. Long before the proclamation, many officers, such as General Henry Halleck, worried about the military burden that freed slaves would impose on the army by flocking to camps and tagging along on marches.[65] Some soldiers cited legal scruples. One Pennsylvania corporal personally opposed slavery but feared that the proclamation violated constitutional guarantees. Start to bend the Constitution, he worried, and "pollitical demagogues" would ignore inconvenient parts at will.[66] Others reasoned that the proclamation would inspire Confederates to fight harder. A private from New England worried that the proclamation "unite[d] the South almost as a unit," minimizing the valuable asset of internal Southern dissent.[67] Meanwhile, some Union troops feared that inevitable disagreement over emancipation might stir up antiwar "revolution in the north," hobbling the Union war effort by heightening disunity.[68]

The Emancipation Proclamation created particular dilemmas for some border state soldiers, many of whom had counted on being able to avoid difficult choices between slavery and union. "It really seems to me that we are not fighting for our *country*, but for the freedom of the negroes," Marylander John Babb grumbled, and that perception was likely to "do more harm than good" to the Union cause in Maryland.[69] David Massey and Phillip Reilly, both from the fiercely divided state of Missouri, resented the war's transformation into what Reilly called a "negro crusade."[70] Massey went further, suggesting, "if old Abe does free the negro I say that the Democrats owt to go in with the south and kill all the Abalitians of the north and that will end this war where nothing else will."[71]

Other Union soldiers blamed slaves for the existence of the war and begrudged the culprits any benefits such as freedom. Cyrus Boyd witnessed such scapegoating in his Iowa regiment, where only a minority opposed emancipation but compensated with a forceful wrath. "The poor African . . . from no fault of his—save in the fact of his black skin," endured "prejudice" and "indignant language" from surly Union soldiers who, in the months following the proclamation, reasoned that if it had not been for slaves, they never would have gone to war.[72] Nobody spoke more angrily or hatefully than Ohioan Chauncey Welton. In one of his outbursts, Welton raged: "When we think it is all for the purpose of raising the poor down troden affrican to a common with an intelligent race of beings[!] My abolition enimys . . . say . . . free the negroe at all hazzards whether the union is saved or not if it takes the last man, yes this is their language. The nigger, nigger, nigger, free him, free him, free him sacrifice money, wealth, treasure, blood, life and country, but free the nigger."[73]

For Welton, racism provided reason enough to oppose emancipation, and it would be easy to leap to the conclusion that all Northern racists shared Welton's feelings. Yet despite obvious exceptions, Union soldiers by and large proved quite capable of looking down on black Americans and supporting the Emancipation Proclamation at the same time. According to Fred Pettit, "nine tenths of the army" supported the proclamation because "a Negro has rights as a dog has rights and [we] think his rights should be respected."[74] Amos Hostetter, who had never thought of freeing slaves before the war, admitted that he and many of his fellow soldiers "like the Negro no better now than we did then but we hate his master worse and I tell you when Old Abe carries out his Proclamation he kills this Rebellion and not before. I am henceforth an *Abolitionist* and I intend to practice what I preach."[75] As Pettit, Hostetter, and countless others saw it, they did not need to believe that black Americans were equal to white Americans in order to support the destruction of the institution that had caused the war.

The habit of separating slavery from race, the passage of time, and soldiers' experiences in the South and on the battlefield helped to change the minds of some who had initially objected to the Emancipation Proclamation. By March 1863, an Ohio soldier reported that "the Pres. Proclamation is gaining favor in the army every day," as troops increasingly recognized it as "the right move at the right time."[76] Even Chauncey Welton reconsidered. He still disliked abolitionists and blacks, but by June, he had come to believe that the proclamation represented a "means of haistining the speedy Restoration of the union and the termination of this war," and he was willing to accept it on those pragmatic grounds.[77]

Ironically, although many Union soldiers could support the Emancipation Proclamation partly because they separated the issues of slavery and race, the proclamation itself made that separation much harder to sustain because it turned millions of slaves into free men, women, and children whose places in the Union would have to be determined. Suddenly, enlisted men such as Stephen Fleharty realized, *"the status of the negro in the future organization of our government"* was a "vexed question" they could no longer ignore.[78] Few soldiers had any clear idea of how a postslavery, biracial society might function. As Pennsylvanian Jacob Seibert pointed out, "we don't want [former slaves] in the north," but whether soldiers liked it or not, the proclamation meant that even reluctant white Northerners could not easily avoid considering the role of black Americans within the American Republic.[79]

Emancipation may have made it difficult for white Union soldiers to evade questions about the place of black Americans in the nation, but the enlistment of black soldiers made it impossible to do so. Caleb Beal asked his uncle, "what do you think of putting the nigger on an equal footing with the white man," and then launched into his own objections to black enlistment, all of which boiled down to an assumption of black inferiority. "No Sir you can never make soldiers of them feller even if you whitewash 'em," Beal claimed.[80] Yet before a year had passed, many white enlisted soldiers changed their minds, including Beal; by June, he saw the wisdom of mobilizing black manpower, since black men were likely to "fight hard."[81] By October, Beal lectured his parents, "there is no mistake they make good soldiers."[82]

White Union soldiers' attitudes grew more favorable toward black enlistment for many of the same reasons that enlisted men had espoused emancipation. "The purpose of employing negroe soldiers is to make them be serviceable to the country," one private pragmatically remarked. As a "war measure," arming blacks who were anxious to fight their former masters offered "the most efficient means that can be brought into action." [83] Especially after Congress passed the first Union draft in March 1863, a number of white soldiers grew "truly glad that they are arming Negroes they are none too good to fight for me, or to die for me, or rather instead of me, if necesary," as an Illinois private cynically reflected.[84] With an equal lack of generosity, Private Milton Bassett favored the mobilization of black troops in Louisiana because stationing "nigger troops" in swamps meant that "the white men can" escape "fever and ague."[85] Others saw the arming of black troops as the most symbolically powerful way to destroy the war's cause, because "Slavery, Rebellion & Chivalry [would] all die together," as Anson Patterson explained.[86] Finally, some Union troops supported black enlistment for idealistic reasons. Carlos Lyman welcomed black enlistment as one of the war's "great steps towards Christianity (*nationally speaking*)."[87]

Black soldiers' performance in the field also changed many of their white counterparts' minds about black enlistment, although black regiments' battlefield successes did not erase all prejudices immediately. Pliny Jewett had entered the army convinced of black cowardice and servility, but after fighting next to a black regiment in Virginia, he praised the determination and bravery of black soldiers, even as he persisted in using derogatory language. "The nigs were on our right they fought like devils," he noted.[88] Shifts in attitude did not always mean that bigotry disappeared. Henry Kircher, a German-born lieutenant with the Twelfth Missouri, declared himself "very much for" arming black soldiers, as long as he did not have to fight next to them and risk being "wounded by the same bullet that first trafficks with a Negro and then pays me a visit." If black and white regiments mixed too closely, "gradually the difference between white and black will show less and less until it has disappeared," warned Kircher. "What is a white who forgets that he stands above the African?"[89]

Tenacious as assumptions of white supremacy proved to be, in the summer of 1863, stubborn racial biases actually began to be called into question. By the Civil War's midpoint, its fury had stripped away romantic visions and forced many soldiers to view the war as God's "curse . . . upon the country for the toleration of that inhuman practice, Human Slavery," as Illinoisan James Jessee reasoned.[90] On July 4, 1863, when the Union won control of the Mississippi River at Vicksburg and Lee's defeated Army of Northern Virginia retreated south after Gettysburg, Union soldiers everywhere interpreted the twin Independence Day victories not as mere coincidence but as proof that "the hand of *God* is in this struggle."[91] Although God's apparent approval encouraged soldiers, the devastation of battles such as Gettysburg suggested that the Union had miles to go before God would be satisfied, and it forced many to confront for the first time what Quincy Campbell called "every vestige" of slavery: Northern complicity in the sin of slavery through racial attitudes that enabled its existence.[92] When draft riots turned into racial rampages in Northern cities, Private Wilbur Fisk knew that white Northerners could no longer duck their own sinfulness. By harboring "wholly wrong, unnatural and unjustifiable" racial prejudices, Northern whites had made slavery possible, and they had kept "the souls of the African . . . down." Now they must face up to their "fearful responsibility."[93]

Especially after Gettysburg and Vicksburg, ordinary white men began to conclude that if God was going to allow the war to continue until Northern whites had atoned for their sinful racial prejudice—which appeared to be the case—they had better reform their own attitudes and those of their fellow white Northerners. As Joseph Scroggs plainly stated, he fought "to assist in removing the unreasonable prejudice against the colored race."[94] Late in the war, Wilbur Fisk wrote a lengthy newspaper column for Northern children and told his young readers that their duties toward black Americans went beyond an occasional "dollar for the Freedmen's Aid Society." White Americans were obligated to abandon the distinctions they drew between themselves and African Americans, and God would frown on anyone who "shall unwittingly despise" blacks rather than treating them like Christ, he warned.[95] Several soldiers went beyond pleas for kindness to demand equal justice. An Ohioan would settle for nothing short of "the equal freedom of all men in this country *regardless of color,*" a goal that few white soldiers could have imagined, let alone advocated, at the beginning of the war.[96] Private Constant Hanks believed that the war would be wasted if it did not place the nation "on the broad firm base of eaqual right" for black Americans.[97] Anything less would betray soldiers' sacrifices, impoverish the Union cause, and disappoint God.

As important as Gettysburg and Vicksburg were in inspiring white troops to consider Northern culpability, black soldiers' day-to-day soldiering skills and their bravery in battle forced white men who fought alongside them to revisit their own racial attitudes.[98] After a former private in an Illinois regiment became a company officer in a regiment of black Louisiana soldiers, he warned his aunt, "I never more wish to hear the expression, 'the niggers won't fight.' Come with me 100 yards from where I sit, and I can show you the wounds that cover the bodies of 16 as brave, loyal and patriotic soldiers as ever drew bead on a Rebel." The battle of Milliken's Bend rivaled Shiloh, yet none of the black enlisted men "offered to leave his place until ordered to fall back. . . . They fought and died defending the cause that we revere."[99]

Not every white Union soldier experienced a racial epiphany, but many ordinary men who had had no interest in racial justice before the war reexamined their own prejudices and assumptions with more critical eyes. The *Mail Bag,* a camp paper created by Ohio soldiers stationed in Kentucky, reflected that the common practice "of calling all negroes boys"—which it had never occurred to most whites to question—"sounds rather strangely."[100] The *Soldier's Letter* of the Second Colorado Cavalry even began to recommend concrete advances in civil rights, including black suffrage, desegregation of public facilities, and the right of black lawyers to argue before the Supreme Court.[101] Such positions would have been considered revolutionary before the war, and only the most radical abolitionists would have endorsed them. Years of grueling warfare—seen by many as the work of a just but angry God—changed the minds of white Northern men who had never before questioned their assumptions of black inferiority. After the events of the summer of 1863, many white members of the Union army expanded the reach of founding ideals such as equality beyond racial limits that had once seemed immovable, and they envisioned a nation that few could have imagined in 1861.

As the war entered its final year, soldiers' commitment to emancipation remained nonnegotiable. "Slavery is the sole cause of the rebellion," insisted Jacob Behm. "Political, civil, moral, and sacred duty" demanded abolition. Any "compromise . . . would give but a breathing spell for a renewed struggle."[102] According to an artilleryman, if the North agreed to "a restoration of this Union upon any other basis than that of the complete and everlasting overthrow of the institution of slavery," it would "have gained nothing."[103] In the election of 1864, 80 percent of Union soldiers voted against George McClellan, former commander of the Army of the Potomac, and in favor of Abraham Lincoln and a platform that was uncompromisingly dedicated to emancipation as a war aim, further emphasizing enlisted men's unwillingness to back down on the question of ending slavery.[104]

Commitment to fighting prejudice and advancing racial justice, in contrast, proved more fragile. Discouraged by the complications bound to arise when an institution so old and deeply embedded in the foundation of the United States disappeared, some soldiers shied away from support for racial advances. "The system of Slavery may suffer material change, yet the negro will not be made practically free," Kentuckian Robert Winn predicted. "The possibility of such a result we push off by mere bravado, not by any good reasoning."[105] Other white Union soldiers soured on the idea of racial progress out of a mistaken belief that blacks received better treatment than whites did. "The negro troops is treeted beter than what we ar in every respect and that dont soot me a bit," complained Ohio soldier Arthur Van Horn.[106]

The progress of the war also influenced racial attitudes. When the war went badly, or when it went so well that it encouraged complacency, many white soldiers retreated from their support of racial justice. In the grim first half of 1864, when the Army of the Potomac suffered appalling defeats at places such as Cold Harbor and every other army seemed stalled, blacks provided targets for whites' frustrations. When a Union plan to crack Confederate lines around Petersburg by exploding a mine underneath them failed, Private Alonzo Rich blamed black soldiers. He remained perfectly "willing the niggers should fight," but from now on he wanted them to do it far away from him.[107] Personal suffering reversed the racial progress made by white Union soldiers such as William Stevens. Emaciated and lice infested, Stevens attributed his prolonged imprisonment to black soldiers, because the Lincoln administration refused to exchange prisoners until Confederate authorities agreed to exchange black and white soldiers equally. Stevens's *abolition principles* did not stand a chance when he knew "that the only reason our Government has for leaving us in such a condition was a miserable quibble, about the '*exchange*' [of] Negroes." In fact, he announced that he "would not willingly endure this again" for the benefit of "every Negro in the Confederacy."[108] Conversely, Union army success could make the need for drastic measures less apparent. The closer Union victory seemed to be, the more quickly Private George Hudson rediscovered old prejudices. "You must have a better oppinion of the Negro than I to leave our Government to their Protection," Hudson wrote to his family in response to a letter from home that spoke approvingly of black suffrage.[109]

Even as some white soldiers regressed, others' views continued to shift. As a result, white Union soldiers displayed a striking multiplicity of perspectives in 1865. Views on race were in flux when the war ended, and the eventual outcome was anything but inevitable. Some men who had interacted with African American soldiers grew in their belief that the reunited nation must continue to work toward justice and equality for black Americans. From Alabama, one white soldier exclaimed, "blistered be the tongue" of Northerners who harped, as he once had, on the dangers of "negro equality." The sight of "5,000 colored . . . soldiers fighting equally . . . for our common country" proved that "the colored man" should be "ELEVATED."[110] Such views demonstrated a real impulse for racial change among some white Union soldiers in the waning days of the war. In contrast, other men abandoned the ideals of racial equality when they saw racial justice as irrelevant to the Union cause or as detrimental to their own well-being, illustrating the existence of countervailing impulses as well. Some soldiers, such as the Kentuckian who supported "*liberty—*but not . . . *equality—*nor *fraternity—*except in the limited sense," could glimpse the possibility of racial justice but fall short of achieving it.[111]

The first Americans to insist on a connection between emancipation and Union victory were black Americans, both free and enslaved, who forced the matter of racial bondage onto the national agenda; the first group of white Americans whose minds they succeeded in changing were enlisted Union soldiers serving in the South. Within months of observing the South and interacting with enslaved men and women, many Union troops decided that only the destruction of slavery could end the war and prevent its recurrence. White Union soldiers were quick to support abolition for a combination of practical, empathetic, and sometimes conflicting reasons, and they served as effective advocates, pushing civilians and political leaders to embrace emancipation. Initially, most of those who championed emancipation paid scant attention to the question of blacks' rights or to their own racial attitudes. As the war progressed, soldiers' growing conception of the war as God's punishment on the entire nation led some to examine Northern complicity in the sin of slavery and to call for steps toward equality, but white soldiers' progressive racial attitudes proved to be tenuous and prone to backsliding. Taken together, Union soldiers' dramatic transformation into advocates of emancipation, the stubborn limits of their racial attitudes, and their fluctuating views on race in 1865 help to explain how the Civil War created a vast potential for racial change in the United States but failed to fulfill it. These phenomena also foreshadow the aftermath of Reconstruction.

NOTES

1. Sgt. E. C. Hubbard, Thirteenth Illinois, to brother, April 12, 1864, Woodville, AL; to brother, August 9, 1861, Rolla, MO; and to sister, December 3, 1861, Rolla, MO, E. C. Hubbard Letters, Special Collections, University of Arkansas.

2. Bell Irvin Wiley, *The Life of Billy Yank: The Common Soldier of the Union* (Indianapolis: Bobbs-Merrill, 1952); "Billy Yank and the Black Folk," *Journal of Negro History* 36, no. 1 (January 1951): 25–52.

3. Reid Mitchell, *Civil War Soldiers* (New York: Touchstone, 1988); James M. McPherson, *For Cause and Comrades: Why Men Fought in the Civil War* (New York: Oxford University Press, 1997).

4. Joseph Glatthaar, *The March to the Sea and Beyond: Sherman's Troops in the Savannah and Carolinas Campaign* (New York: New York University Press, 1985). Glatthaar's *Forged in Battle: The Civil War Alliance of Black Soldiers and Their White Officers* (New York: Free Press, 1989) also looks at the attitudes of the white soldiers who became officers in black regiments.

5. Letters and diaries offer insight into a broad cross section of typical soldiers, not just a privileged few, because more than 90 percent of white Union troops were literate. In addition, camp newspapers were usually collaborative efforts giving voice to enlisted men throughout the regiment; the papers published articles, letters to the editor, and accounts of camp occurrences in which men voted on various topics. Reading letters, diaries, and camp papers from forty-five different archives produced a swirl of voices and plenty of dissent, as should be expected whenever hundreds of individuals share their views. To determine whether any one position dominated, I stipulated that expressions of the prevalent view had to outnumber expressions of dissenting views at the time in question by a factor of three to one.

6. *Liberator,* August 30, 1861, in James McPherson, *The Negro's Civil War: How American Negroes Felt and Acted during the War for the Union* (New York: Vintage Books, 1965), 40. The *Anglo-African,* a black newspaper, agreed, predicting that "no adjustment of the nation's difficulty is possible until the claims of the black man are first met and satisfied. . . . If you would restore the Union and maintain the government you so fondly cherish, make way for liberty, universal and complete" (May 11, 1861, 1).

7. Gen. Benjamin F. Butler to Lt. Gen. Winfield Scott, May 27, 1861, Fortress Monroe, Virginia, in Ira Berlin et al., eds., *Freedom: A Documentary History of Emancipation 1861–1867,* ser. 1, vol. 1, *The Destruction of Slavery* (New York: Cambridge University Press, 1985), 70–71. Despite his apparent deference, Butler actually decided what to do for himself; he famously called runaway slaves "contraband of war" and refused to return them to their Confederate owners. The role of slaves in placing the issue of slavery on the Union's agenda is a major theme of the *Freedom: A Documentary History of Emancipation* series.

8. Sgt. Andrew Walker, Fifty-fifth Illinois, to parents, April 1861, Henderson, IL, Andrew J. Walker Papers, Library of Congress.

9. "How Will It End?" *Advance Guard,* August 28, 1861, Fredericktown,

MO, American Antiquarian Society. The *Advance Guard* was the regimental newspaper of the Seventeenth Illinois.

10. "The Advance into Virginia," *American Union,* July 5, 1861, 3, American Antiquarian Society. The *American Union* was the camp newspaper of the First Rhode Island; Rhode Island Artillery; First Wisconsin; and Second, Third, Eighth, Eleventh, and Twenty-first Pennsylvania.

11. Pvt. Leigh Webber, First Kansas, to friends, the Brown family in Kansas, April 24, 1862, Tipton MO, John S. Brown Family Papers, reel 2, Kansas State Historical Society. See also the *Illinois Fifty-second,* which posed the question, "destroy this Union and what can republics hope for?" *Illinois Fifty-second* 1, no. 1 (January 15, 1862): 3, Stewartsville, MO, Illinois State Historical Library.

12. *Wisconsin Volunteer,* February 6, 1862, 3, Leavenworth, KS, Kansas State Historical Society. The *Wisconsin Volunteer* was the newspaper of the Thirteenth Wisconsin. Five days before his regiment mustered in, an Iowa recruit similarly emphasized that Confederates started the war "to secure the extension of that blighting curse—*slavery*—o'er our fair land." Sgt. John Quincy Adams Campbell, diary, July 9, 1861, Burlington, IA, in Mark Grimsley and Todd D. Miller, eds., *The Union Must Stand: The Civil War Diary of John Quincy Adams Campbell, Fifth Iowa Volunteer Infantry* (Knoxville: University of Tennessee Press, 2000), 2–3.

13. *Cavalier,* July 30, 1863, 2, Williamsburg, VA, Virginia Historical Society. The *Cavalier* was the newspaper of the Fifth Pennsylvania Cavalry.

14. *Traveler,* May 9, 1862, 2, Jacksonport, AR, Illinois State Historical Library. The *Traveler* was the newspaper of the Kane County (IL) Cavalry.

15. Pvt. Edward Dwight, Eighth Wisconsin, diary, August 13, 1861, Pilot Knob, MO, Edward Dwight Papers, State Historical Society of Wisconsin.

16. Lt. E. P. Kellogg, Second Wisconsin, to editor of *State Journal,* November 12, 1861, Camp Tillinghast, VA, E. B. Quiner Correspondence of Wisconsin Volunteers, reel 1, vol. 1, p. 155, State Historical Society of Wisconsin.

17. *First Kansas,* January 18, 1862, 2, Lexington, MO, Kansas State Historical Society. *First Kansas* was the newspaper of the First Kansas and also included contributions by soldiers of the Thirty-ninth Ohio.

18. "Enlisted soldier," Third Wisconsin, to *State Journal,* October 1861, near Harpers Ferry, VA, Quiner Papers, reel 1, vol. 1, p. 176. Similarly identifying slavery as "the cause of all our animosities, and wranglings and this acursed rebellion," a Vermonter in the ranks hoped that "the dark stigma upon our nation may be wiped out." Pvt. Jerome Cutler, Second Vermont, to fiancée Emily, November 11, 1861, Camp Griffin, Fairfax County, VA, Jerome Cutler Letters, Vermont Historical Society.

19. Sgt. John Boucher, Tenth Missouri, to wife, December 7, 1861, Camp

Holmes, MO, Boucher Family Papers, Civil War Miscellany Collection 2nd ser., U.S. Army Military History Institute, Carlisle Barracks, PA. See also Chaplain A. C. Barry, Fourth Wisconsin, to *State Journal,* November 1861, eastern VA, Quiner Papers, reel 1, vol. 1, p. 198.

20. Sgt. John Boucher, Tenth Missouri, to wife, November 30, 1861, Camp Holmes, MO, Boucher Family Papers, Civil War Miscellany Collection, U.S. Army Military History Institute. Sergeant Boucher told his wife that he was "in hopes that this course will be carried out in the present Congress if so we may hope for a speedy conclusion of the war."

21. Sgt. E. C. Hubbard, Thirteenth Illinois, to sister, December 3, 1861, Rolla, MO, E. C. Hubbard Letters, University of Arkansas.

22. Capt. William Dunham, Thirty-sixth Ohio, to wife, October 28, 1861, Summersville, VA, William Dunham letters, Civil War Miscellany Collection, U.S. Army Military History Institute. Missouri soldier A. G. Dinsmore also praised Frémont, "whom we all esteem, and in whose integrity, courage, patriotism and good judgment we all have the utmost confidence." A. G. Dinsmore, Thirteenth Missouri, to unidentified friend, who later published the letter in the Wisconsin *State Journal,* October 14, 1861, Benton Barracks, MO, Quiner Papers, reel 1, vol. 2, p. 11.

23. Pvt. Adam Marty, First Minnesota, to friend, October 10, 1861, Camp Stone, VA, Minnesota Historical Society. See also William Dunham, who could only conclude that Frémont had "been slaughtered by *fogy* politicians." Capt. William Dunham, Thirty-sixth Ohio, to father-in-law, November 15, 1861, Summersville, VA, William Dunham Letters, Civil War Miscellany Collection, U.S. Army Military History Institute.

24. Pvt. Walter Reeder, Thirty-sixth Illinois, to parents and siblings, July 27, 1862, near Rienzi, MS, Walter Reeder Papers, State Historical Society of Wisconsin. George Mowry noted that nothing "would give the soldiers more joy" than hearing that "the Confiscation bill had become a law." Pvt. George Mowry, Seventh Kansas Cavalry, to sister, July 22, 1862, near Corinth, MS, Webster Moses Letters and Diaries, Kansas State Historical Society. Andrew Walker also heralded the First Confiscation Act as "something extraordinary in the history of America." Pvt. Andrew Walker, Fifty-fifth Illinois, to father, December 2, 1861, Camp Douglas, IL, Andrew J. Walker Papers, Library of Congress. Meanwhile, a Norwegian immigrant assured his wife that the Second Confiscation Act "pleases soldiers very much." Cpl. Rollin Olson, Fifteenth Wisconsin, to wife, July 31, 1862, near Jacinto, MS, in "Rollin Olson Civil War Letters" (pamphlet), trans. Morgan Olson, State Historical Society of Wisconsin. The First Confiscation Act of August 6, 1861, allowed the army to confiscate property (including slaves) being used in direct aid of the Confederate military effort, for example, slaves digging fortifications for

Confederate troops. More punitive in nature, the Second Confiscation Act of July 17, 1862, permitted the confiscation of property (including slaves) belonging to anyone disloyal to the Union, whether or not that property directly aided the Confederate military cause. Neither act was very practical in terms of function, but both signaled a stronger stance on slavery. See Silvana Siddali, *From Property to Person: Slavery and the Confiscation Acts, 1861–1862* (Baton Rouge: Louisiana State University Press, 2005).

25. Lt. E. P. Kellogg, Second Wisconsin, to *State Journal,* November 12, 1861, Camp Tillinghast, VA, Quiner Papers, reel 1, vol. 1, p. 155.

26. Pvt. Roland Bowen, Fifteenth Massachusetts, to mother, July 19, 1862, near Harrison's Landing, VA, in Gregory A. Coco, ed., *From Ball's Bluff to Gettysburg . . . and Beyond: The Civil War Letters of Private Roland E. Bowen, 15th Massachusetts Infantry, 1861–1865* (Gettysburg, PA: Thomas Publications, 1994), 115–16. Orderly Felix Brannigan advised "kicking out those legislators who have made the 'nigger' the all-important question," because it seemed to him that Congress paid more attention to the issue of slavery than to supporting the army in its efforts to take the Confederate capital. Sgt. Felix Brannigan, Fifth New York, to family member (probably sister), July 16, 1862, Camp Harrison Landing, VA, Felix Brannigan Papers, *People at War,* collection 22, reel 4, Library of Congress.

27. Enlisted soldier Charles R. Knapp, Twenty-fourth Massachusetts, to brother, March 9, 1863, St. Helena Island, SC, C. R. Knapp Letters, South Caroliniana Library, University of South Carolina.

28. Pvt. Henry Bandy, Ninety-first Illinois, to brother and sister, January 12, 1862, somewhere in KY, Henry Bandy Letters, Illinois State Historical Library.

29. Sgt. John Baldwin, Seventy-fourth Ohio, to wife, Gussie, May 25, 1862, Camp Fool, near Nashville, TN, John W. Baldwin Papers, Ohio Historical Society.

30. QM Sgt. Thomas Low, Twenty-third New York Artillery, diary, March 29, 1862, Washington, DC, Thomas Low Papers and Diary, Special Collections, Perkins Library, Duke University.

31. Pvt. Leigh Webber, First Kansas, to Brown family of KS, June 27, 1862, Trenton, TN, John S. Brown Family Papers, reel 2, Kansas State Historical Society. "If it were not for the curse of slavery [the South] could not be beat," another Northern corporal told a friend. As it was, Southern whites lacked "the thrift and energy that we see in the free States and the baneful effects of slavery are visible everywhere in the lack of enterprise and universal indolence of the inhabitants . . . white men do not work. . . . The land is excellent, but there is little raised." Cpl. S. H. Helmer, Tenth Wisconsin, to a friend, November 1861, Camp Abercrombie, Shepherdsville, KY, Quiner Papers, reel 1, vol. 2, p.

32. See also Sgt. C. Frank Shepard, First Michigan Cavalry, to wife, October 14, 1861, Washington, DC., C. Frank Shepard Papers, Schoff Collection, Clemens Library, University of Michigan; Pvt. George Baxter, Twenty-fourth Massachusetts, to brother Jim, December 14, 1861, near Annapolis, MD, George H. Baxter Correspondence, Massachusetts Historical Society.

32. Sgt. E. C. Hubbard, Thirteenth Illinois, to brother, October 18, 1861, Linn Creek, MO, E. C. Hubbard Letters, Special Collections, University of Arkansas.

33. James Oakes, *The Ruling Race: A History of American Slaveholders* (New York: Vintage Books, 1983), 39.

34. Chaplain William Gibson, Forty-fifth Pennsylvania, to children, March 25, 1862, Otter Island, SC, William J. Gibson Letters, Harrisburg Civil War Round Table Collection, U.S. Army Military History Institute. A Wisconsin soldier similarly claimed that slavery led to a society with "no church bells, no schools, no education," and forced Southerners to live "in a state of mental darkness." C. McD, Eighth Wisconsin, to *Gazette*, November 18, 1861, Pilot Knob, MO, Quiner Papers, reel 1, vol. 2, pp. 22–23. See also M., Eighth Wisconsin, to *State Journal,* November 15, 1861, Pilot Knob, MO, ibid., p. 22; that soldier lamented, "books and newspapers are very rare, and schools and churches are like angels' visit—few and far between."

35. A vast literature exists on the "middle-class culture" of the antebellum and Civil War–era United States, particularly the North. As Mary Ryan showed in *Cradle of the Middle Class: The Family in Oneida County, New York, 1790–1865* (New York: Cambridge University Press, 1981), and as historians too numerous to mention confirmed, a middle class that encompassed much more than simply the appropriate income brackets was imbued with what Ryan and others depicted as "middle-class values," including literacy, self-discipline, domesticity and family life, and especially work. As Charles Sellers put it, "The so-called middle class was constituted not by mode and relations of production but by ideology. . . . A numerous and dispersed bourgeoisie . . . mythologiz[ed] class as a moral category. Scorning both the handful of idle rich and the multitude of dissolute poor, they apotheosized a virtuous middle class of the effortful." Charles Sellers, *The Market Revolution: Jacksonian America, 1815–1846* (New York: Oxford University Press, 1991), 237. That middle-class ideology and values pervaded even western states in the North was demonstrated by Julie Roy Jeffrey, *Frontier Women: "Civilizing" the West? 1840–1880* (New York: Hill and Wang, 1998), especially the introduction and chs. 1 and 4. For the applicability of Northern middle-class ideology to Union soldiers, see especially Reid Mitchell's *Civil War Soldiers* and *The Vacant Chair: The Northern Soldier Leaves Home* (New York: Oxford University Press, 1993) and Earl J. Hess's *Liberty, Virtue, and Progress: Northerners and Their War for the Union* (New York: New York University Press, 1997).

36. For example, Olmsted described pigs wandering around a Southern neighborhood because the dissipated owners could not be bothered, as he saw it, to build a respectable pen. Frederick Law Olmsted, *The Cotton Kingdom: A Traveller's Observations on Cotton and Slavery in the American Slave States* (New York: Knopf, 1962), 31. This work was first published as installments in the *New York Times* and then as three volumes: *A Journey in the Seaboard Slave States* (1856), *A Journey through Texas* (1857), and *A Journey in the Back Country* (1860).

37. Lt. George Landrum, Second Ohio, to sister, May 13, 1862, Huntsville, AL, George W. Landrum Letters, Western Reserve Historical Society. Leigh Webber, who called the owner of a fugitive slave trying to get to Trenton, TN, to see his wife "a perfect *Simon Legree*," was one of many soldiers who referred to *Uncle Tom's Cabin*. See Webber to Brown family, July 11, 1862, Gibson County, TN, John S. Brown Family Papers, reel 2, Kansas State Historical Society. In fact, I found more references to *Uncle Tom's Cabin* in Union soldiers' writings than to any other book except the Bible (even Shakespeare, whose popularity among ordinary, white nineteenth-century Americans Lawrence W. Levine showed in *High Brow/Low Brow: The Emergence of a Cultural Hierarchy in America* (Cambridge, MA: Harvard University Press, 1988).

38. Pvt. Leigh Webber, First Kansas, to Brown family of Kansas, July 11, 1862, Gibson County, TN, John S. Brown Family Papers, reel 2, Kansas State Historical Society. Many other soldiers commented on how actually observing slavery and interacting with slaves forced them to change their minds. A Michigan soldier noted that his senior officer, who had "always been very bitter on the Abolitionists," spent hours in waist-high water "to help 20 contrabands across the river" to reach Fortress Monroe and haven from their masters. The officer explained his apparent change of heart by saying, "they looked so frightened that he had to help them." Lt. Charles Haydon, Second Michigan, journal, March 24, 1862, near Fortress Monroe, VA, in Stephen W. Sears, ed., *For Country, Cause and Leader: The Civil War Journal of Charles B. Haydon* (New York: Ticknor and Fields, 1993), 212. While poking around a North Carolina town, George Baxter and some comrades from a New Hampshire regiment ran across "the old fashioned *stocks and whipping post*" used to punish slaves. "These last named relics of barbarism were not long left standing," Baxter assured his brother, "for the N.H. boys procured an axe and soon leveled with with [*sic*] the ground." Pvt. George Baxter, Twenty-fourth Massachusetts, to brother Jim, March 10, 1862, on steamer *Vidette* off NC coast, George H. Baxter Correspondence, Massachusetts Historical Society.

39. Sgt. Luther Furst, Signal Corps, Thirty-ninth Pennsylvania, diary, May 11, 1862, York River, VA, Luther Furst Diary, Harrisburg Civil War Round Table Collection, U.S. Army Military History Institute.

40. W. D. W., Seventh Wisconsin, to his hometown newspaper, December 16, 1861, Arlington Heights, VA, Quiner Papers, reel 1, vol. 2, pp. 5–6. Many others were bothered by the way slavery allowed the sexual exploitation of women. In his diary, Daniel Thurber Nelson reflected on a visit to a Virginia plantation, where he witnessed a "woman not over 25 years old with 7 children, and 4 or 5 white." When another young mother was asked if she was married, she "hid her face." The whole scene smacked of "degradation and vice" to Thurber, who concluded simply, "this is slavery." Assistant Surgeon Daniel Thurber Nelson, diary, June 16, 1862, on a hospital transport during the Peninsula Campaign, Pamunkey River, VA, Daniel Thurber Nelson Papers, Vermont Historical Society.

41. Peter Kolchin, *American Slavery, 1619–1877* (New York: Hill and Wang, 2003), 126. Soldiers did not have statistical information available, but observation and conversation with slaves told them that family separation was a common fact of slave life.

42. Sgt. Cyrus Boyd, Fifteenth Iowa, diary, February 10, 1863, Providence Lake, LA, Cyrus F. Boyd Collection, Kansas City Public Library.

43. Sgt. J. Q. A. Campbell, Fifth Iowa, to *Ripley Bee*, July 9, 1862, near Rienzi, MS, in Grimsley and Miller, *The Union Must Stand*, 207.

44. Sgt. David Nichol, Battery E, Pennsylvania Light Artillery, to father, February 1, 1862, Point of Rocks, MD, David Nichol Papers, Harrisburg Civil War Round Table Collection, U.S. Army Military History Institute. Meanwhile, an enlisted New Yorker verbally tipped his cap to the bravery of two young runaway slaves who simply "made up their minds not [to] be slaves any longer and therefore left" their master, making their way to Union lines and a future of freedom. Sgt. Uberto Burnham, Seventy-sixth New York, to parents, February 10, 1862, Meridian Hill, Washington, DC, U. A. Burnham Papers, New York State Library.

45. The central point that slaves were primarily responsible for linking emancipation and the Union war effort is not new; its seminal expression appears in Berlin et al., *Freedom: A Documentary History of Emancipation, 1861–1867*, ser. 1, vol. 1, *The Destruction of Slavery*, 1–56. This piece cites white Union enlisted soldiers as the crucial mechanisms by which slaves accomplished that feat. Slaves convinced enlisted soldiers, who modified both their beliefs and their behavior. Meanwhile, enlisted men used letters, camp newspapers, and their own actions to influence the opinions of civilians and leaders, who, lacking soldiers' direct contact with slaves, the South, and the experience of living on the front lines in a war that most people wanted over, lagged behind soldiers in their stances on emancipation. Enlisted men often outpaced their superior officers in opposing slavery. Charles Brewster, for example, reported that his regiment was "almost in a mutiny" because the cap-

tain and major wanted to return runaway slaves to owners, while the enlisted men and some of the junior officers refused to "be instrumental in returning a slave to his master in any way shape or manner." Lt. Charles Brewster, Tenth Massachusetts, to mother, March 5, 1862, Washington, DC, in David W. Blight, ed., *When This Cruel War Is Over: The Civil War Letters of Charles Harvey Brewster* (Amherst: University of Massachusetts Press, 1992), 92. The point, however, is not that slaves convinced soldiers and then soldiers turned around and dutifully passed on their new views to officers. Instead, through a series of overlapping experiences and interactions with slaves, enlisted men changed their ideas and then their behavior, and officers wound up sanctioning the new behavior with policy shifts. Similarly, Mark Grimsley argued in *The Hard Hand of War: Union Military Policy toward Southern Civilians, 1861–1865* (New York: Cambridge University Press, 1995) that interactions with white Southerners led Union soldiers to change their attitudes and then their behavior regarding property policy, which officers were then required to sanction through policy revisions. I would like to thank Aaron Sheehan-Dean for pointing out the parallel with Grimsley's argument.

46. Pvt. Jasper Barney, Sixteenth Illinois, to brother-in-law Capt. John Dinsmore, October 24, 1862, Mound City Hospital, KS, John C. Dinsmore Letters, Illinois State Historical Library.

47. Enlisted soldier, Third Wisconsin, to *State Journal*, October 1861, near Harpers Ferry, VA, Quiner Papers, reel 1, vol. 1, p. 176.

48. *Camp Kettle*, December 30, 1861, 4, Beaufort, SC, Massachusetts Historical Society. One reason for sending the 500 copies north was so that they could be sold and the proceeds donated to the needy wife and children of a soldier, but it seems likely that the paper's creators also hoped that readers would think about what the newspaper had to say.

49. Pvt. Adelbert Bly, Thirty-second Wisconsin, to Anna, November 9, 1862, Memphis, TN, Adelbert M. Bly Correspondence, State Historical Society of Wisconsin.

50. Chip, Eleventh Wisconsin, to hometown newspaper, December 21, 1861, Sulphur Springs, KY, Quiner Papers, reel 1, vol. 2, p. 47. Another soldier smugly noted, "negroes have had more liberties since the army has invaded the State than ever before," but in the same breath he used the derogatory term "coonnesses" to refer to slave women working in the fields. See Marion, First Wisconsin, to *Daily Wisconsin*, May 1, 1862, Mt. Pleasant, TN, Quiner Papers, ibid., p. 162.

51. Capt. William Dunham, Thirty-sixth Ohio, to wife, June 3, 1862, Meadow Bluffs, VA, William Dunham Letters, Civil War Miscellany Collection, U.S. Army Military History Institute.

52. Dunham to wife, January 14, 1862, Summersville, VA.

53. Pvt. Orra Bailey, Seventh Connecticut, to wife, February 16, 1863, Fernandina, FL, Orra B. Bailey Papers, *People at War,* collection 10, reel 2.

54. For a long time, popular assumptions about soldiers' resistance to the Emancipation Proclamation went largely unchallenged by scholarship, and many key works focused on aspects other than soldiers' reactions. John Hope Franklin's *The Emancipation Proclamation* (Garden City, NY: Doubleday, 1963) examines the creation of the document and its impact on the war but concludes that "it is not possible to know the prevailing reaction of the average soldier" (127); it also speculates that the ordinary soldier's reaction was probably "not very important anyway," as long as he spread the news of the proclamation to slaves in the South (128). Louis Gerteis in *From Contraband to Freedman* (Westport, CT: Greenwood Press, 1973) assesses official Union policy toward former slaves and evaluates its impact on postwar conditions for African Americans, but he does not examine soldiers' responses to the proclamation. In "From Preliminary to Final Emancipation Proclamation: The First Hundred Days," *Journal of Negro History* 48, no. 4 (October 1963): 260–76, Roland McConnell discusses the proclamation as a turning point for both Union and Confederate armies but devotes little attention to soldiers' responses. Studies of soldiers often cover their views on slavery but generally do so over the course of the war as a whole, rather than scrutinizing their opinions at any one time. James McPherson finds a notable degree of Union support for emancipation in *Battle Cry of Freedom: The Civil War Era* (New York: Oxford University Press, 1988) and examines soldiers' views on slavery, among other topics, in *For Cause and Comrades.* McPherson also devotes a little space to soldiers' reactions to the proclamation, finding a broad array of opinion in the Union rank and file. He notes that the proclamation "intensified a morale crisis in Union armies" (123) but also argues that a significant portion of the troops endorsed the proclamation, mainly on utilitarian grounds. Reid Mitchell offers a brief but balanced assessment, writing that when the Emancipation Proclamation "made the war an antislavery war, some soldiers were jubilant, others horrified, and still more accepted the war's transformation with troubled minds" (*Civil War Soldiers,* 126). Useful as the insights of McPherson and Mitchell are, they have made little dent in the popular view; each year students enter my class confident in their assumption that Union soldiers hated the Emancipation Proclamation in particular and emancipation generally.

55. Lt. Benjamin Ashenfelter, Thirty-fifth Pennsylvania, to mother, November 12, 1862, near Rappahannock Station, VA, Benjamin Ashenfelter Letters, Harrisburg Civil War Round Table Collection, U.S. Army Military History Institute.

56. Sgt. John Babb, Fifth Maryland, to mother, December 18, 1862, Harpers

Ferry, VA, John D. Babb Family Papers, Special Collections, Woodruff Library, Emory University. Although Babb was personally suspicious of emancipation, he attributed the low spirits among soldiers in general primarily to military setbacks.

57. Pvt. Charles Musser, Twenty-ninth Iowa, to father, February 3, 1863, near Helena, AR, in Barry Popchock, ed., *Soldier Boy: The Civil War Letters of Charles O. Musser, 29th Iowa* (Iowa City: University of Iowa Press, 1995), 28, 25. Although many later historians regard its figures as too high, Ella Lonn's *Desertion during the Civil War* (Gloucester, MA: American Historical Association, 1928; Lincoln: University of Nebraska Press, 1998) remains the most extensive treatment of desertion in the Union army. Lonn estimates that as many as 25 percent of Union troops were improperly absent from the Army of the Potomac on January 26, 1863. Whether men were leaving temporarily, captured by the enemy, or outright deserting, their numbers grew every day. In the West, there were about half as many unaccounted-for soldiers. Despite these high figures, Lonn regards most of these absences as temporary and shows that as 1863 progressed, desertion and straggling dramatically declined to nearly nothing in the Union army (see 145–46, 152, and tables III and V in the appendix). The frequency of desertion varied by region. Lonn reveals comparatively high desertion rates for Illinois, Indiana, and Wisconsin and reports that at "the height of the Copperhead sympathy in 1863," "absenteeism" was especially "brazen" among Indiana and Illinois troops (152, 204).

58. Cpl. Elijah Penny, Fourth New York Artillery, to wife, November 30, 1862, Penny Family Papers, New York State Library.

59. Cpl. Mitchell Thompson, Eighty-third Illinois, to wife, April 10, 1863, Ft. Donelson, TN, Mitchell Andrew Thompson Letters, Tennessee State Library and Archives. Of the first 104 soldiers that I encountered who explicitly addressed the Emancipation Proclamation (or an obvious synonym, such as "the President's Proclamation") in their writings and took a stance on it between September 1862 and June 1863, 79 of them actively supported the proclamation, and 25 opposed it. Others mentioned or noted the proclamation but did not take a definite position on it. Many more soldiers wrote about slavery—mainly to demand its destruction as the only way to end the war—and many others treated the related topic of black enlistment. Most of the 104 wrote about the proclamation more than once, and many claimed that their views represented those of the entire regiment.

60. A private in the Illinois cavalry, to editor, March 26, 1863, Germantown, TN, in *Quincy Whig and Republican*, November 11, 1863, Illinois State Historical Library.

61. Pvt. John Strayer, Twelfth Indiana, to Miss Griggs, March 23, 1863, Camp Bayard, VA, Virginia Southwood Collection, Western Historical Manuscripts Collection, University of Missouri, Columbia.

62. Sgt. James Dodds, 114th Illinois, to friend Miss Lake, March 18, 1863, Helena, AR, John L. Harris Papers, Illinois State Historical Library. Similarly, when the men of the 105th Ohio "heard that there is also a story going the rounds in the north that the soldiers of Ohio, Indiana, Illinois and other western states that are in the army of the west are willing to throw down their arms and let the cause go as it will," they passed resolutions supporting the Emancipation Proclamation and criticizing its opponents as "traitors to our cause and country." Pvt. John Nesbitt, 105th Ohio, to family, February 18, 1863, Murfreesboro, TN, James Nesbitt-Isaac Raub Papers, Western Reserve Historical Society.

63. Pvt. William Lewis, Twenty-sixth Missouri, to wife and children, March 18, 1863, near Helena, AR, William Emmerson Lewis Letters, Western Historical Manuscripts Collection, University of Missouri, Columbia.

64. Gen. George McClellan to President Abraham Lincoln, July 1862, Harrison's Landing, VA, in Stephen Sears, ed., *The Civil War Papers of George B. McClellan: Selected Correspondence* (New York: Ticknor and Fields, 1989), 344–46.

65. McPherson, *Battle Cry of Freedom*, 498.

66. Cpl. John Ellis, 111th Pennsylvania, to nephew, February 1863, Acquia Creek, VA, Ellis-Marshall Family Papers, Harrisburg Civil War Round Table Collection, U.S. Army Military History Institute.

67. Pvt. Edwin Wentworth, Thirty-seventh Massachusetts, to *Argus,* April 4, 1863, near Falmouth, VA, Edwin O. Wentworth Papers, Library of Congress.

68. Sgt. Cyrus Boyd, Fifteenth Iowa, diary, February 9, 1863, on steamer *Maria Downing* in LA, Cyrus F. Boyd Collection, Kansas City Public Library.

69. Sgt. John Babb, Fifth Maryland, to parents and siblings, October 3, 1862, near Harpers Ferry, VA, John D. Babb Family Papers, Special Collections, Woodruff Library, Emory University.

70. Pvt. Phillip Reilly, Twenty-ninth Missouri, to brother, March 31, 1863, before Vicksburg, MS, Philip A. Reilly Letters, Western Historical Manuscripts Collection, University of Missouri, Rolla.

71. Pvt. David Massey, Thirty-third Missouri, to father, January 11, 1863, and to sister, January 26, 1863, near Helena, AR, David T. Massey Letters, Missouri Historical Society. Kentuckian Terah Sampson held the Confederates accountable for the Emancipation Proclamation because, by starting a war to protect slavery, they brought emancipation on themselves and placed Sampson in the disagreeable position of being "in the army for to free nigros." Pvt. Terah Sampson, Sixth Kentucky, to mother, January 9, 1863, near Murfreesboro, TN, Terah W. Sampson Letters, Filson Club.

72. Sgt. Cyrus Boyd, Fifteenth Iowa, diary, February 9, 1863, on board

steamer *Maria Dowling* in LA, Cyrus F. Boyd Collection, Kansas City Public Library.

73. Pvt. Chauncey Welton, 103rd Ohio, to parents, March 7, 1863, Benson Bridge, KY, Chauncey B. Welton Letters, Southern Historical Association, University of North Carolina, Chapel Hill.

74. Pvt. Fred. Pettit, 100th Pennsylvania, to parents and siblings, March 12, 1863, Newport News, VA, in William Gavin, *Infantryman Pettit: The Civil War Letters of Corporal Frederick Pettit, Late of Company C 100th Pennsylvania Veteran Volunteer Infantry Regiment "The Roundheads"* (Shippensburg, PA: White Mane, 1990), 65. Despite the title of this collection, Pettit was not promoted to corporal until June 23, 1864, one month before his death at Cold Harbor.

75. Capt. Amos Hostetter, Thirty-fourth Illinois, to sister and brother-in-law, January 29, 1863, Murfreesboro, TN, Illinois State Historical Library. Thinking along similar lines, David Nichol reassured his parents that he was "no nigger worshiper" but nonetheless welcomed the proclamation for striking "at the root of the Evil" and helping to "end this war." Sgt. David Nichol, Pennsylvania Light Artillery, to parents and siblings, January 4, 1863, near Fairfax Station, VA, David Nichol Papers, Harrisburg Civil War Round Table Collection, U.S. Army Military History Institute.

76. Pvt. Lucius Wood, 121st Ohio, to parents, March 5, 1863, Franklin, TN, E. G. Wood Family Papers, Western Reserve Historical Society.

77. Pvt. Chauncey Welton, 103rd Ohio, to parents, June 15, 1863, Camp Stirling, KY, Chauncey B. Welton Letters, Southern Historical Association, University of North Carolina, Chapel Hill.

78. Sgt. Mjr. Stephen Fleharty, 102nd Illinois, to *Rock Island Argus,* January 23, 1863, Gallatin, TN, in Philip J. Reyburn and Terry L. Wilson, eds., *"Jottings from Dixie": The Civil War Dispatches of Sergeant Major Stephen F. Fleharty, U.S.A.* (Baton Rouge: Louisiana State University Press, 1999), 100.

79. Pvt. and clerk Jacob Seibert, Ninety-third Pennsylvania, to father and all, January 10, 1863, near Falmouth, VA, Seibert Family Papers, Harrisburg Civil War Round Table Collection, U.S. Army Military History Institute.

80. Pvt. Caleb Beal, Fourteenth New York State Militia, to uncle, February 7, 1863, Belle Plain, VA, Caleb Hadley Beal Papers, Massachusetts Historical Society. See also Cpl. William Ross, Fortieth Illinois, to father, February 2, 1863, Davis Mills, MS, William H. Ross Letters, Chicago Historical Society.

81. Pvt. Caleb Beal, Fourteenth New York State Militia, to uncle, June 8, 1863, Brooks Station, VA, Caleb Hadley Beal Papers, Massachusetts Historical Society. After serving with several companies of soldiers from New York and New England, as well as with two companies of white Unionists from North Carolina and a company of black soldiers, Samuel Storrow remarked, "it is very

noticeable that those who have been opposed to arming blacks, have nothing to say *now* against fighting along side of them." Cpl. Samuel Storrow, Forty-fourth Massachusetts, to parents, April 13, 1863, Washington, NC, Samuel Storrow Papers, Massachusetts Historical Society.

82. Lt. Caleb Beal, 107th New York, to parents, October 12, 1863, Elk Springs, TN, Caleb Hadley Beal Papers, Massachusetts Historical Society. Beal transferred to the 107th New York and received a promotion to lieutenant in the spring of 1863, but he was demoted back to private in December 1863.

83. Pvt. John Benson, Fifth Kansas Cavalry, to editor April 15, 1863, Helena, AR, *Rock Island Weekly Union,* May 6, 1863, 1, Illinois State Historical Library. Lt. Peter Eltinge, 145th New York, used similar logic in a letter to his father written from Port Hudson, LA, on May 30, 1863 (Eltinge-Lord Family Papers, Special Collections, Perkins Library, Duke University). A Michigan soldier who believed that western troops looked more favorably on the use of black soldiers than did the Army of the Potomac attributed the difference to the greater practicality of the former. See Capt. Charles Haydon, Second Michigan, journal, June 20, 1863, near Jackson, MS, in Sears, *For Country, Cause and Leader,* 333.

84. Pvt. John Harris, Fourteenth Illinois, to cousin Susan Lake, May 2, 1863, Memphis, TN, John Lindley Harris Papers, Illinois State Historical Library.

85. Pvt. Milton H. Bassett, U.S. Telegraph Service, January 11, 1863, S. W. Pass, LA, Milton Humphrey Bassett Papers, Connecticut Historical Society. Bassett assumed that black soldiers were immune to tropical illnesses because the biting mosquitoes "could not pierce" blacks' darker skin.

86. Lt. Anson Patterson, 100th Illinois, to aunt, June 8, 1863, near Murfreesboro, TN, Anson Patterson Papers, Illinois State Historical Library.

87. Pvt. Carlos Lyman, Sixth Ohio Cavalry, to parents and siblings, March 2, 1863, Camp Ohio, Washington, DC. In another missive, written after Lyman had become a lieutenant in a black regiment, he cheered black soldiers, who "have raised themselves and all mankind in the scale of manhood by their bold achievements." Lt. Carlos Lyman, 100th U.S. Colored Troops, to parents and siblings, June 21, 1864, before Petersburg, VA, Carlos Parsons Lyman Papers, Western Reserve Historical Society.

88. Sgt. Pliny Jewett, First Connecticut Cavalry, to Steve, May 20, 1864, Fredericksburg, VA, Jewett Family Papers, Virginia Historical Society. "Some of the colored troops are the best drilled troops I ever say they make good soldiers, the very best," noted a cavalryman in Virginia. Pvt. William Hill, Ninth New York Cavalry, diary, March 7, 1864, near Williamsburg, VA, William G. Hill Diary, *People at War,* collection 126, reel 49. See also Pvt. Orra Bailey, Seventh Connecticut, to wife, March 13, 1863, Fernandina, FL, Orra B. Bailey Papers, *People at War,* collection 10, reel 2. The importance of black soldiers

in changing whites' opinions is a main argument of Dudley Cornish's classic study *The Sable Arm: Black Troops in the Union Army, 1861–1865* (1966; reprint, Lawrence: University Press of Kansas, 1987), especially ch. 3.

89. Lt. Henry Kircher, Twelfth Missouri, to father, April 19, 1863, Young's Point, LA, Engelman-Kircher Papers, Illinois State Historical Library.

90. Sgt. James Jessee, Eighth Illinois, diary, December 31, 1863, Helena, AR, James W. Jessee Diaries, Special Collections, Spencer Library, University of Kansas. A New Hampshire soldier agreed that God had sent a "durstructive war" as a rebuke to all who, through sins of commission or omission, allowed slavery to woo them away from "the side of truth and rite." Pvt. Roswell Holbrook, Fourteenth New Hampshire, to cousin, January 11, 1864, Washington, DC, Roswell Holbrook Letters, Vermont Historical Society.

91. Lt. J. Q. A. Campbell, Fifth Iowa, diary, November 12, 1863, near Winchester, TN, in Grimsley and Miller, *The Union Must Stand,* 131.

92. Campbell diary, July 4, 1863, near Vicksburg, MS, in ibid., 110.

93. Pvt. Wilbur Fisk, Second Vermont, to *Green Mountain Freeman,* August 13, 1863, near Warrenton, VA, in Emil Rosenblatt and Ruth Rosenblatt, eds., *Hard Marching Every Day: The Civil War Letters of Private Wilbur Fisk, 1861–1865* (Lawrence: University Press of Kansas, 1992), 135. That Fisk wrote this letter to a public forum, his hometown newspaper, suggests that he may have hoped to change the attitudes he wrote about.

94. Lt. Joseph Scroggs, Fifth U.S. Colored Troops, diary, March 30, 1864, near Norfolk, VA, Joseph Scroggs Diary, *Civil War Times Illustrated* Collection, U.S. Army Military History Institute.

95. Pvt. Wilbur Fisk, Second Vermont, to *Green Mountain Freeman,* February 8, 1865, City Point, VA, in Rosenblatt and Rosenblatt, *Hard Marching Every Day,* 308–9.

96. Capt. Carlos Lyman, 100th U.S. Colored Troops, to sister, February 12, 1865, Camp Foster, TN, Carlos Parsons Lyman Papers, Western Reserve Historical Society.

97. Pvt. Constant Hanks, Twentieth New York Militia, to mother and sister, April 1, 1864, near Brandy Station, VA, Constant Hanks Papers, Special Collections, Perkins Library, Duke University.

98. For more, see Glatthaar, *Forged in Battle,* 81–84.

99. Capt. M. M. Miller, Ninth Louisiana, to aunt, June 10, 1863, above Vicksburg, MS, published in *Galena (IL) Advertiser,* reprinted in *Anglo-African,* July 11, 1863, 1.

100. *Mail Bag,* March 28, 1864, Lexington, KY, private collection of Donna Casey. The *Mail Bag* (sometimes called the *Army Mail Bag*) was the newspaper of the Seventy-ninth Ohio and Fifth Ohio Battery.

101. *Soldier's Letter,* June 17, 1865, and February 13, 1865, Fort Riley, KS,

Kansas State Historical Society. The *Soldier's Letter* was the newspaper of the Second Colorado Cavalry.

102. Pvt. Jacob Behm, Thirty-eighth Illinois, to sister and brother-in-law, February 1, 1864, Scottsboro, AL, Jacob Behm Correspondence, *Civil War Times Illustrated* Collection, U.S. Army Military History Institute.

103. Sgt. Henry Hart, Second Connecticut Light Artillery, to wife, October 3, 1864, New Orleans, LA, Henry Hart Letters, Special Collections, Woodruff Library, Emory University.

104. Many soldiers described support for Lincoln in terms of the belief that a vote for Lincoln vindicated emancipation. Quincy Campbell, for example, called Lincoln's electoral triumph a "*glorious victory*" because the lopsided nature of the vote proved "that this war is *not* a failure, [and] that Slavery must die." See Campbell, Fifth Iowa Cavalry, diary, November 16, 1864, Nashville, TN, in Grimsley and Miller, *The Union Must Stand,* 193. McPherson has made this point about the 1864 election results in *For Cause and Comrades,* 129, 146.

105. Pvt. (acting as assistant surgeon) Robert Winn, Third Kentucky Cavalry, to sister, May 3, 1864, Ringold, GA, Winn-Cook Papers, Filson Club.

106. Pvt. Arthur Van Horn, Ninety-fifth Ohio, to wife, February 3, 1864, camp near Memphis, TN, Arthur Van Horn Family Papers, Library of Congress.

107. Pvt. Alonzo Rich, Thirty-sixth Massachusetts, to father, July 31, 1864, in front of Petersburg, VA, Alonzo G. Rich Papers, Civil War Miscellany Collection, 2nd ser., U.S. Army Military History Institute. In Atlanta just over a week later, Charles Bates heard "about the affair at Petersburg" and was even more eager to blame the disaster on black soldiers and to view the incident as justification for racial backtracking. "If Sherman does try to blow up anything I hope he will have sense enough to keep the nigger troops out of the way," he remarked. Sgt. Charles Bates, Fourth U.S. Cavalry, to parents, August 9, 1864, near Atlanta, GA, Charles Edward Bates Papers, Virginia Historical Society.

108. Sgt. William Stevens, Fourth Vermont, to sister, March 26, 1864, "Camp Parole," Annapolis, MD, in Jeffrey D. Marshall, ed., *A War of the People: Vermont Civil War Letters* (Hanover, NH: University Press of New England, 1999), 219. Stevens wrote this letter immediately after his release from a Richmond prison, as he awaited the opportunity to go home.

109. Pvt. George Hudson, 100th Illinois, to folks at home, April 10, 1865, Blue Springs, TN, George A. Hudson Collection, *People at War,* collection 138, reel 54.

110. A. Sanford, white officer of the Fiftieth U.S. Colored Infantry, to editor, April 6, 1865, before Ft. Blakely, AL, *Canton (IL) Register,* October 3, 1864, 1. Few sights cheered Vermonter Rufus Kinsley more than schools for former

slaves in New Orleans; their teachers were "doing for their country a nobler and braver work than has been done on the bloody battle-field of the war," cultivating equality and therefore "sav[ing] the Nation." Lt. Rufus Kinsley, Seventy-fourth U.S. Colored Troops, diary, March 6, 1865, Ship Island, MS, Rufus Kinsley Diary, Vermont Historical Society. Meanwhile, to transform the "land of boasted freedom" from mockery into reality, James Moore argued that neither American ideals nor the will of God allowed anything less than the creation of a nation "based upon equality & freedom to all white, black or copper colored." Assistant Surgeon James Moore, Twenty-second U.S. Colored Troops, to wife, September 25, 1864, Hanscom's Landing, VA, James Moore Papers, Special Collections, Perkins Library, Duke University.

111. Pvt. (acting as assistant surgeon) Robert Winn, Third Kentucky Cavalry, to sister, July 13, 1864, Connestaula River, near Resaca, GA, Winn-Cook Papers, Filson Club.

A Brothers' War?

Exploring Confederate Perceptions of the Enemy

Jason Phillips

Fifty years after Appomattox, Union General Joshua Chamberlain recounted a touching moment in his memoirs. On a cold, gray April morning in 1865, Chamberlain oversaw the ceremony in which General Robert E. Lee's infantry stacked arms, furled flags, and went home. As the remnants of the Army of Northern Virginia passed his men, Chamberlain was deeply impressed by the enemy "standing before us now, thin, worn, and famished, but erect, and with eyes looking level into ours." Their spirit awoke in Chamberlain "memories that bound us together as no other bond," vivid scenes of battlefield glory that united foes. Chamberlain asked his readers, "Was not such manhood to be welcomed back into a Union so tested and assured?" To acknowledge the brotherhood of war, Chamberlain ordered his men to salute the Southerners. Moved by the gesture, Confederate General John B. Gordon commanded his ranks to return the salute. It was "honor answering honor" or, as Gordon remembered, "a token of respect from Americans to Americans."[1]

Chamberlain's recollection evokes a brothers' war that continues to shape the history and memory of the Civil War. Filmmaker Ken Burns showcased the scene in his epic documentary *The Civil War* and considered the salute Chamberlain's "finest hour. . . . In reconciliation, Chamberlain made his greatest contribution to history." Like many others, Burns made sense of the war by viewing it as a "vast and complicated family drama." But as David Blight has cautioned, in a brothers' war, "whoever was honest in his devotion and courage was *right*"; the differences, enmities, causes, and consequences—indeed, the messy reality of the war—can dissolve within a myth of fraternity. The poignancy and necessity of reconciliation cannot be denied, but much evidence shows that the brothers' war was more postwar fabrication than wartime reality.[2]

Chamberlain followed the salute scene with an encounter that is less celebrated but equally important—his confrontation with an unconquered Rebel. When Chamberlain told the Confederate officer that "brave men may become good friends," the Southerner replied, "You're mistaken, sir. . . . There is a rancor in our hearts which you little dream of. We hate you, sir." Although Chamberlain never identified the man, he hinted that the officer was Henry Wise, a former governor of Virginia, fire-eating secessionist, and Confederate general who had lost a son in the war. Wise's remark sparked an escalating series of arguments between the two men over the particulars of a battle, the parole system, and the war's outcome. Tempers flared, and neither man would let the enemy have the last word. Wise told Chamberlain to "go home. . . . You take these fellows home. That's what will end the war." Chamberlain promised to return home after he saw the Rebels home first. "Home!" the Southerner cried. "We haven't any. You have destroyed them. You have invaded Virginia and ruined her. Her curse is on you."[3]

The confrontation reminds us that surrendering was complicated and torturous for Confederate soldiers. Many Rebels refused to acknowledge, let alone salute or embrace, victors who had come to represent evil incarnate. Their reluctance was rooted in powerful abstractions of the enemy that are endemic to warfare. All soldiers fight at least two enemies. On the one hand, they face actual opponents—the individual people, in all their complexities, who fill the ranks and support the other side's war effort. On the other hand, they fight the imagined foes—the caricatures, devoid of complexity and individuality, that animate fear and hatred. Confederates used a spectrum of colorful phrases to identify the enemy, but they usually crammed Unionists into one of two categories: inept, inferior adversaries or evil, barbaric ones. From the time they enlisted to oppose a menace they had not seen, Rebels used these abstractions to motivate themselves and justify their actions.[4]

During the Civil War the idea of a contest between brothers would have undermined Confederate resistance and nationalism. Abhorrence of killing spurs soldiers to abstract the enemy. Hiding the enemy's humanness—his integrity as an individual and his bonds of affection—behind a mask of hatred enables soldiers to kill without considering it murder. Only by denigrating and dehumanizing Northerners could Rebels maintain their sanity in the face of the heaps of dead men for which they were personally and corporately responsible. Enemy stereotypes joined a host of other elements, including group absolution, instinctual action acquired through drilling and experience, the chain of command, a combat "high," and the mechanical and physical distance between a soldier and his target, that diminished individual responsibility. The unprecedented destruction of the war made any real notion of brotherhood across the lines contradictory and absurd.[5]

Confederate nationalism also reinforced the creation and exaggeration of differences. If individual soldiers abstracted the foe to absolve themselves of murder, the whole Confederacy deprecated the Union to justify secession and independence. In wars, particularly civil wars, patriots brand the enemy as an ignoble opposite in order to affirm their right to be hostile and free. Scholars have correctly observed that many white Southerners abandoned the Confederacy as the war worsened. But soldiers' writings and other cultural evidence suggest that hatred for the North and love for the South grew in 1864 and 1865. As the war intensified and its costs increased, Rebel hatred for the Union deepened not only out of vengeance but also because the quest for nationhood required greater justification. Confederates struggled for recognition as a separate people. Viewing the enemy as brothers emphasized the commonalities between North and South, thereby undermining everything for which the Rebels fought and died.[6]

But stereotypes came with a heavy price. Skewed perceptions of the enemy stimulated men to fight and absolved them of guilt. Caricatures also shaped how soldiers interpreted the other side's actions, measured their resolve, and handled defeat. Speaking with the cynicism of a veteran, scholar Paul Fussell admitted that abstractions of the enemy create "a perceptual and rhetorical scandal from which total recovery is unlikely."[7] Enemy stereotypes soured the Rebels on surrendering, because capitulation meant submission to inferiors and reunion with barbarians. Evidence from the Confederacy's last days reveals this bitter reality. On the day he surrendered, a North Carolina captain thought that the worst result of capitulation was not the lost cause of independence but "the fact that these worthless fellows whom we have so often whipped . . . can now lord it over us and ours, can pass with the air of conquerors through our camps and hereafter throughout our whole country." He prayed that God would yet strike "some terrible retribution" against "this motley crew who have waged upon us so unjust so barbarous a warfare." A Tennessean's homeward trek took him through Sherman's destruction in Georgia. He observed, "Many of our men have no homes, their homes having been destroyed by an insolent and barbarous invader, and as yet their only thoughts are those of disappointment at not being able to punish the destroyers."[8] This essay explains why many Confederate soldiers came to see the enemy as barbaric and how this perception colored white Southerners' reactions to surrender. In the process, it challenges the idea of a brothers' war and the notion that widespread fraternity marked the war years.

In the early stages of the war, the image of an inept enemy coexisted with that of a barbaric figure. Antebellum stereotypes combined with war enthusiasm and early Confederate victories to depict Northerners as weaklings. Rebels inflated their own resources and underestimated their adversaries' chances. In this climate, a man who did not boast that he could whip ten Yankees risked being branded unpatriotic or, worse, a coward. Fort Sumter and Manassas convinced many Confederates that pasty Union men were no match for their steel. Federal armies were composed of mumbling immigrants, mill-town boys who had never owned a horse or a gun, urban scum who had enlisted for pay, and New England snobs who polished their buttons and boots but failed as fighters. A Virginia artilleryman considered the enemy "starving Irish who fight for daily bread," and "Western scoundrels . . . spawned in prairie mud." They were unhealthy specimens shrunken by factory work who could not possibly beat legions of Southern men raised in the rustic outdoors.[9]

For many Confederates, the Army of the Potomac embodied this perception of the foe. Lincoln's prized army was a collection of white-gloved recreants who could march in step and impress Washington socialites but withered before Rebel bullets. The slew of commanders who failed to rival Lee—braggarts such as John Pope and Joseph Hooker; the sadly incompetent Ambrose Burnside; and George McClellan, the blood-shy general who aspired to Napoleonic stature—seemed to prove Northern inadequacies. The portrait of an inept enemy fostered a sense that the Confederacy was unconquerable. As a Georgia private expressed it, the "degraded set of Northern people" could never suppress "a noble and respectable squad of Southerners."[10]

The most common name used for the Federals, "Yankee," encapsulated the idea of a pathetic foe. The term lumped all Northerners into a caricature of New Englanders as hypocritical reformers, cold industrialists, money-grubbers, and self-righteous Puritans. Branding men from Maine to Minnesota, regardless of their accent, vocation, or ethnicity, as Yankees perpetuated the Cavalier myth that Northerners were the natural-born adversaries of everything Southern. Only race could discount a Northern soldier from being a Yankee; African American troops were seldom called Yankees or even black Yankees. For Rebels, Yankees were white opponents who represented their mirror opposite, the warped and alien others who had forsaken the Revolution and threatened Southern existence. Some Confederates maintained images of inept Northerners to the very end, underestimating the Union's power and resolve even as its massive armies overwhelmed them. In this way, cultural perceptions of the enemy varied through time and place, thereby complicating simple narratives of change over time.[11]

Nonetheless, a close study of Confederate letters and diaries shows a pattern: as the war intensified, the enemy appeared more frequently (to Rebels and in their writing) as invading hordes. War is terrifying, and even a people as self-confident as the Confederates shivered at the specter of blue columns pouring across the border. Some Rebels imagined this nightmare at the war's inception when Lincoln called for thousands to quell the rebellion. Secession commissioners warned politicians from sister states to join the Confederacy or stand alone against "the same fell spirit, like an unchained demon, [which] has for years swept over the plains of Kansas, leaving death, desolation, and ruin in its track." In other words, the barbaric image of the North did not replace an earlier version of inept Federals halfway through the conflict. These stereotypes coexisted during the war and in the minds of Southerners. As the conflict worsened, however, a barbaric view of the adversary gained currency and influenced how white Southerners viewed the war and faced defeat. That shift had dire consequences. Whereas the caricature of an inept foe promoted ridicule, the figure of a savage enemy evoked hatred. The weak Yankee was fallible and, therefore, human. The barbarian, however, could be demonic or inhuman.[12]

Numberless, mercenary thugs lusting for Southern loot and women composed the minions of this image. If the Army of the Potomac and its carousel of commanders represented the inept foe, Sherman and his grim, unstoppable force embodied the brutal nemesis. Like pestilence, these dusty columns seemed to take everything of value (including slaves) and leave want and destruction in their wake. Their targets seemed to be women, children, and old people—not armed Confederates. Because such behavior disregarded the rules of chivalrous warfare, these men appeared to be demons, vandals, heathens, and animals. Worse still was the foreboding that endless reserves just like them waited at home for their chance to despoil Dixie.

To demonize the enemy, Rebels used savage and racist monikers, including "barbarian," "vandal," "abolitionist," and "miscegenator." In May 1864 a Confederate mother told her son how proud she was that her boy was fighting "the *vilest foe* the sun ever shown on which makes the sacrifice the greater." One Rebel yearned "to sweep from the face of the earth the base and amorous race of Puritans which has so degraded itself and villified and slandered the Southern ladies." He often called the enemy "misceginators" because of his conviction that miscegenation was "the new doctrine which has gained such popularity in Yankeedom." The Confederate religious press also propagated these stereotypes. Historian Harrison Daniel found that "the denominational newspapers referred to Northerners as barbarians—modern-day Vandals, Huns, and Goths—who were seeking to gratify their 'hellish lusts' at the expense of Southern womanhood. On one occasion a religious newspaper printed the letter of a soldier-minister who argued that it was one's religious duty to try to cut the throats of the 'monstrous' Northerners."[13] These barbaric images challenged the North's claims to higher civilization and loftier war aims. According to the Rebels, no Union war aim could conceal the baseness of Northern aggression nor compare with the justness—indeed, the righteousness—of Confederate self-defense. Southerners used scripture, such as Numbers 10:9, to support their case: "go to battle without any fear, and strike boldly for your homes and your altars without any guilt. The right, in such case of self-defense, will be on your side."[14]

The barbaric image of the North drew strength from its diverse sources. Reid Mitchell has argued that Confederates adapted the brutal figure from stock villains of the American past. Sketching a savage enemy mirrored Americans' apprehension of Indian braves and articulated Rebel fears that Federals, like Indians, threatened women and children. Framing Union soldiers as mercenaries harked back to old republican suspicions of the professional soldier-automaton as "the pliant tool of despotism" and expressed Confederate anxieties that the bluecoats would do anything for pay. In other words, both pictures conveyed an invaded people's terror that foes would use warfare to commit monstrous crimes. Savages, by definition, did not know the rules of civilized warfare, and automatons would ignore laws when ordered to do so. Mitchell's analysis is appealing because it highlights Confederates' belief that they were continuing, not forsaking, the American experiment. By painting Yankees with the same brush that colonists and patriots used to mark enemies, Rebels legitimized themselves as the true heirs of the spirit of 1776.[15]

The Union's hardening war policy and the Emancipation Proclamation amplified the barbaric image. Rebels believed that Yankee rulers harbored evil plans behind a facade of reunion and abolition. For many Confederates, restoring the Union seemed to be a Northern excuse to pillage and subjugate the South. Likewise, freeing the slaves really meant the elevation of blacks over whites, miscegenation between Yankee troops and slave wenches, and the rape of Southern ladies by freedmen and Negroes in blue uniforms. These jarring images illuminate Confederate fears that the enemy challenged the foundations of Southern society and manhood. As Southern men, Confederate soldiers drew their identity and authority from the submission of white women, the inferiority of blacks, and the ownership of land. As the war worsened, the enemy threatened to topple these pillars of the Old South. Stories of Union troops raping white women twisted the meaning of female submissiveness and challenged the masculine honor of men who had sworn to protect Southern women. Defiant slaves and black troops upended racial hierarchy. Blue columns occupied and confiscated Southern property. By 1864, it looked like the North was trying to erase Southern civilization and Southern manhood.

Confederate poetry and camp songs voiced these apprehensions while spreading the barbaric image. As a medium, music was particularly effective at glorifying the new nation, demarcating battle lines, and simplifying the issues and stakes involved. Recent histories of the nineteenth century suggest that the sounds of the Civil War profoundly affected how its participants understood the conflict. In particular, music pervaded the soldiers' world: songs wooed men to volunteer, entertained them in camp, sustained them on the march, fostered camaraderie, and consoled them before battle. Some men even sang to calm their nerves within the din of battle. The widespread popularity of music reflected both the sentimentalism of the time and soldiers' search for meaning, comfort, and pleasure in a dreary world.[16]

Confederate songs that called men to arms used the barbaric image to great effect. In July 1861 the newly recruited Kirk's Ferry Rangers held a barbecue in Catahoula, Louisiana. After ladies presented a flag to the unit, a glee club sang "Confederate Song," an anthem written for the men by their captain, E. Lloyd Wailes. The ballad warned the troops that

> Northern Vandals tread our soil,
> Forth they come for blood and spoil,
> To the homes we've gained with toil,
> Shouting "Slavery!"

The slavery Wailes wrote of was a Yankee vow to enslave white Southerners, not an outcry against black bondage.[17] Verses that depicted a Federal onslaught with lurid detail could have sobered Confederates to the odds they faced, but the songs intended and achieved a different result; terror heightened both the urgency of the call and the heroism of those who answered it. By representing the enemy as countless and ghastly, these ballads valorized Confederate regiments as bands of boys willing to oppose a nightmarish force with gallant but mortal hearts.

By darkening Dixie's borders with hordes eager to steal Southern land and women, the songs voiced men's gravest fears and presented them with two honorable options: victory or death. "The Southern Cross," sung to the tune of "The Star Spangled Banner," vilified "the Puritan demon" and envisioned Rebels

> With our front to the field,
> swearing never to yield,
> Or return, like the Spartan,
> in death on our shield.

The tune "Call, All! Call All!" included all Southerners in a sacrificial effort for independence:

Shoulder to shoulder, son and sire!
All, call all! To the feast of fire!
Mother and maiden, and child and slave,
A common triumph or a single grave.

The message was unmistakable: kill or be killed, defend your loved ones or watch them perish.[18]

The enemy appeared in Rebel music as "Yankee despots," "foul mudsills," "rowdies, thieves, vagabonds," "bootblacks, tinkers," "*black-guards*," "Northern scum," "Vandals," "Hessians," "hellish gnomes," "wild fanatic men," and "ruffian hordes."[19] All these slurs elevated Rebels through contrasts: the darker the invaders seemed, the more radiant the defenders felt. In some ballads the comparisons were explicit: "they're *hired* by their master, 'Abe'—*You* fight for *Liberty.*"[20] Such ballads claimed superiority for the Confederacy in three elements that were sacred to white Southerners: blood, cause, and valor.

Soldiers' writings show that music inspired them and helped them express their beliefs. In March 1864 Samuel Meetze, a North Carolina infantryman, swore, "I reather die then be com a Slave to the North." Suspecting that the war was entering its final phase, Meetze used song lyrics to express his views to his sister: "We will conquer or we will die. Tis, for our honer and our names . . . We rais the battle cry." Only weeks before his surrender, Virginia artilleryman James Albright composed a song, "We fight until we die." The central verse sang:

The Yankee thieves have pillaged
Many a Southern home,
And our sweethearts, wives & children
Now penniless do roam. . . .
Let vengeance be our cry
While for Southern Independence
We'll fight until we die!

These lyrics confirm that music offered soldiers more than amusing entertainment.[21] Songs articulated Confederates' deepest fears and strongest convictions. Moreover, finding Civil War music in letters and diaries demonstrates that the period's verse and poetry were more than detached art or imposed propaganda. Melodies emanated from a chorus of sentiment, and when they felt the need, soldiers like Meetze and Albright added their own variations on common themes.

Perhaps the strongest war verse was written by a Confederate prisoner of war, S. Teakle Wallis. From prison, Wallis sent "The Guerillas" to the printers of the *Richmond Examiner* via a paroled comrade. The ballad begins with "a friend" reporting atrocities to a group of Confederate irregulars. First the passerby details how the enemy is harming defenseless civilians:

> The shrieks and moans of the houseless
> Ring out, like a dirge on the gale.
> I've seen from the smoking village
> Our mothers and daughters fly;
> I've seen where the little children
> Sank down in the furrows to die.

Then the narrator stirs racist fears:

> They are turning the slaves upon us,
> And with more than the fiend's worst art,
> Have uncovered the fire of the savage,
> That slept in his untaught heart!
> The ties to our hearths that bound him,
> They have rent with curses away,
> And maddened him, with their madness,
> To be almost as brutal as they.

As a response to these atrocities, the traveler and the guerrillas swear an oath:

> Let every man swear on his blade,
> That he will not sheathe nor stay it,
> Till from point to hilt it glow
> With the flush of Almighty vengeance,
> In the blood of the felon foe.

The threat to women and property, including slaves, pervades Confederate verses and soldiers' writings. The patriarchy of Southern manhood rested on female submission, land ownership, and racial superiority. The Union war effort challenged all these elements of Southern male identity and could revoke a fourth: political rights. For many Confederate soldiers, losing these pillars of manhood doomed them to slavery or subjugation.[22]

In the soldier's world, abstractions not only survived but thrived. On occasion, troops expressed respect for their Northern adversaries. Fraternizing between the lines did occur, but as Randall Jimerson points out, soldiers considered friendly encounters "unusual and paradoxical." According to Jimerson, "most of the verbal exchanges" between combatants "were abusive." James McPherson agrees: "if soldiers' letters and diaries are an accurate indication, bitterness and hatred were more prevalent than kindness and sociability." Denigrating the opposition was too central to the process of warfare for soldiers to give it up. In 1864–1865 many conditions, some unique to soldiers' lives and others common to the white South, perpetuated simple views of the enemy. Union armies validated Rebel caricatures by introducing two features in the final campaigns that were tailor-made for the barbaric image of Yankees: total warfare and black soldiers.[23]

Few actions confirmed the Rebels' views of the enemy and deepened their animosity for Federals as thoroughly as the Union's total war offensives. Overwhelming legions of Yankees trampling crops, wrecking railroads, burning homes, freeing slaves, stealing valuables, and leveling cities actualized white Southerners' greatest fears of the enemy. Marching past General Phil Sheridan's work in the Shenandoah, a Virginia private exclaimed, "The Yankees left their mark of fire behind them." J. Tracy Power noted that Lee's men referred to the enemy as "vandals" and "miscreants" with greater regularity after Sheridan's campaign. When Sherman ordered the expulsion of all disloyal Southerners from Atlanta and refused to exchange prisoners, a Louisiana soldier spouted that such conduct "shows the true Yankee trickery of those inhuman vandals." Across the Mississippi, another Rebel witnessed "the hand of a more savage foe" in 1864. He noted in his diary, "Our camp is the ruins of a magnificent plantation." He slept "amidst a perfect forrest of blackened chimneys." Similar vistas seared Rebels' images of the enemy throughout the South.[24]

The impact of the desolation may have been greater on soldiers who did not witness it firsthand. Anxieties for loved ones and ghastly rumors dogged the minds of far-off veterans. From Richmond in November 1864, a Georgian had "no doubt the hated swarm of Yankees have passed over" his home like a plague of locusts. A member of the Army of Tennessee exclaimed, "citizens that live between here and Dalton sometimes come to us and say that the Yanks treat our people back there as mean as they can. . . . My God what will become of us?" The validity of some reports could not be denied. In June 1864 a Virginian's comrade received ominous mail from his sister: "She says the enemy has been at his father's and have done them an infinite amount of harm. They took all the negroes, all the meat and chickens and broke open every lock in the house and stole everything they could carry away which would be of any use to them or their families." Implausible accounts fanned the gravest fears. Just weeks before his surrender, a Virginia colonel read newspapers "full of details of the Yankees vilanous treatment of the people of North and South Carolina—outrages of the most scandalous character are openly perpetrated by officers and men upon the harmless ladies and beautiful females who may fall into their hands." Deserting was a common response to such stories; deepening hatred for the perpetrators was another. When he received word that some childhood friends had been imprisoned and sentenced to death for desertion by the Confederate army, Reuben Pierson marveled how any man "could not protect an aged parent or a loving sister from the abuses of the rabble" by remaining dutiful soldiers. For Pierson and thousands more, sustaining the Confederate ranks was the only way to protect the people at home. Without the armies, there was no country and thus no defense against Northern aggression.[25]

Federal total war policies fed an already flourishing genre of Confederate propaganda: the atrocity story. Retaliation for atrocities, real or imagined, had motivated belligerents on both sides since the war's inception. In the first years of the conflict, the Southern press claimed that Yankees bayoneted and shot Rebel prisoners, slit the throats and cut out the tongues of Confederate wounded, and even fired at Southerners while they helped wounded Federals caught between the lines. Some stories accused the Yankees of using poisoned bullets.[26]

By the war's final phase, Federal actions and Confederate fears expanded the focus of atrocity stories from the battlefront to the home front. The Southern religious press printed accounts of Federal soldiers beating civilian men and raping their wives and daughters. While

Sherman's army tramped through Georgia, a cavalryman was convinced that "the yankeys are destroying everything before them and ravishing women." Most accounts of sex or rape involved blacks. Historian James Silver noted that a "sure-fire method of creating a feeling of disgust for the Yankees" was to depict them in "captured cities parading up and down the streets with Negro women on their arms." Stories of black soldiers or slaves raping white women produced the greatest loathing. Malinda Taylor wrote to her husband, a soldier in the Army of Tennessee, that "there was a Negro burnt to death in Eutaw the other day for taking a white lady of[f] her horse and doing what he pleased with her." Similar accounts emanated from occupied Atlanta. Arkansan Thomas Key reacted to a "gloomy story of . . . the disgusting equalization of the whites and blacks under Sherman." According to rumor, "a big black negro man" propositioned "one of the most respected young ladies in the city." Key fumed, "The thought of such an occurrence arouses every nerve in my body for vengeance, and I feel like crying: 'Raise the black flag and let slip the dogs of war.'" Whether true or false, these stories vitalized Rebel images of invading hordes and muddied the delineation between legitimate acts of war and crimes, between myth and reality.[27]

Atrocities were important because they seemed to unmask the enemy's intentions. Accounts of miscegenation exposed the "true" impetus behind freeing the slaves: racial amalgamation. Reports of pillage and dominance uncovered the "actual" design for restoring the Union: subjugation of the white South. These perceptions, whether accurate or not, expressed Rebels' gravest fears and elevated their cause and self-identity. Terrible accounts reified the Confederates' self-image as innocent victims, as an oppressed, besieged, and violated minority deserving of independence and free of guilt. War correspondent Michael Ignatieff observed that "people who believe themselves to be victims of aggression have an understandable incapacity to believe that they too have committed atrocities. Myths of innocence and victimhood are a powerful obstacle in the way of confronting responsibility."[28]

The emancipation and Federal enlistment of thousands of former slaves further enraged Confederates and confirmed their perceptions of Yankees. Total warfare proved white Southerners' suspicions that Northerners were barbaric oppressors. Emancipation and black Union soldiers verified Confederate fears that Yankees were racial fanatics. Many Rebels believed that blacks were the victims, not the benefactors, of the Federals' actions. Deceitful Yankees freed slaves merely to provide labor and cannon fodder for the Northern war effort. A Georgia soldier told his wife, "a negro who knows what is for his good will never let the Yanks get him." Another Confederate thought that emancipation spelled doom for the blacks and consoled a friend whose slaves had left, claiming, "they will no doubt regret the day they left their comfortable homes, and kind Master and Mrs—but poor deluded things, they know not [what] suffering is before them." White Southerners mocked the morality of emancipation rather than facing the facts. Believing that blacks were being deceived by Union soldiers was more agreeable than accepting that slaves were justified in fleeing their masters. Expecting a terrible future for runaways was more palatable than anticipating racial equality or superiority for blacks. To denigrate the enemy and ease their own fears, Confederates highlighted evidence of the Yankees' disregard for blacks. A Confederate lieutenant wrote home that the enemy had abandoned blacks during a hasty retreat. During the pursuit, his men found black children "lying in the woods nearly dead." As a punishment, the lieutenant "made the Yankee prisoners carry the little darkies that were broken down. It was an amusing sight to see the little darkies with a leg on either side of a Yankee's neck marching to Petersburg."[29]

As the lieutenant's punishment suggests, Rebels ridiculed Federals' involvement with blacks. One Confederate denigrated the enemy, remarking, "the Yankees marched a line of battle, composed of white negroes and black negroes." In his eyes, white Northerners had descended to blacks' racial status because of their association in a biracial army. A South Carolina soldier laughed at a dream he had in which Henry Ward Beecher and other abolitionists were "married to the blackest, dirtiest, stinkiest . . . negro wench that can be found." A Virginia officer wished that "all the Yanks and all the negroes were in Africa." Some Rebels even hurled racist insults at enemy pickets. At Vicksburg, a defender asked the Union soldiers, "Have you Yanks all got nigger wives yet?" At Atlanta, a Confederate asked, "What niggers command your brigade?" and "Have the niggers improved the Yankee breed any?" Mocking the enemy's racial policies was another way of belittling the North and its war aims.[30]

Rebels' pity and ridicule ended, however, when African Americans entered the fray. Facing black opponents implied a parity between former slaves and Confederate soldiers that many Rebels could not stomach. A soldier manning Lee's trenches confessed that his unit abruptly ended a cease-fire when they realized that black Union troops had replaced white ones. Other Rebels showed no remorse over the murdering of blacks prisoners at Fort Pillow. A South Carolinian was "glad that Forrest had it in his power to execute such swift & summary vengeance upon the negroes, & I trust it will have a good influence in deterring others from similar acts." By killing black prisoners, Rebels revealed not only racist rage but also a chilling psychological distance from their victims. A Confederate song that celebrated Fort Pillow expressed the dehumanizing effects of war:

> The dabbled clots of brain and gore
> Across the swirling sabers ran;
> To me each brutal visage bore,
> The front of one accursed man.[31]

On August 1, 1864, Paul Higginbotham witnessed the horrendous product of these influences at the Crater: "Between 5 & 600 Negroes & white scoundrels now lie buried in the trenches, and in front of them several hundred more are lying there blackening Corpses in solemn warning to the survivors." Viewing the same corpses, John Walters morbidly quipped, "but for their hair and differences of features, the whites could not be distinguished from their colored brothers."[32] For Walters and others, the enemy was a mass of inferior beings who deserved to die terrible deaths for their destructive and radical practices.

The consequences of these perceptions were most evident when the Confederacy faced defeat. Many Confederates considered total war campaigns and the proliferation of black troops evil portents of the South's future should the rebellion fail. Federals increased the destructiveness of their campaigns to persuade Rebels to surrender, and in many respects, this approach worked. But total war also had the opposite effect of convincing many Confederates that surrendering would be worse than death. Many soldiers received letters from parents and spouses who had suffered occupation and devastation. One mother wrote to her son that "death is far preferable to subjugation to the vile Yankees—I know something about it now." As the war intensified, religious propaganda told soldiers to grasp independence or expect extermination at the hands of the brutal North. "What will become of us if defeated?" a Mississippi soldier asked. "Renewed trials, greater difficulties, and almost complete destitution; and withall slavery in its worst forms" was his answer. The destructiveness of Federal forces convinced a Georgia officer that "anything is better for us than to submit to Yankee rule. That people are determined upon our ruin and will carry it out if in their power." When he considered defeat, a South Carolinian thought it "better that every man, woman & child in the South should be buried together in one wide, common grave."[33] By 1865 these Confederates saw the war as an all-or-nothing proposition. If victory or death were the soldier's only honorable choices, independence or mass suicide were the only admirable options for the country.

As the Confederacy faded into oblivion, die-hard Rebels pleaded with their countrymen to persevere against the barbarians. Regiments from across the South sent resolutions to newspapers and to the Confederate Congress reminding their country of enemy atrocities and the hellish vision of submission. McGowan's Brigade of South Carolinians reasoned that if the Rebels had correctly judged four years ago "that the enemy intended to impoverish and oppress us, we *now know* that they propose to subjugate, enslave, disgrace and destroy us." Virginian infantrymen pleaded with the populace to resist "to the last extremity, a foe, subjection to whom would make life itself a burden." Another infantry regiment vowed, "it is better to die freemen than to live slaves." The officers and men of a Virginia regiment reminded citizens that the enemy had committed "the most fiendish outrages and cruelties; has desolated and destroyed our country and committed every barbarity recorded in the past annals of rapacity, wrong and rapine." These resolutions depicted the enemy burning Southern farms, raping Southern women, and elevating blacks over whites. A South Carolina brigade declared that "the outrages upon us by a base and unprincipled foe, in violation of all the usages of civilized warfare, have created an impassable gulf between the two sections, which must forever prevent all union or affiliation between them."[34] Reconciliation was the farthest thing from their minds.

When defeat became a reality, many Rebels expected the worst. After surrendering, a Virginia officer considered himself "a citizen-slave" of the North. Although the military surrenders had been quiet and even respectful, Confederates feared retribution from the government they had defied and from the millions they had enslaved. Many soldiers

summed up scenarios of confiscation, disfranchisement, imprisonment, and miscegenation in one word: subjugation. One Confederate
admitted that the "unknown horrors of *subjugation*" caused him so
much anxiety that his hair was turning gray. The abstractions of a barbaric enemy that had steeled Rebel resolve during the war now spawned
terrible images of the future. Rumors spread that the terms of surrender
included "all Confederate soldiers disfranchised; all property whatever
confiscated & turned over to the Yankees; and all commissioned officers exiled." The Yankees were implementing their plan to dismantle the
South and Southern manhood with it. As one cavalryman explained,
die-hard Rebels vowed to fight against being "ground to death by being
rob[b]ed of all our negroes, and lands and other property—not allowed
to Vote nor hold office any more." He and his comrades suspected that
the Yankees would parcel Confederate farms to freed people or sell the
land to pay Northern war debts. Many Confederates expected a future
that was darker than their worst wartime experiences. Everything they
had fought to prevent, all the nightmarish speculations they had read in
editorials and political addresses, every enemy atrocity they had heard
of, every fiendish act they had sung about darkened their horizon.[35]

   This fear and hatred must be weighed when historians estimate the
fraternity and reconciliation exhibited at Appomattox and elsewhere in
1865. Surely the impulse to forgive, forget, and return to peaceful ways
moved many Southerners. Rebels such as General John B. Gordon agreed
with Walt Whitman that the very word *reconciliation* was as "beautiful
as the sky."[36] But for every Gordon who saluted the victors and implored
his men to accept the terms of surrender, there was a Henry Wise who
insulted the enemy and vowed that the South would win yet. Although
simple disbelief and stubbornness contributed to this die-hard response,
deeper cultural values and the experience of war also shaped unconquered Rebels' reactions to surrender. Confederate perceptions of the
enemy worsened as the war worsened. The cultural change from denigrating the enemy as an inept foe to fearing him as a barbaric horde was
a complicated process that eludes narrative history. Some Southerners
accepted barbaric propaganda at the war's inception. Others acquired
that perspective after the actions of Yankees and slaves actualized such
notions. During 1864, a number of turning points and developments,
especially total war offensives and black troops, transformed the enemy
from inept Northerners to faceless barbarians for thousands of Rebels.

When these barbarians conquered them, Confederates faced an inexplicable defeat and a terrifying future.

The war seared these base perceptions of Northerners into the minds and hearts of millions of Southerners during their formative years. A leg wound received just days before Appomattox kept North Carolinian Reuben Wilson from going home. Stuck in a Union hospital, with "the fire of revenge flying from my eyes like sparks from a furnace," Wilson determined to take the oath of allegiance so that he could help send "good men" to state conventions and Washington. Wilson reasoned that "if every southern state will send two good senators we will . . . be able to check the republican party in their wild schemes." As if to show that his war continued, Wilson wore his Confederate uniform for the rest of his days.[37] Such thoughts and actions epitomized the unconquered loser. Wilson was one of countless Rebels whose refusal to quit marked the South for generations.

Confederates viewed Northerners as barbarians for many reasons. Some of these factors evaporated with capitulation, but others persisted long after the war. Confederates considered the enemy barbaric partly because the Union attacked the pillars of Southern society and manhood: land, women, white supremacy, and political rights. Reconstruction would challenge these pillars more than the war did. Reuben Wilson and other Confederate veterans were willing to do whatever it took to regain control of their society, to affirm their manhood, to defend their position in life, and to beat the barbarians in the end.

NOTES

1. Joshua Lawrence Chamberlain, *The Passing of the Armies: An Account of the Final Campaign of the Army of the Potomac, Based upon Personal Reminiscences of the Fifth Army Corps* (Lincoln: University of Nebraska Press, 1998), 260–61; John B. Gordon, *Reminiscences of the Civil War* (New York: Charles Scribner's Sons, 1905), 444.

2. Robert Brent Toplin, ed., *Ken Burns's* The Civil War: *Historians Respond* (New York: Oxford University Press, 1996), 158, 170; David W. Blight, *Race and Reunion: The Civil War in American Memory* (Cambridge, MA: Harvard University Press, 2001), 96. The success of reconciliation and the brothers' war theme has not only marginalized the significance of race and the war contributions of African Americans but also de-emphasized the hatred and defiance that Confederates felt in 1865.

3. Chamberlain, *Passing of the Armies*, 266–68; Brooks Simpson identifies

Wise in the introduction to this edition (see p. xiii). See also William Marvel, *Lee's Last Retreat: The Flight to Appomattox* (Chapel Hill: University of North Carolina Press, 2002).

4. Numerous studies beyond the field of Civil War scholarship informed this essay on the perceptions of the enemy. In particular, see John W. Dower, *War without Mercy: Race and Power in the Pacific War* (New York: Pantheon Books, 1986); Paul Fussell, *Wartime: Understanding and Behavior in the Second World War* (New York: Oxford University Press, 1989); and Jill Lepore, *The Name of War: King Philip's War and the Origins of American Identity* (New York: Knopf, 1998).

5. This is a subject that deserves greater attention. For soldiers' psychological distance from opponents, see S. L. A. Marshall, *Men against Fire: The Problem of Battle Command in Future War* (New York: William Morrow, 1947); J. Glenn Gray, *The Warriors: Reflections on Men in Battle* (New York: Harcourt, Brace, 1957); Ben Shalit, *The Psychology of Conflict and Combat* (New York: Praeger, 1988); and Dave Grossman, *On Killing: The Psychological Cost of Learning to Kill in War and Society* (Boston: Little, Brown, 1995).

6. Michael Ignatieff, *The Warrior's Honor: Ethnic War and the Modern Conscience* (London: Chatto and Windus, 1998), 51. Scholars of many wars, including King Philip's war, World War I, the Pacific war, and the Falklands war, have shown that diverse cultures fabricate similar sacred-profane dichotomies to mark the enemy. See Paul Fussell, *The Great War and Modern Memory* (London: Oxford University Press, 1975); Dower, *War without Mercy;* Lepore, *The Name of War;* Philip Smith, "Codes and Conflict: Toward a Theory of War as Ritual," *Theory and Society* 20 (February 1991): 103–38.

7. Fussell, *Wartime,* 115.

8. Henry Chambers, diary, April 9, 1865, Henry Alexander Chambers Papers, 1832–1925, Southern Historical Collection, University of North Carolina, Chapel Hill (hereafter SHC UNC); William E. Sloan, diary, May 3, 1865, Civil War Collections, Tennessee State Library and Archives.

9. C. G. Chamberlayne, ed., *Ham Chamberlayne—Virginian: Letters and Papers of an Artillery Officer in the War for Southern Independence, 1861–1865* (Richmond: Dietz Printing, 1932), 186. For more on the Yankee image, see Reid Mitchell, *Civil War Soldiers: Their Expectations and Their Experience* (New York: Touchstone, 1988).

10. Quoted in Randall C. Jimerson, *The Private Civil War: Popular Thought during the Sectional Conflict* (Baton Rouge: Louisiana State University Press, 1988), 127. Diverse events and figures in the war supported Rebels' perception of an inept foe. In addition to Lee and Jackson, Confederate cavalry leaders often provided the most colorful evidence that Southern intelligence, courage, and ability surpassed that of their Northern counterparts. When

Nathan Bedford Forrest, John Morgan, John Mosby, and J. E. B. Stuart humili-
ated Federal opponents, they produced an entire genre of legends. Ralph
Semmes, captain of the *Alabama*, mimicked these men's successes on the high
seas against overwhelming odds. In addition to Fort Sumter and Manassas,
Jackson's Valley Campaign and Lee's defense of Richmond during the Seven
Days' battles were offered as proof of Rebel military superiority.

11. At the Crater, one Rebel noted, "the negroes fought better than their white
Yankee brethren." Thomas Elder to Anna Fitzhugh (May) Elder, July 30, 1864,
Thomas Claybrook Elder Papers, Virginia Historical Society (hereafter VHS). See
also Milton Barrett to his brother and sister, August 1, 1864, in J. Roderick Heller
III and Carolynn Ayers Heller, eds., *The Confederacy Is on Her Way up the Spout:
Letters to South Carolina, 1861–1864* (Athens: University of Georgia Press, 1992),
123; and Edmund Fitzgerald Stone letter, date unknown, VHS.

12. Stephen F. Hale to Governor Beriah Mogoffin, December 27,
1860, quoted in Charles B. Dew, *Apostles of Disunion: Southern Secession
Commissioners and the Causes of the Civil War* (Charlottesville: University of
Virginia Press, 2001), 95. For how Union strategy affected Confederate civil-
ians' perceptions of the enemy, see Mark Grimsley, *The Hard Hand of War:
Union Military Policy toward Southern Civilians, 1861–1865* (Cambridge:
Cambridge University Press, 1995).

13. Mother to Dunbar Affleck, May 21, 1864, Thomas Affleck Correspondence and Writings, Hill Memorial Library, Louisiana State University (hereafter LSU); Thomas Key, diary, April 10, 1864, in Wirt Amistead Cate, ed., *Two
Soldiers: The Campaign Diaries of Thomas J. Key, C.S.A. and Robert J. Campbell,
U.S.A.* (Chapel Hill: University of North Carolina Press, 1938), 70. Key uses
"misceginator" in his December 7, 1864, entry (p. 164). It is worth noting that
Democrats used the term *miscegenator* to demonize Republicans during the
1864 presidential campaign. W. Harrison Daniel, *Southern Protestantism in the
Confederacy* (Bedford, VA: Print Shop, 1989), 39.

14. Ronald Glenn Lee, "Exploded Graces: Providence and the Confederate
Israel in Evangelical Southern Sermons, 1861–1865" (master's thesis, Rice
University, 1990), 145–46.

15. Mitchell, *Civil War Soldiers*, 24–25. For English impressions of Native
Americans, see Richard Slotkin, *Regeneration through Violence: The Mythology
of the American Frontier, 1600–1860* (Middletown, CT: Wesleyan University
Press, 1973), and James Axtell, *The European and the Indian: Essays in the
Ethnohistory of Colonial North America* (New York: Oxford University Press,
1981). For American views of standing armies during the Revolutionary era,
see Charles Royster, *A Revolutionary People at War: The Continental Army and
American Character, 1775–1783* (Chapel Hill: University of North Carolina
Press, 1979).

16. Civil War poetry and music provide examples of how popular culture shaped soldiers' perspectives, yet military historians seldom used them. Alice Fahs's cultural study of wartime literature points the way: *The Imagined Civil War: Popular Literature of the North and South, 1861–1865* (Chapel Hill: University of North Carolina Press, 2001). For the influences of music and the aural world in general on Civil War participants, see Mark M. Smith, *Listening to Nineteenth-Century America* (Chapel Hill: University of North Carolina Press, 2001). For Confederate music, see Willard A. Heaps and Porter W. Heaps, *The Singing Sixties: The Spirit of Civil War Days Drawn from the Music of the Times* (Norman: University of Oklahoma Press, 1960), and Francis A. Lord and Arthur Wise, *Bands and Drummer Boys of the Civil War* (New York: Da Capo Press, 1966). For music in battle, see Earl J. Hess, *The Union Soldier in Battle: Enduring the Ordeal of Combat* (Lawrence: University Press of Kansas, 1997), 112. For a comparative look at Japanese war songs, see Dower, *War without Mercy*, 213–14.

17. Frank Moore, ed., *Songs and Ballads of the Southern People, 1861–1865* (New York: D. Appleton, 1886), 109–10.

18. Ibid., 15, 16, 30–33.

19. Ibid., 66, 83, 72, 93, 97, 102, 131.

20. Ibid., 158.

21. Samuel S. Meetze to his sister, Mary, March 13, 1864, Confederate Papers, SHC UNC; James W. Albright, books, March 1, 1865, SHC UNC.

22. Moore, *Songs and Ballads*, 166–69. Perhaps the most remarkable atrocity song was James R. Randall's "At Fort Pillow." See Charles W. Hubner, ed., *War Poets of the South and Confederate Camp-fire Songs* (Atlanta: Charles P. Byrd, n.d.), 105–8. Randall justifies the Confederates' slaughter of hundreds of prisoners as retribution for numberless Federal offenses.

23. Jimerson, *The Private Civil War*, 175; James M. McPherson, *For Cause and Comrades: Why Men Fought in the Civil War* (New York: Oxford University Press, 1997), 152. Regiments of former slaves fought in 1863, but most Confederate soldiers did not oppose them until 1864. Rebels' savagery toward African Americans in blue can be reconciled with their support for enlisting slaves in their own army; many Confederate soldiers voiced a greater commitment to independence and victory than to the institution of slavery. For this debate, see Robert F. Durden, *The Gray and the Black: The Confederate Debate on Emancipation* (Baton Rouge: Louisiana State University Press, 1972), and Philip D. Dillard, "Independence or Slavery: The Confederate Debate over Arming the Slaves" (Ph.D. diss., Rice University, 1999).

24. Creed Davis, diary, October 6, 1864, Creed Thomas Davis Diary, VHS; J. Tracy Power, *Lee's Miserables: Life in the Army of Northern Virginia from the Wilderness to Appomattox* (Chapel Hill: University of North Carolina Press,

1998), 142–43; James Adams to parents, September 16, 1864, Israel L. Adams and Family Papers, LSU; William Heartsill, diary, July 31 and August 11, 1864, in Bell I. Wiley, ed., *Fourteen Hundred and 91 Days in the Confederate Army* (Jackson, TN: McCourt-Mercer Press, 1954), 211, 212.

25. Edgeworth Bird to Saida Bird, November 30, 1864, in John Rozier, ed., *The Granite Farm Letters: The Civil War Correspondence of Edgeworth & Sallie Bird* (Athens: University of Georgia Press, 1988), 218; Grant Taylor to Malinda Taylor, June 21, 1864, in Ann K. Blomquist and Robert A. Taylor, eds., *This Cruel War: The Civil War Letters of Grant and Malinda Taylor, 1862–1865* (Macon, GA: Mercer University Press, 2000), 262 (Taylor's apprehension for the region was heightened by the destruction he saw that corroborated stories from Dalton); Charles Blackford to Susan Leigh Blackford, June 18, 1864, in Susan Leigh Blackford, Charles Minor Blackford, and Charles Minor Blackford III, eds., *Letters from Lee's Army, or Memoirs of Life in and out of the Army in Virginia during the War between the States* (Lincoln: University of Nebraska Press, 1998), 257; Richard Launcelot Maury, diary, March 27, 1865, VHS; Reuben Pierson to William Pierson, ca. January 30, 1864, in Thomas W. Cutrer and T. Michael Parrish, eds., *Brothers in Gray: The Civil War Letters of the Pierson Family* (Baton Rouge: Louisiana State University Press, 1997), 226–27.

26. James W. Silver, *Confederate Morale and Church Propaganda* (Tuscaloosa, AL: Confederate Publishing Co., 1957), 85–86; Mitchell, *Civil War Soldiers*, 25–28. It is interesting to note that both Americans and Japanese accused the other side of similar atrocities in the Pacific war; see Dower, *War without Mercy*, 115–29. Bell Irvin Wiley, *The Life of Johnny Reb: The Common Soldier of the Confederacy* (Indianapolis: Bobbs-Merrill, 1943), 311. See also U.S. War Department, *The War of the Rebellion: A Compilation of the Official Records of the Union and Confederate Armies* (Washington, DC: Government Printing Office, 1880–1901), ser. 1, XII, pt. 2, 202–3; XX, pt. 1, 880; and LI, pt. 2, 329.

27. Daniel, *Southern Protestantism in the Confederacy*, 40; John Cotton to wife, ca. November 1864, in Lucille Griffith, ed., *Yours Till Death: Civil War Letters of John W. Cotton* (Birmingham: University of Alabama Press, 1951), 120; Silver, *Confederate Morale and Church Propaganda*, 87. Silver asserted, "the triple-edged combination of horrors at the North, atrocities of Northerners in the South, and the threat of overwhelming barbarism if the Confederacy failed, moved into high gear in the last two years of the war. Stories of desecrated churches, desolated homes, and outraged women became common." Malinda Taylor to Grant Taylor, September 2, 1864, in Blomquist and Taylor, *This Cruel War*, 280; Thomas J. Key, diary, September 23, 1864, in Cate, *Two Soldiers*, 138–39.

28. Ignatieff, *Warrior's Honor,* 176. Dower illuminated a similar relationship between atrocity myths and perceptions of the enemy in the Pacific war: "atrocities and war crimes played a major role in the propagation of racial and cultural stereotypes. The stereotypes preceded the atrocities, however, and had an independent existence apart from any specific event" (*War without Mercy,* 73).

29. Edgeworth Bird to Sallie Bird, August 28 and August 4, 1864, in Rozier, *Granite Farm Letters,* 196, 181; John Doyle to Maggie Knighton, August 26, 1864, Josiah Knighton and Family Papers, LSU; Charlie DeNoon to his parents, July 8, 1864, in Richard T. Couture, ed., *Charlie's Letters: The Correspondence of Charles E. DeNoon* (Bolling Island Plantation: R. T. Couture, 1982), 226.

30. Thomas Key, diary, December 7, 1864, in Cate, *Two Soldiers,* 164; James Brannock to Sarah Caroline (Gwin) Brannock, March 29, 1864, James Madison Brannock Papers, VHS; Henry Robinson Berkeley, diary, September 23, 1864, in William H. Runge, ed., *Four Years in the Confederate Artillery: The Diary of Private Henry Robinson Berkeley* (Chapel Hill: University of North Carolina Press, 1961), 101; Bell Irvin Wiley, *The Life of Billy Yank: The Common Soldier of the Union* (Indianapolis: Bobbs-Merrill, 1952), 352–53.

31. Edmund Fitzgerald Stone to Samuel Marion Stone, n.d., Edmund Fitzgerald Stone Letter, VHS; James Madison Brannock to Sarah Caroline (Gwin) Brannock, March 29, 1864, James Madison Brannock Papers, VHS; James R. Randall, "At Fort Pillow," in Hubner, *War Poets of the South,* 108.

32. Paul Higginbotham to Aaron Higginbotham, August 1, 1864, Paul Higginbotham Letters, VHS; John Walters, diary, August 1, 1864, in Kenneth Wiley, ed., *Norfolk Blues: The Civil War Diary of the Norfolk Light Artillery Blues* (Shippensburg, PA: White Mane, 1997), 140. For more Confederate accounts of the Crater, see Power, *Lee's Miserables,* 135–40. Some Confederates were sickened by the massacres.

33. Parents to Fred Fleet, June 12, 1864, in Betsy Fleet and John D. P. Fuller, eds., *Green Mount: A Virginia Plantation Family during the Civil War: Being the Journal of Benjamin Robert Fleet and Letters of His Family* (Lexington: University Press of Kentucky, 1962), 332; Silver, *Confederate Morale and Church Propaganda,* 82–84, 90–91; William L. Nugent to Eleanor Smith Nugent, May 5, 1864, in William M. Cash and Lucy Somerville Howorth, eds., *My Dear Nellie: The Civil War Letters of William L. Nugent to Eleanor Smith Nugent* (Jackson: University Press of Mississippi, 1977), 174; Edgeworth Bird to Wilson Bird, January 17, 1865, in Rozier, *The Granite Farm Letters,* 236–37; James Madison Brannock to Sarah Caroline (Gwin) Brannock, March 29, 1864, James Madison Brannock Papers, VHS. Brannock had a similar reaction after the fall of Atlanta; see Brannock to Brannock, September 12, 1864, Brannock Papers, VHS.

34. Resolutions Adopted by McGowan's Brigade, South Carolina Volunteers (Richmond, 1865); Resolutions Passed at a Meeting of the Ninth Virginia Infantry (Richmond, 1865); Resolutions Passed at a Meeting of the 14th Virginia Infantry (Richmond, 1865); Resolutions Adopted by the Officers and Men of the 57th Virginia Regiment (Richmond, 1865); Resolutions Adopted by Bratton's Brigade, South Carolina Volunteers (Richmond, 1865). See also Resolutions Adopted by Company "H," "I" and "K" Thirteenth Virginia Infantry, January 28, 1865 (Richmond, 1865): "we ridicule, as absurd, the idea of reconstruction; for we believe re-union would subject us again to the government of that sectional majority which is confined to the abolition States, and which is alike a stranger to our institutions, feelings and habits of thought as a people, and foreign to our territory."

35. Giles Cooke, diary, April 13, 1865, Giles Buckner Cooke Diary, 1864–1865, VHS; Jared Y. Sanders II to "Bessie," May 11, 1865, Jared Y. Sanders and Family Papers, LSU; Samuel T. Foster, diary, May 4, 1865, in Norman D. Brown, ed., *One of Cleburne's Command: The Civil War Reminiscences and Diary of Capt. Samuel T. Foster, Granbury's Texas Brigade, CSA* (Austin: University of Texas Press, 1980), 174.

36. Walt Whitman, "Reconciliation," in *Drum Taps* (New York: Bunce and Huntington, 1865).

37. Reuben Wilson to his aunt, Mrs. Beverly Jones, May 13, 1865, Jones Family Papers, SHC UNC. For Confederate civilians' reactions to defeat, see Anne Sarah Rubin, *A Shattered Nation: The Rise and Fall of the Confederacy, 1861–1868* (Chapel Hill: University of North Carolina Press, 2005).

"THE ARMY IS NOT NEAR SO MUCH DEMORALIZED AS THE COUNTRY IS"

Soldiers in the Army of Northern Virginia and the Confederate Home Front

Lisa Laskin

By the last year of the Civil War, many soldiers in the Army of Northern Virginia (ANV) still believed that their army offered the best opportunity to save the Confederacy's fortunes. Despite the increasing stream of deserters, enough men stayed in the ranks and remained committed to the cause (albeit for a range of reasons) to maintain the ANV as a formidable presence on the eastern battlefields. Commitment to Confederate war aims, a common feeling of superiority over the enemy, and pride in their army and its leadership contributed to ANV soldiers' unity and high morale and supported an esprit de corps that persisted, even if dimmed by dire circumstances, until the last days of the war.[1]

Yet the strains on ANV soldiers were significant and worked against the ties of honor, pride, and commitment that kept men in the fight. Long years of camping and campaigning took a physical and emotional toll on every ANV soldier, as did longing for their families. The single most persuasive argument for deserting came from the home front: for many soldiers, their families' situations were more dire and compelling than the state of Confederate cause. The threat of punishment deterred some from making this risky choice; others cited personal and family reputation as the reason for not leaving their posts. Whether they approved of desertion or not, many soldiers were particularly critical of those at home who were not fully supporting the war effort. An examination of soldiers' contemporary writings about their relationships with Southern civilians illuminates this paradox: the people to whom soldiers looked for emotional support also proved to be the group most capable of sabotaging soldier morale.[2]

Over the course of the war, soldiers were in constant contact with Southern civilians, forging sometimes intimate, usually short-term, but often complicated relationships with local citizens encountered while on the march or in camp. Such engagements both boosted and depressed soldier morale, but in the end, it was declining home-front morale that caused a rift between soldiers and the society they were fighting to preserve. This divide served to strengthen soldiers' primary self-identification as members of the ANV rather than as citizens of the Confederacy. Soldiers did not entirely forsake the cause for which they were fighting; to follow the ANV was, of course, to fight for the Confederacy, and many would remain committed to this goal until the end. But the Confederacy as represented by the fractious home front became more challenging for soldiers to support. Consequently, they shifted their loyalties toward the simpler but no less powerful symbols of their army and its charismatic leadership.

The narrator of the post–Civil War song "The Old Unreconstructed" makes this change in priorities clear: "We fought a fight to tell about," he says, "and I am here to say / I'd climb my horse and follow Marse / To hell come any day."[3] By the end of the war, this old Rebel fought not necessarily for the Confederate States of America, nor for Jefferson Davis, nor even for his state or his own family, but for his army and his commander, Robert E. Lee. Such loyalty was not just a postwar phenomenon of the Lost Cause (although the ANV is certainly central to that understanding of the Civil War). Instead, soldiers in the ANV developed a strong sense of group identity during the conflict itself, thanks in no small part to their changing views of the home front. In the end, the men of the ANV found themselves bound together by the dual, awesome, and sometimes crushing responsibility to maintain not only their own spirits but those of Confederate society as well.

Although far from their own families, soldiers were not isolated from civilians; they had regular contact with them while on the march, traveling to and from furlough, in hospitals, and in winter camp. Unlike today's highly secure and rigidly separate military compounds, the boundary between nineteenth-century military operations and the home front was porous, and soldiers had ample opportunity to interact with local communities. The reception soldiers received varied greatly and depended in large part on the political leanings of the area and the amount of local destruction wrought by both the Union and Confederate armies.[4]

At first, a strong affection for Virginia, the state in which the ANV did much of its fighting, was not limited to its native sons. Men from all over the Confederacy were impressed with the generosity of the Old Dominion's civilians, and this enhanced soldiers' affection for the army that bore that state's name. Following the Confederate victory at Second Manassas, for example, Lieutenant John Tyler, too ill to travel any farther, simply stopped at a house near Leesburg, Virginia, where "we were attracted by the sight of the truly benevolent countinances of some ladies. Here [his traveling companion] was told that although they had two or three sick there already still they would take another and do their best."[5] Tyler stayed with the family for several weeks, writing often in his journal of their kind and generous treatment. Other soldiers on this campaign described similar treatment from grateful (usually female) Virginians, who pressed flowers, food, and water into the men's hands.[6]

Although such generosity had a positive effect on soldier morale, negative treatment had a more profound impact. There were two types of civilian animosity toward soldiers: political disapproval and citizens' attitudes about the impact of the military presence. The political response, present from the beginning of the war, came from those who had never supported secession and viewed any Confederate army as representative of an unwelcome government. Citizens in areas that were Unionist in political sentiment, such as the westernmost parts of Virginia and along its northern border, were less than thrilled with the ANV's presence, even if it was only temporary.[7]

Unionist pockets also existed in other states visited by the ANV, as Fred Fleet discovered while on duty in South Carolina in September 1863.[8] "I am very much surprised to find that there are some Union men about here," he wrote from Camp Wappoo, on the Stono River just outside of Charleston, "men who will neither sell nor give potatoes, of which there is a great abundance in this region, to the soldiers, and say they would rather the Yankees should have them than our own men." Fleet's comrades exacted their own revenge on such disloyalty, and he remarked that "some of the potato patches or fields, have suffered since we have been in the neighborhood."[9] Fleet thought that such stealing was wrong, but as he pointed out, "to take the other view, it looks hard that we are here defending their property and they will neither give nor sell anything to us."[10] Similarly, James Blackmon Ligon reported from Tennessee that "sometimes I Meet with an old union man that treats us pretty rough but his Bee-gums and chickens repay for the damage done. I could tell some interesting anecdotes that has taken place with me and the unionists," he added cryptically.[11]

North Carolinians in particular, known for their uneven devotion to the Confederacy, generally impressed ANV soldiers as much with their self-interest as with their antagonism toward the Confederate cause. On passing through the port city of Wilmington in September 1863, Chaplain William Edward Wiatt wrote in his journal that he "had a very disagreeable time last night . . . paid $3- for a very ordinary dinner &c &c. Was thoroughly disgusted with W[ilmington] and the people; almost everything outrageously dear and the people very selfish; want to get away."[12] The state's ongoing political turbulence and vocal critics of the war did not help matters, as Virginian William Henry Cocke wrote distastefully from Kinston, North Carolina, a month later. In addition to their criticism of the war, Tar Heels "profess to hate Virginians & say it is because they have always treated Carolinians so badly in Va. driving them from their doors & refuseing to feed them &c but they can never point out a single case."[13] Whether such behavior represented an intensified antebellum rivalry or an emerging wartime dissatisfaction, by January 1864, Virginian Jimmie Booker could declare with certainty that "the soldiers dont like the N.C., nor the N.C. dont like the Va soldiers."[14]

The issue for Fred Fleet and his comrades was not so much the politics of the local population; rather, it was the community's unwillingness to help the soldiers. After all, soldiers went out of their way to be polite guests, as South Carolinian David Crawford reported from Bull's Gap, Tennessee, in early 1864. In the last house he stayed, "the old woman charged us eight dollars for staying there eight nights. We gave her some corn, and hauled her a load of wood. We made up our beds every morning too. She cooked our rations two days, we did the rest." Nevertheless, in addition to her lack of hospitality, this woman had a political motive. "She is a great Union Woman, and has her husband and two sons in the Yankee army."[15] Crawford may have been determined to demonstrate proper behavior toward the locals, but the evidence suggests that few soldiers met this kind of civilian reluctance with such equanimity. Citizens with Unionist political leanings might refuse to help Confederate soldiers, but anecdotes such as those from Fleet and Ligon made it clear that they would pay a stiff price for their convictions.

Dislike was one thing, but active hostility made the situation more dangerous. While in the politically fractious and violent state of Tennessee, members of Longstreet's corps had to keep an eye out for bushwhackers (citizens operating as Unionist guerrillas fighting against Confederate forces), as well as deal with a generally hostile population. In February 1864, Georgian William J. Rheney casually reported that on his most recent march his unit "did no execution I believe except killing of a few bushwackers," and Abram Young recounted how a company mate had been shot at by the same.[16] Bushwhackers did not pose a serious threat to the Confederate military effort, but they did make life difficult and, in some cases, unexpectedly short for individual soldiers.[17]

Despite its obvious intent to disable those fighting for the Confederate cause, guerrilla activity generated surprisingly little strong emotion among soldiers. Men like Rheney and Young remarked on bushwhackers more as a feature of the landscape than as a serious threat, yet they were clearly upset by the poor treatment they received from local citizens. Why the discrepancy in their reactions to noncombatants and guerrilla fighters? It suggests that what soldiers could not stand was poor *personal* treatment—the refusal of a place to sleep, the reluctance to share food, the unwillingness to provide basic creature comforts. When a citizen turned them down face-to-face, in a direct encounter, the soldiers saw it as an affront to their personal honor. Bushwhackers, in contrast, were a largely anonymous group that ANV soldiers seldom confronted directly (their presence being less common in the eastern than the western theater). But even when they did encounter guerrilla fighters, as long as the saboteurs kept their distance, they caused no particular problems. The bushwhackers were, in effect, an extension of the Union army, easy to fight and kill in a largely anonymous manner and presenting no challenge to a soldier's sense of personal honor. Civilians who refused to provide basic assistance, however, were not only disavowing the Confederate cause but also personally insulting the soldier. Harsh civilian attitudes were, in a sense, breaking the contract about fair treatment between soldiers and civilians. Just as soldiers in the ANV prided themselves on their relatively polite treatment of civilians during the Pennsylvania invasion of 1863, so they expected Southern civilians to at least return the favor.[18]

Political differences were not the only reason that locals treated soldiers with suspicion. The second source of civilian animosity was the mere presence of a military force. Even where civilians otherwise supported the Confederate cause, an army's presence was physically and emotionally traumatic for the local population. Like those in Tennessee, the citizens of northern Virginia were particularly taxed for resources, as both Confederate and Union forces camped in their area for extended periods and fought huge, destructive battles nearby. Soldiers were aware that their presence was highly destructive. "You have no idea what a distruction to a country an army is," wrote Joel Wright to his mother in mid-June 1862 from Harrisonburg, Virginia. "The plantations are robed of their fences & large wheat fields where the wheat is maturing we ride in columns & knock it down and distroy it. It makes me sorry for there people out here to see their property all distroyed," not only by Confederates but also by "the Yankees [who] stoled a heap of there negroes." Such knowledge made Wright hope that "an army will never pop through our country, but I cant see where will be the end of this war."[19] Historian Daniel Sutherland details the plight of Culpeper County, Virginia, through which Confederate and Union armies passed repeatedly during the war. In addition to physical destruction, he notes that the presence of Confederate armies was ominous to civilians for another reason: where the ANV was, the Yankees were likely to follow.[20]

Although a campaigning army left a swath of destruction (or, at the very least, disarray) in its wake, it was the more permanent presence of a camp that created acute problems for civilians. Daniel Brown of Duplin County, North Carolina, wrote to his wife from winter camp in March 1863 to say that "hit is the hardest times that I ever saw in my life the soldiers is stealing horses [every?] thing tha can Get that hand on." He advised her and their friends to hide everything they could because "if this regment was thar tha would steal every thing you all had in one night. I want you all to watch for soldiers," he concluded darkly, "for tha are the meanest thing that ever lived."[21] Even those recuperating in the hospital were not to be trusted, according to Harry Lewis. "I was not pleased with the idea of establishing a Hospital in our native town," he wrote to his mother in Mississippi, "for it seem to me that wherever sol-diery predominates decay and scarcity follow; and a certain appearance of cheerlessness (as far as the inhabitants are concerned) seems to exist in proportion as the number of soldiers (locusts) increases. This is the case in Va. but I hope it won't prove so in Woodville."[22]

Both sources of negative civilian response—politically motivated antagonism and that generated by an army's adverse impact on the community—had a debilitating effect on soldier morale. Whereas the former was a more or less constant presence during the war, the latter increased over the years as the war's physical hardships weighed more heavily on soldier and civilian alike. When even the ANV proved to be less than dominant on the battlefield, it became harder for civilians to countenance the physical damage that its presence inflicted on the countryside and the population.

Despite such antagonism between soldiers and civilians, continued contact with local citizens could also reinforce soldiers' commitment to the Confederate cause. Friendly treatment from Virginians was not lim-ited to the first years of the war, and soldiers continued to remark on it in their letters, reporting generous meals in private homes, warm recep-tions as they marched through towns, and gifts of clothes and food.[23] In addition to gratitude for a kind reception, soldiers were motivated by stories and sights of Union destruction. Men such as Harry Lewis noticed a correlation among secessionist sentiment, support of soldiers, and Yankee depredations. In June 1863 the Mississippian described a warm reception (possibly in Charlestown), telling his family that view-ing such a sight "would do any patriot heart good. And these people have suffered unspeakable misery from the tyrants who have oppressed them so often; and who have beggared them of all except honor and love of country."[24] Just as the sight of Northern civilians had steeled men to fight harder, so too did the hardships experienced by their own people.

On New Year's Day 1865, when few could point to anything posi-tive about the Confederate cause, citizens around Petersburg and Richmond attempted to organize a feast for the soldiers protecting their cities. Lacking resources and clearly unable to feed the tens of thou-sands of men who were expecting an actual feast, the residents did their best, although the effort was deemed "somewhat a failier" by most sol-diers. Nevertheless, "it was a Large undertaking and goes fare to Show the generasity of the Virginia people," wrote South Carolinian Henry Calvin Connor. Virginian Jefferson Stubbs remarked that "it was the will and not the deed that pleased the Army. All, all seemed to be highly pleased and satisfied."[25]

Throughout the war, civilians in some of the hardest-hit areas went out of their way to support the soldiers, even if only by token demonstrations. Yet overall, positive encounters with Southern civilians declined over the course of the war. The ANV generally campaigned in Virginia and Maryland, but as the war carried on, soldiers visited other areas of the Confederacy, such as North Carolina and Tennessee, where local populations were less committed to the Confederate cause. Increasing shortages made the competition for resources all the more fierce, and strained emotions caused negative encounters that often concluded with the civilian coming up short. In the end, contact with local civilians provided ANV soldiers with a stark example of the inconstancy of home-front support.

The Petersburg New Year's feast mentioned earlier was undertaken largely by the city's women, and female civilians in general were given particular notice by soldiers. Despite negative treatment by some individuals, soldiers described the commitment of Southern women as a group as unparalleled and heaped praise on them. Such idealization may not have matched the reality of women's experiences, because the evidence suggests that women were not shy about venting their frustration and despair at soldiers' actions. But as the men in the ranks saw it, Southern women's devotion to the cause was the brightest spot on the home front.

From the soldiers' perspective, there were two kinds of women's patriotism. The first was an active, service-oriented one that manifested itself in activities such as nursing. The other consisted of moral and emotional support. The aftermath of the battles at Seven Pines and the Seven Days sent thousands of wounded men to Richmond hospitals, and they were uniformly effusive in their praise of the women who tended them. Marylander John O'Farrell visited several hospitals in June 1862 and observed that "it was very touching, in deed, to see the attention paid [soldiers] by the good ladies of Richmond, hovering around them like angels ministering to their every want." It was not only touching but also inspirational: "the devotion exhibited was enough to excite every soldier to braver deeds."[26] Often described as angels, women in hospitals provided a welcome note of grace, as well as much-needed services such as bandage changing and letter writing.[27]

Outside of hospitals, women supplied a broader range of services, including passing out water to thirsty soldiers on the march, making clothes, or baking a soldier's flour ration into bread.[28] The availability of such assistance might vary, depending on the politics of the region and the devastation caused by previous occupying forces. But over the course of the war, women provided enough help to cause many soldiers to conclude their descriptions of such generosity with their highest acclaim: "God bless the ladies."

As much as the physical comforts, however, soldiers appreciated the moral support that women provided both to them and to the Confederate cause. In asking his sister to pass on his regards to the local ladies, Reuben Pierson remarked that "if it were not for them patriotism would be a humbug & speculation would undermine and destroy our newly organized confederacy. They are the ones who implore the aid of man in behalf of the poor soldiers who are fighting to substantiate the rights of the most valuable property of our land." He concluded with a familiar-sounding flourish: "Woman is mans Guardian angel on earth & always clings to what is right let the excitement be what it may."[29] Commentary like this began to appear more regularly in soldiers' correspondence in the winter of 1862–1863. Although victory still seemed possible for the Confederates at this point, the costly battle at Antietam that fall had dampened enthusiasm, and it was clear that the war would last for some time. Thus soldiers were grateful for any morale boost.

Women's patriotism served two important purposes: it goaded men on the home front into joining the fight, and it provided soldiers with a powerful symbol of the Southern way of life. As Lewis noted, "The women of the South have proved themselves its bravest defenders, and the firmest enemies of our enemy. Let such of those whose hard lot it is to be left in the Yankee lines finish their good and glorious Mission by spurning from among them such men as are able to bear arms." Lewis was confident that with the help of such women, "the enemy can never hold our territory."[30]

Such pressure did not always work, and it was certainly not uniformly applied. Nevertheless, soldiers like Charles Fenton James knew that "the women of the Confederacy have the power, if they have the will and determination to save the country. They can do more towards recruiting the army than all the measures of Congress."[31] It is doubtful that James's wordy appeal (the portion of his letter on women's roles alone is several pages long), written to his sister in the last weeks of the war, would have had much influence on its recipient by then. But combined with earlier statements by like-minded soldiers, it demonstrates that soldiers recognized the powerful influence that women had over shirkers and stay-at-homes.

While preparing for the Pennsylvania campaign in the summer of 1863, South Carolinian Taliaferro Simpson hoped that "when the time comes, we all as one man may prove ourselves worthy sons of the gallant and patriotic daughters of the South."[32] The most important thing that women did during the war, in the opinion of many soldiers, was to symbolize the Confederacy; women embodied home and sacrifice, and their vulnerability shone like a beacon to guide men on the bloody path to Confederate independence. Honor, with its patriarchal aspect of protecting one's dependents, played a part as well. Soldiers felt a strong need to protect their families—and womenfolk in particular—from both enemy invader and the vaguer but no less threatening specter of black equality. As a result, women, especially those who publicly supported the Confederacy, became a powerful symbol of the goals of this war.

In August 1863 James Magruder wrote to his cousin Eva, illuminating this theme of the particular risks for women and the important role they played in maintaining Southern morale. "Until now, I think the women of the South have shown very little despondency, in spite of the great stakes they have in the game, even greater than we have, For in no event will we have to live under the despot's rod, while for them there is no escape, in case we fail to sustain our cause with our arms." Magruder's letter then took a didactic turn: "I hope never to live to see the day when they [women] will lend their influence to the support of a weakly & submissive policy, for while we are away in the army, the management of affairs at home is in a very great measure dependant upon them and their influence, and remove that influence, or give it in behalf of weakness & submission, & where would our country & cause be hurried in a very short time, left in the hands of such men as are most remaining at home?"[33] Only women, with their superior patriotism and commitment (compared with that of stay-at-home men), could keep the Confederacy on its track toward independence.

The material support that women provided in the form of food and lodging, combined with the moral support of their patriotism, prompted many a soldier to express sentiments similar to those of James Albright, who, after marching through Petersburg and seeing crowds of women on the street handing out food and drink, wrote in his journal, "God bless such womanhood! Who would fail to do and dare for their welfare and safety?"[34] Such discussions of women's patriotic zeal demonstrate soldiers' gratitude for the support of at least one segment of the home-front population. There is an obvious discrepancy, however, between soldiers' idealization of women's patriotism and the aforementioned hostility sometimes displayed by civilians. By placing women (as a group) on such a patriotic pedestal, some soldiers failed to understand that women (as individuals) might grow discouraged and act out against the Confederate cause—thus their surprise and indignation when encountering someone like David Crawford's reluctant hostess in Bull's Gap, Tennessee.

Group action by women was even less comprehensible. In the spring of 1863, as home-front food shortages became acute, women across the Confederacy took matters into their own hands, participating in riots both large and small to demand food and other support.[35] The Confederate government tried (largely unsuccessfully) to suppress newspaper reports of the most serious disturbance in Richmond, and just a handful of soldiers remarked on the event in their writings.[36] Soldiers may not have known about the bread riots that swept through the Confederacy in the spring of 1863, but they certainly knew of civilians' dire food situation, being on half rations themselves at that point. Those who discussed the riots saw them as a class issue; they uniformly disparaged the rioters as a lawless, marauding mob incited by foreigners.[37] Louisiana Chaplain Louis-Hippolyte Gâche (who, it should be noted, strongly disputed the idea that foreigners were involved because, being Catholic, they would have been in church at the time) described the crowd as made up of "one thousand women of all ages, but not of all classes," who "screamed at the top of their voices for food and clothes," and he sarcastically referred to them as "representatives of the fair sex."[38]

Others took a similar down-the-nose approach, and there is little indication of any sympathy or understanding of what might have driven these women to such desperate action.[39] Despite Gâche's pointed remark about the class makeup of the mob, at least one soldier from the opposite end of the economic spectrum criticized the participants as being too well-off to act in such a manner. Milton Barrett wrote, "There was women that live in the serverbs [suburbs] of the citty and the head leders was wimen that ther husmen [husbands] was imployed in the government shop at ten Dollars per Day." Yet, among those who described the riots, Barrett was the only soldier to give any credence to the idea that civilians might be suffering to such a drastic extent. "The fack is to wel known to be disputed what we ar a runing short of suplyes . . . the cearsity [scarcity] of provishons is a cosing a grate deal of uneasiness a mong the soldiers."[40] From the way soldiers described the Richmond bread riots, it appears that they could not—and, more importantly, would not—reconcile the hungry armed hordes who stormed through the city with their images of loyal Southern womanhood. To look too closely at the mob might have knocked female patriots from their pedestals and shattered one of the few strong ties that kept soldiers connected to civilians.[41]

In early April 1863 Marion Hill Fitzpatrick noted that "if it were not for the patriotism and industry of the women, the southern Confederacy would soon come to nothing. Many a soldier can now realize the value of a woman's work that thought but little or nothing about it before the war commenced."[42] He was referring specifically to the day-to-day duties of cooking, sewing, and cleaning that soldiers (those without servants) had to learn to do for themselves in the army. But his reference to patriotism and the value of women's work to the Confederacy suggests that he, and perhaps others, was profoundly grateful that at least one segment of Confederate society held goals similar to the soldiers' and was willing to sacrifice almost as much in the achievement of those goals. Although most historians agree that women's support of the war waned over time, soldiers in the ANV laid the blame for declining morale on the home front in general, rather than specifically on women.[43] From the soldier's perspective on the battlefield, in camp, or on the march, women remained an important symbolic and tangible force in the shaping of military morale throughout the war.

Despite localized demonstrations of patriotism and support and the superior example of Confederate women, declining home-front morale over the second half of the war was increasingly frustrating to ANV soldiers.[44] Three types of home-front attitudes were particularly disturbing: the avoidance of wartime responsibilities on the part of civilians (mostly men), wartime profiteering, and, by the last years of the war, a rising tide of general despair. Unlike the relatively constant politically based antagonism in certain locales, these factors were temporal, influenced by the course of the war itself.

Whereas women on the home front were generally viewed sympathetically as bearing a uniquely difficult burden, men who stayed out of the fight were harshly criticized by soldiers. Such commentary was bound to increase as the reality of combat set in, especially after the spring and summer of 1862. In November 1862 Georgian Jasper Gillespie remarked that "men at home know nothing about the suffering of those in the army."[45] Yet as the war carried on, it is hard to imagine how anyone in the Confederacy could *not* be aware of the harsh conditions of soldiering. Those in the line of fire assumed that civilians who avoided service were afraid of the obvious consequences. "How can so many stout and healthy young men of our country remain at home while this state of things are in existance?" asked Tennessee Private Ben Coleman incredulously in April 1863. "Are they cowards? Had they rather endure the wounds to their feelings than risk them in their body? If so, let them remain where they are as they would be worthless in the field."[46] The implication was that the army was the place for men of courage and honor; the rest should not debase the ANV with their presence. During the calamitous summer of 1863, as the Yankees closed in on Charleston and other coastal cities, Mississippian J. J. Wilson hoped that "every man that is capable of bearing arms will rush forward and fight of their country and homes," but he knew that "there is a good many young men about these cities and towns that had rather die than to face the yankee bullets."[47]

It was no surprise that such feelings increased among soldiers in the summer of 1863. They had just been through several months of hard campaigning, culminating with Gettysburg and the difficult retreat into Virginia. Earlier that spring they had lost a beloved commander in Stonewall Jackson, and his service and death provided soldiers with an almost mythic example of bravery against which they could compare the lack of enthusiasm from other quarters. In addition, the loss of Vicksburg and the threat against Charleston with the attack on Battery Wagner showed that the Confederacy was vulnerable everywhere. Once they had recuperated from their invasion campaign, soldiers in the ANV started to believe that they were the only ones who could pull the nation through this crisis. Just as home-front support for the war began to disintegrate in earnest, those who had survived the campaigns of 1862 and 1863 were now hardened to make light of fear and inured to the sacrifices of military life. They saw themselves as fighting for the Confederacy's very existence and had no patience for those who chose not to participate out of some (as they perceived it) quaint notion of self-preservation. Courage and one's reputation among one's fellow soldiers took priority in the Southern conception of personal honor, and the men in the ANV considered themselves the final repository of the Confederacy's honor. They would not have turned away anyone who wanted to join their army, but they were united in their condemnation of those who could not live up to their ideals of courage and manhood.

Soldiers' assumption of the stay-at-homes' cowardice demonstrates the widening gulf that separated soldiers from civilians as the war went on, particularly their diverging notions of manhood. Although some soldiers discussed the issue in practical terms, as essentially a manpower shortage, more treated it as a moral defect on the part of the shirkers. On Christmas Day 1863, North Carolinian R. Conley wrote home: "I have no trouble getting along with my men nor any one else. The worst disturbance I have is to see how some of our men who are at home remain there & leave us to carry on the war alone this I dislike; I never can respect such principals." He explained that the men in his regiment, the Sixth North Carolina, were "as good Soldiers as I would ask & if all would do their part, this war could be easily borne by our people for a long time, without such distress as many predict." Conley knew that there was a difference between his outlook and that of the stay-at-homes. "I am confident all will end right; but I am sorry so many of our country men are giving way" to immoral principles that would lead to the ruin of their country.[48] There were two processes at work here, supporting each other. Soldiers saw themselves as different from civilians, especially those who refused to participate in the war effort. This feeling created a rift between soldiers and the home front because it appeared that soldiers supported the war, whereas those at home (with the exception of women) did not. At the same time, this distancing enhanced soldiers' sense of solidarity within the ANV, because they came to see themselves as the only Southern men brave enough to take on the enemy. In other words, as a shared sentiment among soldiers, contempt for stay-at-homes may have strengthened ANV unity, morale, and dedication to the Confederate cause, even as it distanced soldiers from civilians.[49]

Other than simply avoiding military service, which became harder to do as the war continued, the most visible sign of civilian breakdown was the fast rise in wartime profiteering. "Extortioners" and "speculators" were the pejorative terms commonly used to describe those who viewed the war as a financial opportunity. Civilians charged higher prices for basic necessities as supplies became tighter, demanded higher payments for services than before the war, traded across Union lines, or smuggled and sold luxury goods, all with the goal of personal gain.[50] By the time the ANV came into being in June 1862, such behavior was already widespread, and soldiers were vocal in their complaints and condemnations.[51]

Soldiers' anger about profiteering covered a variety of topics. To begin with, Confederate soldiers were barely paid enough to support themselves in the field, much less help their families. Soldiers supplemented their meager rations of food and clothing by purchasing necessary items locally, and as prices rose, enlisted men's salaries did not keep pace with the rampant inflation in the Confederate economy. "It is a shame how we have to pay for things here," wrote Georgian Eli Pinson Landers from a camp near Richmond. "Some people is making a fortune off of us soldiers."[52] Enlisted soldiers were paid $11 a month, and it was not issued regularly; often months would pass before soldiers received what they were owed. The spiraling inflation of the Confederate dollar made this amount worth less and less as time passed, but it was not until June 1864 that Congress authorized a $7 per month raise—still barely enough to make ends meet, and still rarely doled out on schedule.[53] Long before that, Virginian Charlie Baughman warned that "they had better increased the pay of the soldiers than that of the clerks who have all the comforts of home while we poor privates are risking our live for our country and do not get enough pay in a month to buy a pair of boots."[54]

Herein lies another obvious division between civilians and soldiers. From the soldiers' perspective, civilians saw the war primarily as a way to make money and to advance themselves financially, whereas soldiers had sacrificed their comfort, their financial security (or at least their financial status quo), and perhaps even their lives to secure the independence of the new nation. With such divergent goals, it is no wonder that soldiers began to draw away psychologically from the very communities for which they were fighting. That men of means were able to get out of the war with greater ease than poor folks only made matters worse and created yet another sore spot. "Sister the rich men are all leaving the army and the poor men will have to fight for their property," wrote Alabamian Lewis Branscomb from winter camp in December 1862.[55]

But in 1863, as military defeat began to show its dark face to the Confederacy, an increasing number of soldiers thought that profiteering was a major cause for the downturn in Southern fortunes. Virginian James Wright believed that "the Speculators are doing more to ruin our once-happy country than the Yankees are and are more dreaded by our Soldiers," and by October, Charles Kerrison observed that in Richmond, "Everybody is speculating and looking after number one." He was coming to the same conclusion that many of his comrades had reached: "that patriotism no longer exists a lust after riches having extinguished the last spark in the breast of the people."[56] The "greedy avaricious Money maker" was responsible for many social woes, according to Georgian Josiah Blair Patterson, who hoped that "the day will come when a just retribution will be visited upon all such as have amassed money in this way by extortionate speculation."[57]

Soldiers' condemnation of profiteering continued to be both practical and ethical throughout the war. On the pragmatic end, James Wright was concerned about the kind of revenge that Patterson hinted at, about soldiers "taking matters in their own hands" to deal with speculators on the home front.[58] Others worried about civilians having enough to eat, while Georgian Shepard Pryor wondered how the army itself would be able to eat if prices kept going up. "I am now gitting to believe that if wee are ever whiped out at all it will be done by our friends at home breaking down the government with high prices for provisions in the army." After noting some of the exorbitant prices that North Carolina counties were charging for corn and bacon, Pryor concluded gloomily that "no government can feed an army long at those prices those noble patriotic souls at home are letting the allmighty dollar influence them to help the north to subdue and break down the government that their fathers brothers & husbands are now in the field trying to establish."[59]

Ethical condemnation of profiteering was both societal and moral. Some critics saw profiteering as reflective of one's social worth and con-

sidered it a behavior to be looked down on, regardless of the specu-
lator's position in the community. J. W. McLure, for example, advised
his wife Kate that the behavior of such individuals should "excite your
contempt rather than your indignation."[60] This kind of indictment was
also tendered in early 1863 by the aristocratic Virginian James DeWitt
Hankins, who was pleased to learn that his father would not sell necessities to poor folks at any price higher than cost. "How rare it is to meet
with a generous hand in this day of speculation and vile extortion," he
wrote. "There is nothing so low-born as this detestable spirit that lives
and grows fat upon the life blood of the country."[61] Societal criticisms
like this tended to come from the elite and well educated.[62] For these
men, who were not personally affected by profiteering, such activity
demonstrated a vulgar interest in money and was a transgression of the
elite's traditional leadership role in Southern society.

During the second half of the war, many soldiers also came to see
overpowering civilian self-interest as a religious sin, and they condemned profiteering not only as a social transgression but as a moral
evil as well. After hearing that his father-in-law's family was engaging
in speculation, South Carolinian Theodore Augustus Honour wrote to
his wife in April 1863, "Let me beg of you for the sake of humanity,
and your own peace of mind afterwards, do not in any way engage in
this terrible vice. I believe the curse of God will rest upon all who do
it . . . because others do wrong to make money and worship mannon,
it is no reason why we should."[63] Such duplicity, manifested by supposedly upstanding members of the community who were in fact making
money off the poor and defenseless, enraged soldiers almost as much as
Yankee depredations did.

What Micahjah Woods had called a "morbid, unnatural state of
affairs" in 1862 had become the order of the day on the home front by
the last year of the war, in the view of many soldiers.[64] Poorer soldiers
wondered how they and their families would eat, while wealthier or
more educated men debated the effect such avariciousness would have
on Southern society. Regardless of their approach, it is clear that soldiers
were infuriated by the idea of some people profiting at home, probably
at the expense of soldiers who were risking their lives and livelihoods in
battle. Although their criticisms demonstrate different interpretations
of wartime economic woes, Southern soldiers of all classes could unite
in their condemnation of profiteering on the home front.

Soldiers came to consider inhospitable treatment from civilians, avoidance of the war effort, and profiteering as symptoms of declining civilian morale. While they did their best to save the Confederacy on the battlefield, it appeared that the home front was sabotaging their hard work. By 1863, this split between soldiers and civilians in terms of dedication to the war effort was beginning to be noticed by those in the army. John Shaffner of North Carolina learned from visitors that "there is amuch despondency at home, as to the length of the contest, and even regarding the final result." He assured his correspondent that "this does not exist here. All is life and animation."[65] Just a few weeks before Gettysburg, James Branscomb noticed that his correspondent seemed "to be discouraged about the war." This was not surprising, he thought, since "patriotism is near about played out every where only in the army and there is as much of that there now as there every was."[66] These soldiers were clearly determined to remind the folks at home that if the ANV, which was actually fighting the war, was not despairing of the Confederacy's future, then neither should they.

Some soldiers expressed anger about this apparent abandonment by those at home, an attitude that was absolutely antithetical to what they believed about the war. "I wish the feelings of our friends at home were the same that exists in the Army," wrote South Carolinian Peter McDavid. "It wounds the feelings of our soldiers to hear of despondency at home. Why should citizens despair? You who are at home living as well as ever you did in halcyon days of peace ought to be mute on this subject." McDavid lectured his sister about the confident, buoyant spirits of ANV soldiers, "ever ready to sacrafice their lives in defence of all that is dear. This is the way we are rewarded—our own people forsake us in the trying hour. . . . Degrading wretched unpatriotic infamous thoughts."[67]

The difference in living conditions, alluded to by McDavid, was particularly galling and was tied to soldiers' resentment of those who avoided service. Edgeworth Bird was "astonished at the state of public feeling in Georgia as represented by the returned furloughed men." They claimed that "Georgia is almost whipped, and she has hardly ever had an armed heel on her soil."[68] From the midpoint of the war, soldiers' remarks about the home front were permeated with anger and frustration over the lack of understanding by those at home, and by 1864, sympathy was in short supply for any but their own immediate families. "It puts me all out of patience," snapped Mississippian William Ker, "when I see people giving up our cause in despair and abusing in most bitter and outrageous terms our President, Government, and military leaders simply because they (the aforesaid functionaries) cannot in *every* instance accomplish *miracles,* and because *their* homes are left undefended and consequently fall into the hands of the Yankees." Ker thought that civilians were essentially selfish, claiming, "there is no excuse for people thinking that their own homes are of as vital importance as the whole *Confederacy* or expecting that we can always be victorious."[69]

Of course, the unheard voices in all this belong to the thousands of ANV soldiers who deserted. They may have left little record of their opinions, but they provided clear indications that selfishness was not limited to civilians.

By the last year of the war, it was increasingly apparent to soldiers that the ANV was becoming the main repository of strong morale and support for the Confederate war effort. "Thank God! we still have an Army that is still confident by this blessing and favor to gain our independence," wrote Virginian John Sale in January 1865. He admonished his correspondents not to disseminate despair in the army. "If any of your acquaintance are weak and wavering bid them do as suits themselves but in Heaven's name don't write to discourage those who are resolved to follow the fortunes of our Confederacy."[70] Soldiers wrote about the spirit of the army and the mood of the men for several reasons—to raise spirits on the home front, perhaps to convince *themselves* of why they were still fighting the war, and certainly to remind their families of the importance of their continued presence in the army, as opposed to at home. But remarks like Sale's also demonstrate the extent to which soldiers and civilians differed in their views by 1864. Rather than trying to bring his correspondents around to his and the army's way of thinking, Sale accepted their despair and simply asked that they not infect the army with it. His recognition of this difference in morale had a finality to it. In his desire to protect the army and his fellow soldiers from the disease of despondency, Sale demonstrated that his allegiance lay ultimately with the ANV, which was the only hope left to the Confederate nation.

Criticism of the Confederate government and its leaders was not a major theme in soldier correspondence, despite the government's imperfect support of its soldiers. In contrast, unsupportive civilians were the target of much soldier criticism and anger. In response to news of recent Yankee raids in his neighborhood, for example, Alabamian Jimmie Simpson was not particularly sympathetic. "I am in hopes it will do good in some way," he wrote in August 1864; "it should for one thing, arouse our citizens to a sence of their duty and teach them that they cannot depend entirely on us in a distant field to defend their homes and property."[71] By citing the physical distance between the army and the home front, Simpson's blunt response was indicative of the growing psychological distance between soldiers and home. From the soldiers' perspective, civilians did not understand what the army was going through, and they did not support the army; other than maintaining their personal relationships and acquiring basic necessities, soldiers increasingly wanted little to do with civilians.

By the final months of the war, soldier commentary about the state of the home front was filled with descriptions of disheartened civilians. Despite the tightening of enlistment laws in early 1864, stay-at-homes continued to provoke soldiers' ire. Henry Connor called those who would not fight "soulless . . . no appeal from thair country can bring them out and induce them to do thair duty but would rather remain at home and Speculate of the [necessities?] of the orphans and widows of Soldiers who have sealed their devotion to thair country cause with their blood." Connor thought that such men were "more objects of pity than contempt," emphasizing the idea of the home front as lost to the cause for which soldiers were still fighting.[72] William Hinson agreed and described in his journal his mother's agony at having to send him back to the army after his furlough. He wished that "all mothers in our land were like her, for there is a great deal of 'shirking' and I almost think at times that as a people we are not worthy of our 'freedom.'"[73] Clearly, the lack of home-front support made men like Hinson wonder whether there was any value to their efforts, and whether there was any Confederacy worth saving.

In early March 1865, Georgia surgeon Abner McGarrity remarked with some understatement that "our people are not the same as they were four years ago. Their courage, spirit and pride is gone." He feared that if despair were not stopped, it "will prove fatal to our people and nation."[74] The word choice is significant—not only would the effort to establish Confederate independence fail; in addition, Southerners would lose their society and their way of life if they were not successful in achieving independence. McGarrity's diagnosis came too late, of course; the civilian will to fight had been disintegrating since at least 1863, and by 1865, few Southerners held out much hope for victory. Soldiers in the ANV who maintained even a remotely positive attitude tended to do so out of a conviction of their own invincibility, or that of their army, rather than out of a strong belief in Southern society.

Historian Gary Gallagher has argued persuasively that the ANV was critical to maintaining Confederate civilian morale, but this essay suggests that the relationship was not entirely reciprocal.[75] At the very least, it was complicated. There is no question that the ANV's impressive battle record helped boost the spirits of the folks at home, but it could never entirely overcome the inherent friction in soldier-civilian relations. Some of these antagonisms were present throughout the war, such as long-standing political opposition in Unionist areas. Others were generated by the war itself, such as increasing competition for resources. From the soldiers' perspective, the downward slide of civilian morale and its manifestations (shirking, speculating) were difficult to comprehend. Even as women's patriotism—whether realistically interpreted or not—became an increasingly important totem for soldiers, nothing frustrated those in the ranks more than the growing reports of civilian apathy or antiwar activities.

Ultimately, soldiers' commitment to the war—or at least to seeing the job through—was in stark contrast to the wavering commitment of those at home. Soldiers' own devotion to the Confederate cause was not without its complexities. But as a troublesome divide deepened between soldiers and civilians, men in the ANV appear to have shifted their loyalty away from the society they were fighting *for* and toward the army they were fighting *in*. Long before the Lost Cause helped the "Old Unreconstructed" climb his horse, ANV soldiers considered themselves and their army the final repository of Confederate spirit.

Notes

The quotation in the title is from Whitfield G. Kisling to cousin, August 26, 1863, W. G. Kisling Collection, Eleanor S. Brockenbrough Library, Museum of the Confederacy, Richmond, VA (hereafter MOC).

1. There are many elements that contributed to the unique sense of solidarity and group identity within the army, including shared ideas about the preservation of the racial status quo, a view of the enemy as inferior, honor

(also understood as public reputation), and devotion to the leadership and record of the ANV itself. These assumptions and this essay are drawn from research done for my dissertation, "Good Old Rebels: Soldiering in the Army of Northern Virginia, 1862–1865" (Harvard University, 2003). For that study, I examined the writings of a geographically representative sample of 647 soldiers in the ANV. In addition to a database of sources, I created a database drawn from company rosters for a similarly representative sample of ten ANV companies, including infantry, artillery, and cavalry companies, from around the Confederacy.

2. Although the source base for this study is vast, it is important to understand its limits. A study based on soldiers' letters is naturally limited to those who wrote letters and those whose letters were saved after the war. This means that my source sample is probably slightly more affluent than the general population (if literacy and the means to preserve written materials are associated with socioeconomic status), slightly younger than the general soldier population (many of these letters are found in university archives throughout the South, with a healthy proportion being there because the letter writers or family members attended that school), and, probably most important, generally more positive about their participation in the war. To illustrate this last point, one need only think of the number of desertions from Confederate armies. We know that thousands of men from all walks of life did it, but one searches almost in vain for a letter from a deserter himself. Many soldiers comment on the phenomenon, but it is very difficult to find written evidence of the act from deserters themselves. Similarly, letters that have been saved in families and then donated to archives or published tend to demonstrate a slightly higher level of patriotism and pride in service than is found in the general soldier population. Nevertheless, soldiers' letters are one of the best sources we have for learning about this cataclysmic experience. When used carefully and in conjunction with other evidence, such as the demographic material previously cited, such letters provide an incomparable view into the spectrum of opinions and experiences of Civil War soldiers.

3. Author unknown, "The Old Unreconstructed," lyrics cited from the liner notes to *Songs of the Civil War,* Columbia Records, 1991.

4. The growing area of Southern community studies offers ample evidence of the complex relations between civilians and the armies that moved through their communities. For example, in *Seasons of War: The Ordeal of a Confederate Community, 1861–1865* (Baton Rouge: Louisiana State University Press, 1995), Daniel E. Sutherland examines in minute detail the war world of Culpeper County, Virginia, one of the most fought over patches of land in the Confederacy. William Blair's *Virginia's Private War: Feeding Body and Soul in the Confederacy, 1861–1865* (New York: Oxford University Press, 1998) is

another excellent example of a deeply researched community study relevant to the ANV. The narrow focus of such works makes it problematic to apply their conclusions to the entire nation, but they do emphasize the range of Confederate wartime experiences.

5. John Tyler, journal, September 4, 1862, Diary of Lt. John Tyler, MS 6150, Special Collections, Alderman Library, University of Virginia, Charlottesville (hereafter UVA).

6. Tyler's experience came early in the war, but many soldiers continued to describe gratefully their treatment at the hands of Virginia civilians.

7. See, for example, Harvey Black to wife, September 26, 1862, in Glen McMullen, ed., *A Surgeon with Stonewall Jackson* (Baltimore: Butternut and Bine, 1995), 43.

8. Regional differences in support for the Confederacy are well known, with the violence in Missouri being the most prominent example; sections of Alabama, Georgia, North Carolina, and Tennessee harbored strong Unionist, or at least antiwar, sentiment. For Missouri, see Michael Fellman, *Inside War: The Guerilla Conflict in Missouri during the American Civil War* (New York: Oxford University Press, 1989). For more on Alabama, Georgia, North Carolina, and Virginia, see Paul D. Escott, *After Secession: Jefferson Davis and the Failure of Confederate Nationalism* (Baton Rouge: Louisiana State University Press, 1978), especially ch. 4.

9. A. Frederick Fleet, September 28, 1863, in Betsey Fleet and John D. P. Fuller, eds., *Green Mount: A Virginia Plantation Family during the Civil War, Being the Letter of Benjamin Robert Fuller and His Family* (Lexington: University Press of Kentucky, 1962), 272.

10. Ibid., October 8, 1863, 275–76.

11. James Blackmon Ligon, January 25, 1864, James Blackmon Ligon Papers, South Caroliniana Library, University of South Carolina, Columbia (hereafter SCL).

12. William Edward Wiatt, journal, September 16, 1863, in Alex L. Wiatt, ed., *Confederate Chaplain: William Edward Wiatt, an Annotated Diary* (Lynchburg, VA: H. E. Howard, 1994), 103.

13. William Henry Cocke, October 21, 1863, Cocke Family Papers, Virginia Historical Society, Richmond, VA (hereafter VHS). Among those critics was newspaper editor William Holden, whose call for peace sounded increasingly attractive to civilians who were tired of the war's hardships.

14. James Booker to cousin, January 1, 1864, Civil War Letters of John and James Booker, UVA.

15. David Crawford, March 22, 1864, Crawford Family Papers, SCL.

16. William J. Rheney to mother, February 5, 1864, William J. Rheney Papers, SCL; Abram Hayne Young, April 2, 1864, Abram Hayne Young Papers, SCL.

17. Noel C. Fisher, "Definitions of Victory: East Tennessee Unionists in the Civil War and Reconstruction," in *Guerillas, Unionists, and Violence on the Confederate Home Front,* ed. Daniel E. Sutherland (Fayetteville: University of Arkansas Press, 1999), 100–101.

18. For ANV soldiers' pride regarding their conduct toward enemy civilians, see Reid Mitchell, *Civil War Soldiers: Their Expectations and Their Experiences* (New York: Touchstone, 1988), 155–57. None of the essays in Sutherland's *Guerillas, Unionists, and Violence* addresses the Confederate soldier's response to guerrilla violence; instead, they focus on its sources, proponents, and civilian victims. Even though soldiers in the Army of Tennessee surely experienced guerrilla targeting more frequently than did those in the ANV, Larry J. Daniel does not address the topic in his *Soldiering in the Army of Tennessee: A Portrait of Life in a Confederate Army* (Chapel Hill: University of North Carolina Press, 1991). The subject is likewise absent from Bell Irvin Wiley, *The Life of Johnny Reb: The Common Soldier of the Confederacy* (Indianapolis: Bobbs-Merrill, 1943); James McPherson, *For Cause and Comrades: Why Men Fought in the Civil War* (New York: Oxford University Press,1997); and Georgia Lee Tatum, *Disloyalty in the Confederacy* (Chapel Hill: University of North Carolina Press, 1934; reissued, Lincoln: University of Nebraska Press, 2000). Mitchell considers Union soldiers' reactions to Rebel guerrilla activity but does not address the issue from the Confederate perspective (*Civil War Soldiers,* 132–38).

19. Joel Wright to mother, June 15, 1862, James M. Wright Papers, Rare Book, Manuscript and Special Collections Library, Perkins Library, Duke University, Durham, NC.

20. Sutherland, *Seasons of War,* 98, 264.

21. Daniel M. Brown to wife, March 17, 1863, Isaac Brown Collection, North Carolina Department of Cultural Resources, Archives and History Division, Raleigh (hereafter NCDAH).

22. Harry Lewis to mother, February 15, 1863, Harry Lewis Papers, #1222, Southern Historical Collection, University of North Carolina at Chapel Hill (SHC).

23. See, for example, Richard Henry Watkins to Mary, January 12, 1864, Richard Henry Watkins Papers, reel 42, Joseph T. Glatthaar, ed., *Confederate Military Manuscripts Series A: Holdings of the Virginia Historical Society* (hereafter *CMM/A*); Henry F. Wilson, journal, March 14, 1864, Henry F. Wilson Mobile Rifles Diary and Notebook, Alabama Department of Archives and History, Montgomery, AL (hereafter ADAH); William Hawkins Welch to mother, May 21, 1864, Elliott Stephen Welch Papers, Duke University; Fred A. Brodé, November 19, 1864, Fred A. Brodé Letters, MOC; Edwin Kerrison to sister, September 30, 1862, Kerrison Family Papers, ms. 6209, SCL; Sutherland, *Seasons of War,* 359–60.

24. Harry Lewis to mother, June 22, 1863, Harry Lewis Papers, SHC.

25. Henry Calvin Connor to Ellen, January 4, 1865, Henry Calvin Conner Papers, SCL; Jefferson Stubbs to father, January 5, 1865, Jefferson W. Stubbs and Family Papers, reel 18, Joseph T. Glatthaar, ed., *Confederate Military Manuscripts Series B: Holdings of the Louisiana and Lower Mississippi Valley Collection, Louisiana State University* (hereafter *CMM/B*).

26. John O'Farrell, journal, June 5, 1862, John O'Farrell, diary, Diary Collection, MOC.

27. Women were more ambivalent about nursing; for them, it was hard, ugly, and horrifying, not to mention the fact that it caused social conflict by putting them in contact with men and women of other classes. For a description of women's nursing experiences, see George Rable, *Civil Wars: Women and the Crisis of Southern Nationalism* (Urbana: University of Illinois Press, 1989), 121–28. Drew Gilpin Faust analyzes the meaning of nursing and administrative work for elite women in *Mothers of Invention: Women of the Slaveholding South in the American Civil War* (Chapel Hill: University of North Carolina Press, 1996), 92–112.

28. Bartlett Yancey Malone, journal, May 8, 1863, in William Whately Pierson Jr., ed., *Whipt 'em Everytime: The Diary of Bartlett Yancey Malone, Co. H, 6th N.C. Regiment* (Jackson, TN: McCowat-Mercer Press, 1960), 81; Fred A. Brodé, November 19, 1864, Fred A. Brodé Letters, MOC; Mark Holland to father, December 3, 1864, Holland Family Papers, MS 902, UVA; see also Robert A. Moore, journal, September 14, 1863, in James W. Silver, ed., *A Life for the Confederacy: As Recorded in the Pocket Diaries of Pvt. Robert A. Moore, Co. G, 17th Mississippi Regiment, Confederate Guards, Holly Springs, Mississippi* (Jackson, TN: McCowat-Mercer Press, 1959), 166; William Hawkins Welch to mother, May 21, 1864, Elliott Stephen Welch Papers, Duke University.

29. Reuben Allen Pierson to sister, December 23, 1862, in Thomas W. Cutrer and T. Michael Parrish, eds., *Brothers in Gray: The Civil War Letters of the Pierson Family* (Baton Rouge: Louisiana State University Press, 1997), 140.

30. Jno. Lewis to mother, July 21, 1863, Harry Lewis Papers, #1222, SHC.

31. Charles Fenton James to sister, February 13, 1865, Charles Fenton James Letters, VHS.

32. Taliaferro Simpson to Ma, June 13, 1863, in Guy R. Everson and Edward H. Simpson Jr., eds., *"Far, Far from Home": The Wartime Letters of Dick and Tally Simpson, Third South Carolina Volunteers* (New York: Oxford University Press, 1994), 245.

33. James M. Magruder to Eva, August 8, 1863, John Bowie Magruder Papers, Duke University.

34. James W. Albright, journal, June 8, 1864, James W. Albright Books, #1008, SHC.

35. For the most detailed investigation into the Richmond riot, see Michael B. Chesson, "Harlots or Heroines? A New Look at the Richmond Bread Riot," *Virginia Magazine of History and Biography* 92 (April 1984): 131–75. For shorter accounts, see, for example, James McPherson, *Battle Cry of Freedom: The Civil War Era* (New York: Oxford University Press, 1988), 617, and E. Merton Coulter, *The Confederate States of America, 1861–1865,* vol. 7 of *A History of the South* (Baton Rouge: Louisiana State University Press, 1950), 422–23. Chesson, however, correctly criticizes most discussions of the riot as too brief and shallow. Studies of women's lives during the war tend to give a more sympathetic but similarly brief reading of the incident. See, for example, Rable, *Civil Wars,* 108–11.

36. I should note that Chesson finds no basis for the oft-cited claim that the government suppressed reporting of the incident. He points to the *Richmond Examiner*'s April 4, 1863, account as being remarkably similar to that of several writers on the topic. Soldiers' descriptions of the mob, though similar to one another, bear no resemblance to the *Examiner*'s, with the exception of referring to the foreign makeup of the crowd ("Harlots or Heroines?" 132).

37. Drew Gilpin Faust suggests that the foreign connection to mass misbehavior is also evident in condemnations of profiteering. "'Sliding in the World': The Sin of Extortion and the Dynamic of Confederate Identity," in *The Creation of Confederate Nationalism: Ideology and Identity in the Civil War South* (Baton Rouge: Louisiana State University Press, 1988), 41–57; see especially 49–50.

38. Louis-Hippolyte Gâche, March 8, 1863, in Cornelius M. Buckley, ed. and trans., *A Frenchman, a Chaplain, a Rebel: The War Letters of Pere Louis-Hippolyte Gâche, S.J.* (Chicago: Loyola University Press, 1981), 159–61. I believe that this source has incorrectly dated the letter; it is clearly referring to the Richmond riot, which took place in early April, not March.

39. I would like to make clear that this is how soldiers viewed the event at the time, not how it has been interpreted in recent years. For other examples of soldiers' negative opinions, see Robert P. Tutwiler to Nettie, April 3, 1863, T. C. McCorvey Papers, #452-z, SHC; Charles Kerrison to sister, April 9, 1863, Kerrison Family Papers, ms. 6209, SCL; Daniel M. Brown to wife, April 12, 1863, Isaac Brown Collection, NCDAH; William Lyne Wilson to parents, April 17, 1863, in Festus P. Summers, ed., *A Borderland Confederate* (Pittsburgh: University of Pittsburgh Press, 1962), 55; and John Francis Shaffner to friend, April 21, 1863, Shaffner Diary and Papers, PC 247, NCDAH. Historians have taken good advantage of hindsight and a broader range of sources to demonstrate that the Richmond riots, though containing a lawless element, were in fact driven by real hunger and need. See, for example, Chesson, "Harlots or Heroines?" 170–74. Blair argues in *Virginia's Private War* (74–76) that the riot

had a positive impact on the government's benevolent activity and was in fact a turning point in the Confederacy's general response to the plight of the poor.

40. Milton Barrett to brother and sister, April 14, 1863, in J. Roderick Heller III and Carolyn Ayres Heller, eds., *The Confederacy Is on Her Way up the Spout: Letters to South Carolina, 1861–1864* (Athens: University of Georgia Press, 1992), 96.

41. Drew Faust applies this idea of an accepted narrative about women's sacrifice and patriotism more broadly in "Altars of Sacrifice: Confederate Women and the Narrative of War," *Journal of American History* 76, no. 4 (March 1990): 1200–28; for the bread riots in particular, see 1225–27.

42. Marion Hill Fitzpatrick to Amanda, April 17, 1863, in Henry Vaughan MacRea, *Red Dirt and Isinglass: A Wartime Biography of a Confederate Soldier* (privately published, 1992), 404–5.

43. Such demoralization is well documented in studies of women and the home front during the war. Rable's *Civil Wars* makes an effort to consider the patriotism of white women of all classes, while Faust's *Mothers of Invention* focuses on the shifting roles of elite women in Southern society. For a more condensed version of Faust's argument on the decline of women's patriotism, see "Altars of Sacrifice." Contradicting Faust somewhat is Berlin, who suggests that although Southern women greeted defeat with relief, their anger was directed at the North rather than at the Confederacy itself. Jean V. Berlin, "Did Confederate Women Lose the War? Deprivation, Destruction, and Despair on the Home Front," in *The Collapse of the Confederacy*, ed. Mark Grimsley and Brooks D. Simpson (Lincoln: University of Nebraska Press, 2001), 168–93.

44. Declining home-front morale during the second half of the war manifested itself in a variety of ways, and some twentieth-century historians focused on it as a critical element of Southern defeat. See, for example, Charles H. Wesley, *The Collapse of the Confederacy* (Washington, DC: Associated Publishers, 1937; reissued, Charleston: University of South Carolina Press, 2001), ch. 3; Charles W. Ramsdell, *Behind the Lines in the Southern Confederacy* (Baton Rouge: Louisiana State University Press, 1944); Coulter, *Confederate States of America*, 566–67; Bell I. Wiley, *The Road to Appomattox* (Memphis: Memphis State College Press, 1956), ch. 10; Escott, *After Secession*, chs. 4–7; Emory Thomas, *The Confederate Nation, 1861–1865* (New York: Harper and Row, 1979), ch. 11; and Richard E. Beringer, Herman Hattaway, Archer Jones, and William N. Still Jr., *Why the South Lost the Civil War* (Athens: University of Georgia Press, 1986). Although these historians may focus on different aspects of the civilian experience or propose slightly different timing, they all generally agree that the South's waning will to fight was an important factor in its defeat. Rable attempts to paint a more complex picture of Southern morale and suggests that those who engaged in positive thinking were increasingly delu-

sional in the last months of the war; see George C. Rable, "Despair, Hope and Delusion: The Collapse of Confederate Morale Reexamined," in Grimsley and Simpson, *The Collapse of the Confederacy*, 129–67. Blair provides the counter-argument in *Virginia's Private War*, 4. He proposes that morale in the Virginia counties he studied collapsed only at the end of the war, when the presence of the Union armies and the lack of resources could no longer be withstood. Though limited in its applicability to the entire Confederacy, Blair's thought-provoking study adds a welcome nuance to the overall argument about declining morale.

45. Jasper A. Gillespie, November 27, 1862, Jasper A. Gillespie Civil War Letters, 2351–18c, ac 65–404, Georgia Department of Archives and History, Morrow (hereafter GDAH).

46. Ben W. Coleman to parents, April 26, 1863, Ben W. Coleman Letters, *Civil War Collection, Confederate*, Tennessee State Library and Archives.

47. J. J. Wilson to father, August 10, 1863, J. J. Wilson Papers, 677mf, Mississippi Department of Archives and History, Jackson.

48. R. Conley to father and family, December 25, 1863, Conley Civil War Letters, Civil War Soldiers Letters, LPR 78, Box 1, ADAH.

49. Gerald Linderman also made an argument about Civil War soldiers' alienation from civilians, proposing that the experience of combat simultaneously forged a bond between soldiers (both in their own army and on the other side) and created a gulf between them and civilians. In his view, the divide came in part from civilians' clinging to their romantic notions of war, which soldiers quickly learned were useless in helping them understand the reality of such ferocious fighting on such a vast scale. In other words, soldiers came to share an understanding of combat that excluded civilians, who were still wrapped up in old-fashioned notions of chivalric battle. By the end of the Civil War, soldiers knew better. This is a valid argument about soldiers' reaction to combat, but it differs (albeit subtly) from my point here, which is that civilian disenchantment with the war fueled soldiers' resentment of the home front and their subsequent identification with the ANV. See Gerald F. Linderman, *Embattled Courage: The Experience of Combat in the American Civil War* (New York: Free Press, 1989). For a similar comparison of Linderman's thesis and the argument presented here, see McPherson, *For Cause and Comrades*, 141–42.

50. Soldiers never mentioned profiteering in the ranks, although there were surely some who took advantage of opportunities to make a quick dollar by providing services or supplies. Discussion of profiteering was most often combined with condemnation of the stay-at-homes who were engaging in avaricious activity.

51. Although none considers the impact of profiteering on soldiers' morale, a few historians of the Southern home front address the topic of profiteering

and see it as a key element in the decline of Southern civilian morale. See, for example, Wesley, *Collapse of the Confederacy,* 68–71, and Coulter, *Confederate States of America,* ch. 11. The best examination of the moral concerns associated with Southern profiteering on the home front is Faust, "'Sliding in the World.'"

52. Eli Pinson Landers to mother, July 31, 1862, in Elizabeth Whitley Roberson, ed., *In Care of Yellow River: The Complete Civil War Letters of Pvt. Eli Pinson Landers to His Mother* (Gretna, VA: Pelican Publishing, 1997), 91.

53. Wiley, *The Life of Johnny Reb,* 136.

54. Charles C. Baughman, November 19, 1862, Charles Baughman Papers, MOC.

55. Lewis Sylvester Branscomb to sister, December 2, 1862, Branscomb Family Letters, 1851–65, ADAH.

56. James M. Wright to sister, April 4, 1863, James M. Wright Papers, Duke University; Charles Kerrison to sister, October 24, 1863, Kerrison Family Papers, SCL.

57. Josiah Blair Patterson to daughter, August 18, 1863, Josiah Blair Patterson Civil War Letters, mf 147, ac 61–210, GDAH.

58. James M. Wright to sister, April 4, 1863, James M. Wright Papers, Duke University.

59. Shepard G. Pryor to Penelope, April 25, 1863, Mills Bee Lane IV Papers, ms. 1291, box 1, Georgia Historical Society, Savannah.

60. J. W. McLure to Kate, July 19, 1862, McLure Family Papers, SCL.

61. James DeWitt Hankins, February 12, 1863, Hankins Family Papers, sections 6, 13, and 14, VHS.

62. Hankins is one example, as are more modest but still comfortable slaveholders like Shepard Pryor and J. W. McLure. This could simply be reflective of the source sample's bias toward more affluent soldiers, however.

63. Theodore Augustus Honour to wife, April 6, 1863, Theodore Augustus Honour Papers, SCL.

64. Micahjah Woods, journal, November 5, 1862, Micahjah Woods Papers, UVA.

65. John Francis Shaffner, March 20, 1863, Shaffner Diary and Papers, NCDAH.

66. James Zachariah Branscomb to sister, June 8, 1863, Branscomb Family Letters, 1851–65, ADAH.

67. Peter McDavid to Nellie, August 15, 1863, Peter McDavid Papers, Duke University.

68. Edgeworth Bird to Sallie, August 28, 1863, in John Rozier, ed., *The Granite Farm Letters: The Civil War Correspondence of Edgeworth and Sallie Bird* (Athens: University of Georgia Press, 1988), 145.

69. William H. Ker to sister, July 14, 1864, William H. Ker Letters, reel 10, *CMM/B*.

70. John F. Sale to aunt, January 23, 1864, John F. Sale Papers, Library of Virginia, Richmond.

71. J. M. Simpson to wife, August, 4, 1864, Allen-Simpson Family Letters, M-929, SHC.

72. Henry Calvin Connor to Ellen, October 18, 1864, Henry Calvin Connor Papers, SCL.

73. William G. Hinson, journal, January 27, 1865, in Joseph Ivor Waring, ed., "The Diary of William G. Hinson during the War of Secession," *South Carolina Historical Magazine* 75, no. 2 (January, April 1974): 115.

74. Abner Embry McGarrity to wife, March 6, 1865, in Edmund Cody Burnett, ed., "Letters of a Confederate Surgeon: Dr. Abner Embry McGarrity, 1862–65, Part 4," *Georgia Historical Quarterly* 30, no. 1 (March 1946): 62.

75. Gary Gallagher has made a small industry out of his excellent studies of the ANV and its famous leadership, but perhaps his most relevant works on this topic are "Lee's Army Has Not Lost Any of Its Prestige: The Impact of Gettysburg on the Army of Northern Virginia and the Confederate Home Front," in *The Third Day at Gettysburg and Beyond* (Chapel Hill: University of North Carolina Press, 1994), and especially *The Confederate War* (Cambridge, MA: Harvard University Press, 1997).

"No Nearer Heaven Now but Rather Farther Off"

The Religious Compromises and Conflicts
of Northern Soldiers

David W. Rolfs

I do not understand what I do. For what I
want to do I do not do, but what I hate I do.

—*Romans 7:15*

As Northern Christians enthusiastically marched off to war in the spring
of 1861, few imagined how severely their faith would be tested over the
next four years. Separated from their families and churches, deprived
of regular opportunities for worship, and forced to live in an exclusively
male society that was apathetic if not openly hostile to organized religion and believers, religious soldiers struggled to resist the traditional
temptations of army life and the demoralizing spiritual climate of their
wartime camps. Richard Gould, one of seven deeply religious brothers
from New York who volunteered to fight for the Union, explained the
Christian soldier's predicament in a letter to his sister: "Hannah, this is
a hard place for one to serve the Lord. I will try to serve him but I do a
great many things that [I] ought not to do and leave undone things that
I ought to do."[1] Robbed of their traditional spiritual supports and surrounded by unbelievers, many Christians found it difficult to avoid sins
of commission and omission. Those who yielded to sin knew that they
could always obtain forgiveness from a Savior who had also experienced temptation, but many could not escape the terrible sense of guilt
they felt for having been unfaithful. In a highly emotional letter to his

Indiana fiancée, "Miss Mirriam," in May 1864, Sergeant Amos Weaver could "scarcely refrain from crying" when he contemplated the various "temptations and inducements" he had to contend with in the Union army: "I wished that I was as pure and upright in heart as you are."[2]

Disappointed with the obvious moral failures of their comrades in the camps and their own spiritual shortcomings, religious soldiers were even more troubled by the terrible scenes of destruction that greeted them on the battlefield. Private J. A. Dernten was obviously still processing his first awful encounter with the enemy when he tried to describe it to a girlfriend back home: "The sights and sounds of horror that crowded those days I hope may never come before your experiences." Although "some had prophesied that if the two hostile armies should ever meet in battle array, they would drop their weapons and rush into each other's arms," Dernten sadly observed that his battlefields told "a terribly different story."[3] Caught up in the vicious guerrilla war that was ravaging Tennessee, Private Gasherie Decker of the Third Wisconsin Artillery Battery was equally disturbed by the unprecedented violence and hatred: "You at home may read the papers till you are grey and never fully realise the horrors of this war. Neighbor against neighbor. Brother against Brother and Father against Son."[4]

Regardless of the justice of their cause, Christian combatants in both armies had to reconcile their faith in a good and just God with the unprecedented evils they experienced on the battlefield, their families' and friends' grievous wartime sacrifices, and their own problematic role in the violence. Surprisingly, most Northern Christians had little difficulty reconciling their wartime experiences with their faith. Although some Civil War historians, such as Gerald Linderman, have argued that Northern soldiers gradually became demoralized during the war, especially after the 1864–1865 eastern campaigns, even Linderman acknowledges that "the drift from religious faith should not be exaggerated. . . . There were few renunciations of belief in God, or even expressions mistrusting God's control of the evolution of the war."[5] Indeed, the research of numerous other distinguished Civil War historians, including James McPherson, Reid Mitchell, Phillip Shaw Paludan, and, most recently, Steven Woodworth, seems to suggest that, if anything, Northern soldiers became more religious during the war.[6]

Most religious soldiers rationalized the killing using traditional just-war or holy-war arguments, which essentially maintained that the horrors of war were sometimes justified as a last resort or a necessary evil to combat even greater injustices, such as slavery, rebellion, and moral anarchy. There was, however, always a small but significant minority of religious soldiers who struggled to reconcile their religious values with their military duties. These soldiers either concluded that they would have to compromise some of their religious beliefs to wage a successful war against the South or experienced serious spiritual conflict when they perceived that a certain battlefield duty, their army's conduct, or some other personal sin was somehow transgressing God's laws and thus forfeiting his special favor and perhaps even their own salvation. This essay explores the rich diversity of Northern Christians' theological responses to the conflict and the degree to which they ultimately relied on their personal faith to process the meaning of their wartime experiences.[7]

Those who struggled to reconcile their wartime participation with their spiritual beliefs generally fell into two camps. The first and largest camp included those who consciously or unconsciously compromised certain prewar religious beliefs that seemed to conflict with their military duties—such as the prohibitions against hating one's enemies, seeking vengeance, or killing human beings made in God's image. The second, far smaller camp consisted of soldiers who experienced a spiritual epiphany when they suddenly realized that their wartime conduct, or that of their armies, was somehow violating God's law. Although they often expressed feelings of guilt concerning such conduct, they did not abandon their morally troublesome duties or the religious beliefs that convinced them that such behavior was evil. As a result, these soldiers were frequently burdened with various degrees of spiritual conflict and guilt for the duration of their wartime service.

Although religious soldiers may have experienced more spiritual compromises and conflicts than previously suspected, these spiritual responses must be placed in their proper historical context. First, only a small minority of religious soldiers had difficulty reconciling their faith with their military duties. Second, those who expressed doubts about their wartime actions rarely renounced their faith or abandoned their military duties. As long as they were physically capable of doing so, most continued fighting to the bitter end. Even though his faith sometimes caused a religious soldier to question the morality of his military duties, it also apparently provided him with the spiritual strength to complete his wartime mission. Finally, although this essay focuses exclusively on religious soldiers' spiritual compromises and conflicts, it is important to recognize that other non-Christian Union soldiers likely experienced similar ethical dilemmas as they wrestled with the moral implications of their battlefield duties. After all, Christians have never enjoyed a monopoly on matters of conscience. Thus, the religious soldiers' temptations and compromises might represent—at least in some respects—a microcosm of every good man's struggle to combat evil in a just manner.

There are several possible explanations as to why some religious soldiers decided to ignore or compromise certain key scriptural doctrines during the war. The simplest answer is that, like many modern believers, Civil War soldiers pragmatically adapted their faith to the popular culture around them. Sensing that their religious beliefs were no longer compatible with prevailing behaviors and attitudes, the soldiers simply changed their beliefs to fit the new wartime realities. This could be done by ignoring certain religious prohibitions or reinterpreting their previous meaning. In other cases, these modifications may have represented the natural evolution of an individual's religious beliefs, as a young man's childlike faith, previously sheltered by family and church, was transformed by the realities of life in an often harsh and unforgiving world. Those who were not well grounded in the faith before enlisting may have already been searching for reasons to discard beliefs that they had never understood or embraced in the first place.

More than anything else, however, it was the soldiers' spiritual demoralization in their wartime camps and gradual desensitization to the wartime violence that probably set the stage for many subsequent spiritual compromises. During one of the most difficult times of their lives, Northern Christians were deprived of their traditional spiritual mentors, resources, and support mechanisms. Removed from their former religious society, soldiers were thrust into a new one that often ignored or even openly mocked their religious sensibilities. Indeed, the army could not have designed a better system for demoralizing orthodox believers. While they were still struggling against the unwholesome influences of their camps, religious soldiers were suddenly thrust into their first battles, horrifically violent affairs that permanently scarred the minds of impressionable young men. The war's violence and apparent injustice undoubtedly provoked spiritual doubts and moral questions that some young believers—deprived of adequate spiritual resources—could not address on their own. Like other Union soldiers, religious troops also became increasingly desensitized or hardened to the wartime violence and suffering. When combined with their earlier spiritual demoralization in the camps and traumatic initiation into combat, this hardening probably made it difficult for some Christian soldiers to retain beliefs that hindered them in the performance of their military duties or that no longer seemed to make sense in the context of a bloody civil war.

The first major compromise made by religious soldiers was the abandonment of the prewar practice of attending weekly religious meetings and observing a strict Sunday Sabbath. Although the very nature of army life made it difficult for soldiers to continue these practices, most religious soldiers tried to create suitable substitutes for such meetings, and if they could not physically observe the Sabbath as a day of rest, they consciously observed its spirit as best they could under the circumstances. Others, in contrast, noted the loss of the Sabbath in their letters but then never raised the issue again. Those who expressed little concern over the loss of their religious meetings and the Sunday Sabbath often compromised on other major tenets of their faith as well. The loss of religious support mechanisms, such as competent chaplains, weekly religious services, and the Sabbath, no doubt contributed to this religious devolution, but the most decisive factor behind these spiritual compromises may have been the war itself. As the war continued and casualties mounted, each side became increasingly frustrated with its opponent's stubborn refusal to abandon a costly and illegitimate cause. Increasingly embittered by their so-called Christian enemies' recalcitrance and the death of family members and friends, some Northern Protestants abandoned their religious framework for waging war so that they could impose what they considered to be a more appropriate punishment on their Southern enemies. This spirit of frustration and bitterness set the stage for the religious soldiers' most egregious wartime compromises: hating their Southern adversaries, seeking personal vengeance for their enemies' "crimes," and disregarding the moral distinction between killing and murder.

Warfare was clearly sanctioned in the Old Testament and was not specifically condemned by Christ in the Gospels, but he clearly defined the proper attitude of the Christian warrior. In the scriptures, Christ instructed believers to love their enemies, forgive their sins, and do good to those who hated them. Indeed, a constant refrain in Northern wartime sermons was that although war was a necessary evil in a wicked world, God still expected soldiers to retain their Christian identities and values in battle. Religious soldiers were not supposed to fight with a spirit of hatred. Because Christ had mercifully spared other sinners who deserved to die, they were to both spare the lives of enemy soldiers who surrendered and pray for their opponents' repentance, even as they fought and killed them on the battlefield.[8]

Even though the passionate anger and dreadful carnage unleashed during the Civil War seem to completely contradict these noble religious sentiments, surprisingly, most Northern believers sincerely struggled to observe this Christian code of warfare throughout the conflict. There were certainly exceptions, but most religious soldiers did not passionately hate their sectional counterparts, seek personal vengeance against their foes, or boast about the number of Rebels they had killed. Indeed, given the context of a bloody and protracted civil war, Northern Protestants could be remarkably merciful to wounded Southern soldiers and prisoners whom they had been trying to kill just a few hours earlier. The pioneer of common soldier studies, Bell Irvin Wiley, marveled at the numerous "indications of friendly sentiment" and "acts of kindness" among the opposing participants, ironically noting that if the desperate battles "could be overlooked, it might be inferred that good feeling outweighed hostility."[9] The numerous friendly meetings of opposing pickets during the war also seem to confirm the fact that off the battlefield and away from their officers, Billy Yank and Johnny Reb genuinely enjoyed each other's company and rarely harbored any deep hatred for their sectional counterparts. As Bruce Catton observed, the war was fought between men "who when left alone, got along together beautifully."[10] My own survey of hundreds of religious soldiers' collections revealed that what was true of the average Billy Yank was even more true of his religious comrades. Most religious soldiers directed their anger and vituperation toward the Confederate leadership, not their common soldier counterparts on the other side.

When the violence escalated, however, especially in the last three years of the war, and as soldiers lost more and more family and friends to a seemingly endless war, some Northern Christians embraced a new-found hatred for their Southern foes. The religious soldiers' experiences in the South often fueled this growing hatred. Increasingly exposed to Southern intransigence on and off the battlefield—in the form of bullets, curses, glares, and other indignities—there was a gradual hardening of Northern hearts toward Southerners. Private Sylvester Bishop told his mother that he had "learned a great deal Since coming South." At first, Bishop thought that "all we had to do was to treat the Secesh well to gain them over to the Union. Experience has taught better, the milder you treat a Secesh the more bold and insolent he is." Likening Southerners to disobedient dogs, Bishop seemed to believe that it was the Northern armies' job to discipline them. Although he reassured his mother that he would not personally molest any Southern citizens or property, he confessed that his "sympathies are not so tender for Secesh who lose a little property as they were a few months ago."[11] Private Michael Branniger also found it increasingly difficult to respect his Southern neighbors as he became better acquainted with their sins: "Pen nor Tounge can not express the half that I have seen men that have been hunted for weeks by men and dogs and that dare not go near their homes for fear of being shot or hung and all because they loved the old flag and would not fight against it." Southern atrocities against Unionist neighbors in places such as Tennessee and Missouri seemed to confirm the abolitionists' prewar prophecy that those who treated Africans like animals would someday do the same thing to whites. In any event, other religious soldiers probably would have heartily endorsed Branniger's sentiment: the "longer I stay in the Army the more I hate the Rebs and there proceedings."[12]

As some Northerners came to despise Southerners for instigating a wicked war and killing their friends and relatives, their passionate hatred fueled an intense desire for revenge. The scriptures repeatedly admonished believers that vengeance belonged to the Lord and that by taking matters into their own hands, believers would be subjected to a host of other evils. But with the entire country now paying the price for the South's prewar sins, some Northern Christians were determined to make Southerners bear the brunt of the wartime judgment. For example, when General William T. Sherman ordered Atlanta evacuated so that it could be more easily defended from Southern counterattacks, Private John Siperly told his fiancée that although he once might have felt sorry for the "thousands of families" who would have to "leave home and property" and be "exiled from all that is dear to them," he now believed that the good citizens of Atlanta were merely reaping what they had sown. "To the superficial observer," Siperly noted, the forced evacuation might seem "cruel, and in fact it is hard," but to those better acquainted with the South's wartime crimes, it seemed like an appropriate punishment: "Look at the resting places of over half a million victims—look at as many more hobling about cripled for life—and wasting away in hospitals . . . look at the 18 acre pen at Andersonville. . . . I say look at and think of all this . . . and then can you say it is unjust?"[13] Convinced that the South alone was responsible for these wartime evils, for some religious soldiers, vengeance became the order of the day.

This was certainly true for some of the religious soldiers locked in a merciless guerrilla war against Confederate partisans in Missouri and Tennessee. After Confederate irregulars burned several local bridges near his Missouri camp, Private Edwin Sackett of the Fifty-second Illinois told his family, "they are a pack of cowards they are like a theif in the night if they are pursed by troops they cut + run to their homes if you go to their houses to question them + they are good union men. . . . I don't know any other way to subdue them only to shoot them down or hang them up." Stationed a couple hundred miles to the southeast in Nashville, Tennessee, Captain Alexander Ayers told his wife that if he were in charge, "I would put the torch to every house in the state—the women may look out for themselves." Irish Private David King Jr. of the Sixty-eighth Illinois was equally incensed with the cowards who used the cover of darkness to stab unsuspecting Union pickets and stage night-time ambushes outside Cairo's Fort Defiance: "Just such *conduct* makes me feel like going through the war and shoot[ing] every rebbell in the field." Although he thought the war was "horable," Private John Barnard wanted those "that brought it on" to suffer its evil consequences: "I do not want any compromise I want them Subdued or exterminated."[14]

Religious warriors battling Confederate guerrillas were not the only Protestant soldiers who usurped God's authority over the dispensation of vengeance. Just like Herman Melville's Captain Ahab, religious soldiers who lost family members or relatives in the war or who heard about alleged Southern atrocities sometimes embarked on their own personal quests for revenge. As in most tribal blood feuds, the preferred form of retribution was invariably life for life—or better yet, as many enemy lives as possible. A year after the Rebels killed his brother in battle, Private John Lindley Harris's heart was still consumed with vengeance. To comfort his heartbroken father, Harris assured him that he would avenge his brother's death "by getting some of them to bite the dust before the war ends."[15]

Although Private John Jones's early letters sound as though they were written by a long-suffering preacher, in the fall of 1863 he apparently embraced a different Gospel when he learned that some of his comrades had allegedly been shot in cold blood after surrendering to the enemy: "What they did on that day will not be forgotten, they will be repaid. Many of our men had surrendered to them, only to be mowed down like grass. It made our blood boil, and it will be a sorry day for the rebs when we get at them."[16] With some religious soldiers beginning to nurse a spirit of vengeance against their Southern enemies, it was not much of a leap for others to lose sight of the traditional Christian distinction between justified killing in combat and the murder of one's enemies. Organized wartime violence was supposed to be dispassionate, anonymous, limited, and conducted for public, not private, reasons. But those who pursued vengeance personalized the violence by killing their victims with premeditation and malice. Victims were singled out in blind hatred, guilty or not, and furiously dispatched, on or off the battlefield, with little or no regard for their common humanity. In short, whereas the evangelical Protestant worldview recognized that there were some subtle but important differences between legitimate wartime killing and murder, in their terrible quests for personal vengeance, some religious soldiers obviously ignored these distinctions.

Nineteenth-century evangelicals did not believe that it was immoral to kill enemy soldiers, but they thought that the motives, attitudes, and methods of those who did the killing could conceivably be sinful. Christians were not supposed to take pleasure in the physical act of killing or celebrate the death of enemies made in God's image. In his righteous judgment, God might destroy the wicked, but he took no pleasure in their death. Ideally, Christian soldiers were to kill their enemies without malice on the battlefield and then care for their wounded opponents afterward.[17]

Perhaps twentieth-century Christian apologist C. S. Lewis summarized this traditional Protestant understanding of just warfare best when he explained that the greatest challenge confronting Christian warriors was not the physical act of killing or even justifying the violence, but rather ensuring that one always fought with the right attitude: "We may kill if necessary, but we must not hate and enjoy hating. . . .

Even while we kill . . . we must try to feel about the enemy as we feel about ourselves—to wish he were not bad, to hope that he may, in this world or another, be cured: in fact to wish his good." Those who failed to check their darker passions in combat would likely be consumed by the terrible hatred and violence accompanying such warfare. According to Lewis, failing to love and forgive—even one's wartime enemies—would gradually cause the soldier to see everything—God, friends, family, and even himself—"as bad, and [he would] not be able to stop doing it." He would, in effect, be "fixed for ever in a universe of pure hatred."[18]

In addition to entertaining proper attitudes about the enemy, in the early stages of the war, some religious soldiers seemed anxious to ensure that their method of killing the enemy did not violate God's laws. The government had clearly authorized soldiers to serve as instruments of retributive justice, but the scriptures enjoined them to exact such retribution in a just and carefully circumscribed manner. They were to punish evildoers, but in a manner that respected their special status as creatures made in God's image and that avoided engendering a spirit of greater anger and revenge in the hearts of their enemies. Although it was their duty to defeat—and, if necessary, destroy—their enemies in battle, soldiers were to employ only the minimal amount of force needed to achieve that end. Given this Christian understanding of warfare, Protestant soldiers generally concluded that it was morally justifiable to kill enemy soldiers threatening their homes, families, and God-ordained government as long as they were serving in official, government-sanctioned armies.

Even when armed with the government's authority to kill, most religious soldiers were still extremely anxious about possibly violating the Sixth Commandment. To ensure that they did not transgress God's law, religious soldiers tried to distinguish between certain methods of killing that were morally justified and others that were not. Since it was every soldier's duty to help defeat the opposing army in battle, religious soldiers generally believed that shooting enemy soldiers on the battlefield was morally justified but that other methods of killing, such as sharpshooting, bushwhacking, and shooting pickets, were nothing short of murder. These latter methods of killing were illegitimate because they did not significantly influence the outcome of battles and, more importantly, they did not give enemy soldiers an adequate opportunity to either defend themselves or make appropriate spiritual preparations for death. In the first two years of the war, it was relatively easy for religious soldiers to observe this Christian code of warfare.

As the fighting continued, however, and religious soldiers became increasingly hardened by the prolonged violence, some found it increasingly difficult to uphold such a code and maintain the distinction between justifiable killing and murder. For example, by 1864, an early and idealistic Union volunteer named Richard Gould had grown so accustomed to the Rebel sharpshooters that were constantly "pecking away" at him that he no longer minded them as he watched in fascination as Pennsylvania coal miners burrowed under a Confederate fort at Petersburg "for the purpose of blowing it up." Gould had also apparently lost whatever respect he once had for the common humanity of his Southern adversaries. As he coldly informed his loved ones back home, when the engineers detonated the subterranean explosives, "We will send a few Johnnies nearer Heaven than they would ever get [on their own?]. . . . We are getting just right now to fight. The men are hardened to it." Although the resulting explosion (which launched the disastrous battle of the Crater) killed nearly 300 unwary Confederates without offering them any chance to prepare for death or defend themselves, there is no evidence that Gould, a devout Christian, regretted the circumstances surrounding their murder.[19]

Perhaps to ease their troubled Christian consciences, some religious soldiers who were obsessed with killing their sectional enemies began to depict Southerners as somehow less human than their Northern counterparts. Rather than uphold the Noahidic Covenant concerning man's unique moral status as a creature made in the image of God, these soldiers began to dismiss their Southern enemies' common humanity. This was not difficult for some Northerners, who had always viewed themselves as culturally superior to the poorer, less-educated Southern rank and file.[20] Transforming men into brute beasts made it easier for Christians to disregard scriptural warnings about murdering those who bore God's image. After all, if religious soldiers were merely hunting primitive savages or animals, their motives, methods, and attitudes were of little consequence.

After witnessing the results of Confederate guerrilla activity in eastern Tennessee, another pious Gould brother named William told his sister that Southerners were worse than savages: "I have seen enough of southern chivelry. They are the most Barbarious race of people in the civilized world. They are worse than the red man of the forest for they will use a friend well." Just as earlier U.S. administrations had labeled Native Americans "uncivilized savages" to justify robbing them of their lands, vindictive religious soldiers were now stripping away Southerners' humanity to justify their destruction.[21]

Soldiers who ignored their Southern enemies' special moral status sometimes revealed their own inhumanity when they confessed that they were not troubled by the killing or that they even enjoyed it. Although he was very anxious before his first major battle, Private William Onstot felt much better when he recalled that he was fighting for a holy cause and "against a treasonable horde. . . . After this I was troubled no more with unpleasant feelings." As Onstot boasted to his sister, "I felt as cool as though I was *shooting chickens*." Private George Squier told his wife, Ellen, that when he began to return the Rebels' fire at Shiloh, he was "as cool and composed as if sitting down for a chat or shooting squirrels." A few months later, while defending Union supply trains from Confederate irregulars in Tennessee, Squier shared that there was "something rather exciting in shooting, and particularly at one's fellow beings." Other religious soldiers began to take perverse pleasure in the death throes of their enemies. After telling his brother that his unit had been justified in sacking a local Southern town, Arthur Lee Bailhache admitted that in the most recent battle, "It was a sad sight and yet a not unpleasant one to see those infernal rebels lying on the field—Kicking like a flock of dead partridges."[22] Although religious soldiers embraced may compromises during the war, surely one of the worst was deriving satisfaction from the death of other human beings.

Whereas a significant minority of religious soldiers ignored or compromised various morally problematic or inconvenient beliefs during the war, a much smaller number stubbornly clung to their beliefs throughout the conflict—even as they failed to live up to them. Those who chose to retain their prewar religious principles, despite a growing conviction that their personal actions were betraying them, experienced varying degrees of spiritual conflict as they struggled to continue performing their duty in spite of a guilty conscience.

These religious soldiers often began to express spiritual doubts about the morality of certain military duties, the escalating violence, and other personal sins during the last year of the war, when Ulysses S. Grant dramatically accelerated the pace of the fighting with his "On to Richmond" campaign and inadvertently subjected his men to even greater wartime stresses. The resulting battle fatigue, exhaustion, and unprecedented casualties undoubtedly contributed to some religious soldiers' subsequent spiritual crises in the final stages of the war. These spiritual conflicts posed a serious moral dilemma for the soldiers. Torn between an intense desire to please God and assure their place in heaven and an equally strong commitment to their country and comrades, these soldiers probably experienced a certain degree of cognitive dissonance.

Webster's Dictionary defines *cognitive dissonance* as a "psychological conflict resulting from incongruous beliefs and attitudes held simultaneously." According to the theory of cognitive dissonance, most people naturally seek consistency between their beliefs and their attitudes and behaviors. When an individual's behavior or attitude contradicts one of his or her beliefs, the person experiences dissonance, or a profound sense of physical discomfort. This moral dissonance often causes the person to feel a profound sense of moral tension or guilt. Because dissonance always makes the individual feel uncomfortable and stressed, the natural reaction is to try to restore consistency by reducing or removing the inconsistency in life. However, because the individual often cannot avoid the behavior, the best way to do this is by altering the individual's beliefs about the deviant behavior. Although an individual can also reduce dissonance by changing his or her self-perception, this is not encouraged because it can sometimes lead to highly destructive attacks on the individual's self-concept.[23]

Protestant soldiers who experienced cognitive dissonance—or a growing conviction that their combat duties or some other personal sin was somehow transgressing God's laws—were caught in a terrible dilemma. They could remove that sense of guilt by either abandoning their deviant military behavior or changing their beliefs concerning that behavior, but given their strong commitment to faith, cause, and comrades, they considered both options immoral. This left Protestant soldiers with only one option for relieving their growing dissonance: changing their perceptions of themselves. This was the least desirable solution for restoring moral consistency, because it caused soldiers to question or, in some cases, seriously attack their self-concepts. For deeply religious soldiers who believed in the depravity of human nature and thus probably had a negative self-image already, this process of self-evaluation was particularly harmful because it only reinforced their sense of guilt at having failed to live up to God's laws. This intense moral scrutiny often burdened soldiers who were already suffering from the emotional consequences of cognitive dissonance with new doubts about themselves and the sincerity of their faith. In some of the more extreme cases of spiritual conflict, religious soldiers may have become depressed as they began to question some of their former religious certainties.[24]

It may not be possible to properly diagnose a soldier's psychological state on the basis of a few letters, but one can certainly make a reasonable hypothesis based on the evidence. In many cases, soldiers who expressed spiritual doubts about the morality of their wartime activities seemed to be manifesting the classic symptoms of depression: loss of interest in the events of everyday life, general irritability and fatigue, recurrent thoughts about death, and inappropriate guilt.[25] For example, while traveling aboard the steamboat *Empress* in January 1863, Private Daniel Webster observed that many of his comrades no longer seemed interested in the war or in the ultimate fate of their cause: "We do not see that enthusiasm among our soldiers that we did one year ago. All appear to merely exist and act as if they go into battle because they were obliged to, and not because they felt any interest in it or cared whether our cause succeeded or not." Unfortunately, such disillusionment often proved to be highly contagious. As Webster complained to his wife, "I tell you what, it is a very hard matter for a man to keep up good courage and spirits with such a manifest feeling existing around him."[26] In an army largely composed of citizen-soldiers, such apathy could prove highly deleterious to both the soldiers' morale and the cause for which they were fighting.

Even the most ardent patriots' health suffered when they kept fighting despite their increasingly troubled consciences. In January 1864 Sergeant Amos Weaver informed a family friend that the emotional and physical demands of the war were ruining him and his comrades. Wishing "to turn away from the sad battlefield scene" because he abhorred "the ferocious atrocities perpetuated during this cruel war," Weaver sadly noted that the war was "frightfully shortening our lives and hurrying us off to the Tomb many of us will be if we are so fortunate as to escape the battlefield . . . disqualified and so indisposed that home comforts will never restore us to our former condition."[27] Although the hardships Weaver described were primarily physical in nature, given our increasing understanding of the interrelationship between stress and human illness, one can only imagine how much additional stress was created by these soldiers' spiritual conflicts and what the long-term impact was on their health.

In their physically exhausted and depressed states, some religious soldiers had already begun to dwell unhealthily on the subject of death. While awaiting the next major attack on Vicksburg in early 1863, a Wisconsin private named Robert Steele seemed increasingly disillusioned and worried that he might not survive the battle: "I am sick of this cursed war and it is enough to make any one sick that has a heart to see the way thing[s] are carried on. I hope throug the mercy of God to see the end and be permited to return to our home in safety."[28]

Other religious soldiers' thoughts also turned increasingly to death. When he learned that his favorite aunt back home had passed away, Private John Jones became almost obsessed with what he believed was his own imminent death and repeatedly inserted the text of Matthew 22:44, a verse about Christ's Second Coming, into his loved ones' letters. After surviving Sherman's first disastrous attack on Vicksburg, Jones quoted the passage in a letter to his parents: "You probably know better than we do how many were lost. I know that a very large number had to face the last judgment and eternity. We are daily warned 'Therefore be ye also ready: for in such an hour as ye think not the Son of man cometh.'" Three weeks later, Jones cited the ominous passage again as he penned a letter near one of his regiment's improvised graveyards. After recording the verse, Jones gloomily noted, "We are being daily forewarned by seeing others from our regiment being buried." One wonders whether Jones was prepared for his own final judgment when he was killed a year later near Jackson, Louisiana.[29]

Other religious soldiers seemed unhealthily preoccupied with guilt. In 1864 a veteran Union artilleryman who had recently lost a brother in the war shared his religious views with a Wisconsin girlfriend. Although he claimed to share his friend's Christian faith, he now rejected the concept of "eternal damnation" because he could not imagine a worse punishment "than a guilty conscience." To flush out his vision of hell, the soldier invoked the words of the Old Testament prophet Isaiah: "'God saith' There is no peace for the wicked, 'a guilty conscience will dent[?] Its sting.' We may try all the pleasures of the world in turn; but we cannot be happy. We may plunge deeper and deeper into the wildest excitements but we cannot drown that conscience." Was he just speaking in abstract theological terms, or was he describing the personal demons that tormented believers who thought that they had somehow failed God?[30]

The principal cause of these religious soldiers' depression was not the thought that they might be killed in battle but rather the distinct possibility that God might not forgive them or their side for violating his commandments. Over time, some had come to realize that the scriptures were a double-edged sword: the same Bible that soldiers used to justify their holy crusade against the South also condemned the violence of war. The scriptures warned that God would demand a special accounting for "whoever sheds the blood of man . . . for in the image of God has made man."[31] Other passages, such as Christ's admonition to Peter to put back his sword, "for all who draw the sword will die by the sword," also seemed to condemn the violence of war.[32] Warfare, bloodshed, and ruin were the fruits of evildoers, and numerous Old Testament and New Testament passages urged believers to live peaceful lives.[33] The apostle Paul was explicit on this point in his epistle to the Romans: "Do not repay anyone evil for evil. . . . If it is possible, as far as it depends on you, live at peace with everyone."[34]

Religious soldiers who were convinced of these biblical truths but kept fighting anyway questioned whether a good God would ever forgive them for consciously continuing to do something that they knew was evil. Gerald Linderman touched on this theme in *Embattled Courage*. He noted that by 1865, even the renowned Christian veteran Colonel Joshua Chamberlain had begun to doubt that Union "soldiers were doing the work God intended them to do. . . . The carnage perplexed him and he was no longer sure that by killing rebels he and his men continued to execute God's will."[35] After a particularly savage battle outside Petersburg, Chamberlain observed all the shattered bodies littering the battlefield and rued: "We had with us . . . more than five hundred bruised bodies of men,—men made in the image of God, marred by the hand of God, and must we say in the name of God? And where is the reckoning for such things? And who is answerable? One might almost shrink from the sound of his own voice, which had launched into the palpitating air words of order—do we call it?—fraught with such ruin. Was it God's command we heard, or His forgiveness we must forever implore?"[36]

In the afterword to *Religion and the American Civil War,* James McPherson also shared a poignant example of a conscience-stricken officer concerned about the eternal consequences of knowingly violating God's laws: "Even after two years of combat experience, the lieutenant colonel of the 57th Indiana continued to agonize about the question: 'How can a soldier be a Christian? Read all of Christ's teachings, and then tell me whether one engaged in maiming and butchering men—men made in the express image of God himself—can be saved under the Gospel.' He had still not resolved the question when he was killed at Resaca in May 1864."[37]

By substituting the gospel of war for the Gospel of Christ, had religious soldiers somehow forfeited their place in heaven? After surviving another "close call" in battle in the fall of 1862, Lieutenant John Blackwell had his doubts and confided his deepest fears to his wife: "I am not happy. You know how often I fell doubts of my safety, how dark my soul is + how sin mars all my happiness. . . . Business drives me all day long but at quiet hours, in the stillness of the night conscience wakes and stings me. Dearest I'm afraid that just so near as that bullet was to my heart just so near I was to eternal ruin + yet [it] has made so little impression on me that I fear I am no nearer heaven now but rather farther off. But drops of grief care not or pay the doubt I own + besides I make you sad. Keep these things as our secrets. God knows them."[38]

Increasingly troubled by his own spiritual doubts, Private Hamlin Coe of the Nineteenth Michigan Volunteers also lost his former certainty concerning salvation. After a furious midsummer battle in Georgia, where "many a poor fellow fell, and we gained nothing but a little ground," Coe reflected on the horrors of war and asked his wife, "Will God forgive men for such work is a question I often ask myself, but I receive a silent reply and utter my own prayers for the safety of my poor soul and my country."[39] Although Coe never received the heavenly reassurance he so earnestly sought, like most other religious soldiers, he apparently retained his faith in a just and sovereign God.

Although only a minority of religious soldiers failed to reconcile their military service with their faith, the preceding survey illustrates the remarkable diversity of their theological responses to the dilemma. When soldiers perceived that there was a conflict between their faith and their duty, they generally concluded that duty to country came first and adapted their faith accordingly. Although these compromises took various forms and were probably both conscious and unconscious, principled and pragmatic, once implemented, they were rarely retreated from. Perceived incompatibilities between faith and duty, however, did not always result in a compromise of religious principles—at least in the heart of the believer. A handful of believers refused to abandon either their beliefs or a growing conviction that their combat duties were immoral and might rob them of their temporal and eternal salvation.

This essay also demonstrates that Northern Christians took their faith far more seriously than previously imagined. Popular stereotypes concerning the irreligious nature of Northern soldiers probably originated in the work of postwar Southern apologists such as William W. Bennett and J. William Jones, whose one-sided histories of the late-war revivals in the Southern armies played an important role in creating the Lost Cause legend of the Christian Southern soldier. Although professional historians eventually rejected most of this Lost Cause apologia, for some reason, the myth of the irreligious Yankee persisted. Perhaps part of the problem is that, until relatively recently, the subject of religious faith in the Civil War, especially as experienced by the common soldier and his family, was generally overlooked by historians of religion.

But as the writings of Steven Woodworth, Reid Mitchell, and others have increasingly emphasized, many Northern soldiers were intensely religious.[40] Religion was the prism through which they viewed and interpreted all their wartime experiences. As historian Edward L. Ayers noted, "Religion lay at the heart of who Americans were even as they killed one another. . . . Faith, theology, and church constituted the very language of self-understanding, defined the limits of sympathy and imagination, [and] provided the terms of vengeance and solace."[41] In a period that religious historian Mark Noll characterizes as the golden age of Protestantism, most antebellum Americans were raised in a society steeped in evangelical values and traditions. With their own identity and worldview so firmly rooted in a commonsense reading of the scriptures, it was only natural that when confronted with the terrible suffering and chaos of a protracted civil war, antebellum believers turned to God for the meaning and strength they needed to weather the storm. Soldiers' faith provided a rationale for the terrible violence and suffering, comfort to those victimized by the fighting, meaning to otherwise senseless wartime tragedies, and hope that the soldiers' sacrifices were not in vain and would someday be rewarded.

One of the problems with the postwar literature about religious soldiers, which is often unintentionally perpetuated in today's limited literature on the subject, is that it often defines their faith too simplistically. Christian soldiers are erroneously portrayed as otherworldly saints whose naïve faith never wavered in the face of constant wartime temptations, dangers, hardships, and military reverses. This study, and particularly the examples of soldiers who experienced spiritual conflicts during the war, belies this one-dimensional stereotype of soldiers' faith by demonstrating that even devout soldiers could have spiritual doubts when confronted with the tragic circumstances of a civil war.

The common soldiers' faith was actually far more realistic and complex than previously portrayed—realistic, in that it was a practical faith that seriously addressed the everyday problems believers encountered living in a fallen world, and complex because it was a comprehensive faith that encompassed a wide range of changing religious sentiments, from the steadfast certitude of the seasoned saint to the despair of a less mature believer suddenly confronted with doubts. If their faith's realism anticipated human frailties and failures, its complexity provided believers with a means of overcoming such problems—or at least coping with them effectively. In times of crisis, Christian soldiers' faith assured them that a loving Heavenly Father would graciously give his children the strength to endure their temporary trials until, one way or another, he eventually delivered them from evil. That so many of them ultimately weathered their wartime spiritual crises is a testimony to the tremendous resiliency, practicality, and adaptability of their Christian faith.

So if faith played such an important role in sustaining Northern Christians on the battlefield, what impact did these soldiers' spiritual compromises and conflicts have on the war effort or their own military service? Since only a small minority of religious soldiers embraced such compromises or doubts, it is unlikely that their religious decisions significantly influenced the Northern war effort. As far as their actual battlefield performance is concerned, soldiers who compromised certain prewar beliefs rarely expressed any subsequent spiritual doubts about their wartime activities and seemed to perform their military duties as well as the next soldier. But could the same be said of soldiers who experienced spiritual crises—those who continued to fight despite a growing personal conviction that their wartime service was an affront to God? These soldiers experienced varying degrees of spiritual conflict, and some of them were undoubtedly deeply disturbed by their seemingly irreconcilable spiritual conflicts. But did these cognitive distractions undermine their military performance or place them at greater risk on the battlefield? Although this is a plausible conclusion, the limited nature of the evidence I have compiled thus far precludes any definitive answer to this question. Perhaps the best that can be said about these soldiers' faith is that it cut both ways. It imposed a terrible emotional burden on some soldiers by convincing them of their wartime sins, but as McPherson noted in his study of common soldiers' motivations, it also made them more courageous by dispelling their fear of death.[42] The same faith that raised doubts about the morality of their wartime actions instructed soldiers that life on earth was fleeting at best and that an infinitely more satisfying eternal existence awaited those who ultimately proved faithful to God and country. Unfortunately, this hope did not spare soldiers from the dangers of the battlefield or the heartache of a wounded conscience.

Those who experienced spiritual crises as they sincerely struggled to fulfill their moral obligations to both God and country undoubtedly suffered more cognitive dissonance than did soldiers who ignored or compromised their beliefs. Although the former faithfully executed their duties to the end, their seemingly irreconcilable moral dilemmas burdened these soldiers with spiritual conflicts and guilt that caused many of them to either become depressed or experience serious doubts about their faith. Soldiers who compromised their beliefs, meanwhile, experienced little if any such dissonance during the war. These compromises certainly proved expedient at the time, but their long-term spiritual costs may have been high, for as Christian soldiers knew better than anyone else, there is nothing worse than a guilty conscience.

NOTES

1. Richard Gould to sister, in *Dear Sister: The Civil War Letters of the Brothers Gould,* ed. Robert F. Harris and John Niflot (Westport, CT: Praeger, 1998), 64.

2. Amos C. Weaver to Mirriam, May 13, 1864, Amos C. Weaver Letters, Indiana State Historical Society.

3. J. A. Dernten to Kittie Crandall, October 29, 1862, Crandall Family Correspondence, State Historical Society of Wisconsin.

4. Gasherie Decker to sister Gertrude, August 22, 1863, Gasherie Decker Diaries and Letters, State Historical Society of Wisconsin.

5. Gerald F. Linderman, *Embattled Courage: The Experience of Combat in the American Civil War* (New York: Free Press, 1989), 255. Linderman may have overstated his argument concerning the religious disillusionment of the Northern armies. Other scholars' work, such as James M. McPherson's *For Cause and Comrades: Why Men Fought in the Civil War* (New York: Oxford University Press, 1997), Gardiner H. Shattuck Jr.'s *A Shield and Hiding Place: The Religious Life of the Civil War Armies* (Macon, GA: Mercer University Press, 1987), and Steven E. Woodworth's *While God Is Marching On: The Religious World of Civil War Soldiers* (Lawrence: University Press of Kansas, 2001), do not support Linderman's claim that the Northern armies became increasingly disillusioned with religion at the end of the war. Perhaps it would be more accurate to state that less time and energy were devoted to religious worship and private religious activities after Grant assumed command of the Union armies and unintentionally inaugurated a grinding war of attrition and an almost continuous period of fighting in the east. It was this nonstop fighting, not general disillusionment with religion or with the Union cause, that caused an increasing number of soldiers to physically and spiritually break down. Once the fighting ended, the religious revivals returned—something that would not have happened if the eastern troops had truly abandoned their religion. A dramatic increase in the membership of Northern churches between 1860 and 1866, despite the wartime deaths of more than 300,000 Northerners, also seems to belie Linderman's disillusionment argument. See also Timothy L. Smith, *Revivalism and Social Reform: American Protestantism on the Eve of the Civil War* (New York: Harper and Row, 1957), 20–21.

6. See McPherson, *For Cause and Comrades,* 62–76; Reid Mitchell, "Christian Soldiers? Perfecting the Confederacy," in *Religion and the American Civil War,* ed. Randall M. Miller, Harry S. Stout, and Charles Reagan Wilson (New York: Oxford University Press, 1998); Phillip Shaw Paludan, "Religion and the American Civil War," in ibid., 24–25; and Woodworth, *While God Is Marching On.*

7. This essay is drawn from a larger manuscript, "No Peace for the Wicked: How Northern Christians Justified Their Participation in the American Civil War." I have spent the better part of the last decade studying the lives of the common soldiers of the Civil War and, more specifically, serious Christian believers serving in the Union army. All the cited quotes are drawn from the collections of Union soldiers that I identified as religious or, in some cases, deeply religious. Since even Christians would acknowledge that only God knows the state of a man's soul, it was extremely difficult to come up with an objective formula for identifying such soldiers. Church rolls could provide many names but would not necessarily identify men of serious Christian faith, and they would exclude too many Christian soldiers. For various reasons,

many serious nineteenth-century believers never formally joined churches, and thousands of additional soldiers converted to Christianity during the war. The final, rather laborious formula I devised was to read a soldier's entire collection and observe how often he employed obvious religious language in a serious way to discuss the war or interpret his wartime experiences. If a given collection included at least three incidences of such religious expression, I included this soldier in my "religious" sample. Soldiers who did not discuss religion in their letters or who used only popular religious phrases and images in passing or superficially were excluded as nonreligious. I generally adhered to this rule of three except when citing soldiers who had previously been identified as religious by other historians or when the collections contained only a couple of letters or fragments. Admittedly, this process was somewhat subjective, but the result represents my best efforts to fashion an objective formula for distinguishing the more religious Union soldiers from non-Christians or those of nominal faith.

8. See Matthew 5:38–44, Luke 6:27–35; these and all subsequent biblical quotations are from the New International Version. For example, after the war, the South's premier Christian general, Robert E. Lee, claimed that he had never harbored any bitter or vindictive feelings toward his Northern enemies and that he had prayed every day for the repentance of those people who were waging war on his beloved Virginia.

9. Bell Irvin Wiley, *The Life of Billy Yank: The Common Soldier of the Union* (Indianapolis: Bobbs-Merrill, 1952; reprint, Baton Rouge: Louisiana State University Press, 1978), 351, 356–57.

10. Bruce Catton and John Leakley E. B. Long, *Reflections on the Civil War* (Garden City, NY: Doubleday, 1981), 46.

11. Sylvester C. Bishop to mother, July 21, 1862, Sylvester Bishop Papers, Indiana State Historical Society.

12. Michael Heyes Branniger to wife, May 10, 1864, Michael Hayes Branniger Cunningham Letters, State Historical Society of Wisconsin.

13. John R. Siperly to Jennie, September 21, 1864, Jennie Safford Smith Correspondence, Robert M. Woodruff Memorial Library, Emory University.

14. Edwin C. Sackett to family, December 27, 1861, Edwin C. and John H. Sackett Papers, Illinois State Historical Library; Alexander Miller Ayers to wife, November 11, 1862, Alexander Miller Ayers Papers, Robert W. Woodruff Library, Emory University; David King Jr. to sister, July 1, 1861, King Family Papers, Illinois State Historical Library; John M. Barnard to wife, March 19, 1863, John M. Barnard Letters, Indiana State Historical Society.

15. John Lindley Harris to father, April 6, 1863, John Lindley Harris Papers, Illinois State Historical Society.

16. Private John G. Jones to parents, November 21, 1863, John G. Jones Letters, State Historical Society of Wisconsin.

17. Ezekiel 18:23, 32; Ezekiel 33:11; Psalms 11:5; Isaiah 59:6–7.

18. C. S. Lewis, *Mere Christianity: A Revised and Amplified Edition, with a New Introduction, of the Three Books "Broadcast Talks," "Christian Behavior" and "Beyond Personality"* (San Francisco: HarperCollins, 2001), 119–20, 118.

19. Richard Gould, *Dear Sister,* 74, 130.

20. McPherson, *For Cause and Comrades,* 154. Wiley, *The Life of Billy Yank,* 98–99.

21. William Gould, *Dear Sister,* 81.

22. William H. Onstot to sister, November 16, 1861, William H. Onstot Papers, Illinois State Historical Library; George W. Squier, *This Wilderness of War: The Civil War Letters of George W. Squier, Hoosier Volunteer,* ed. Julie A. Doyle, John David Smith, and Richard M. McMurry (Knoxville: University of Tennessee Press, 1998), 11, 24; Arthur Lee Bailhache to brother, October 22, 1861, Bailhache-Brayman Papers, Illinois State Historical Library.

23. *Webster's Ninth New Collegiate Dictionary* (Springfield, MA: Merriam-Webster, 1987), 257; Jeff Stone, "Behavioral Discrepancies and the Role of Construal Processes in Cognitive Dissonance," in *Cognitive Social Psychology: The Princeton Symposium on the Legacy and Future of Social Cognition,* ed. Gordon B. Moskowitz (Mahwah, NJ, and London: Lawrence Erlbaum Associates, 2001), 41–44, 46–49, 51–52, 57; see also Social Influence Theories at http://osru.orst.edu/instruct/comm32/gwalker/influence.htm.

24. Herbert C. Kelman and Reuben M. Baron, "Inconsistency as a Psychological Signal," in *Theories of Cognitive Consistency: A Source Book,* ed. Robert P. Abelson, Elliot Aronson, William J. McGuire, Theodore M. Newcomb, Milton J. Rosenberg, and Percy H. Tannenbaum (Chicago: Rand McNally, 1968), 332–34; Eva M. Pomerantz, Jill L. Saxon, and Gwen A. Kenney, "Self-Evaluation: The Development of Sex Differences," in Moskowitz, *Cognitive Social Psychology,* 63.

25. David E. Larson, ed., *Mayo Clinic: Family Health Book* (New York: William Morrow, 1990), 1018.

26. Daniel Webster to Gertrude, January 6, 1863, Daniel Webster Letters, State Historical Society of Wisconsin.

27. Amos C. Weaver to Miss Wills, January 22, 1864, Letters, Indiana Historical Society.

28. Robert Steele to wife, January 31, 1863, Robert Steele Papers, Wisconsin Historical Society.

29. Private John G. Jones to parents, January 5 and 24, 1863, John G. Jones Letters, State Historical Society of Wisconsin.

30. Will Crandall to Kitty, November 3, 1864, Crandall Family Correspondence, State Historical Society of Wisconsin.

31. Genesis 9:5–6.

32. Matthew 26:52.

33. Isaiah 59:1–8; Romans 3:15–17; Psalms 120:6–7; Isaiah 32:17–18; Psalms 34:12–14; Mark 9:50; Hebrews 12:14; 1 Peter 3:11.

34. Romans 12:17–21.

35. Linderman, *Embattled Courage,* 256.

36. Joshua Chamberlain, *The Passing of the Armies: An Account of the Final Campaign of the Army of the Potomac, Based upon Personal Reminiscences of the Fifth Army* (Lincoln: University of Nebraska Press, 1998), 55.

37. James M. McPherson, "Afterword," in Miller et al., *Religion and the American Civil War,* 410.

38. John Blackwell to wife, October 11, 1862, John A. Blackwell Letters, Indiana State Historical Society.

39. Quoted in Linderman, *Embattled Courage,* 256–57.

40. See, for example, Mitchell, "Christian Soldiers? Perfecting the Confederacy"; Phillip Shaw Paludan, *"A People's Contest": The Union and the Civil War, 1861–1865* (Lawrence: University Press of Kansas, 1996); and Woodworth, *While God Is Marching On.*

41. Edward L. Ayers, *Journal of Southern Religion, 1998–99,* review cited from Internet posting at http://jsur.as.wvu.edu/ayers.htm.

42. McPherson, *For Cause and Comrades,* 68.

"STRANGERS IN A STRANGE LAND"

Christian Soldiers in the Early Months of the Civil War

Kent T. Dollar

On December 15, 1862, two days after the bloody fighting at the battle of Fredericksburg ended, Marion Hill Fitzpatrick, a private in the Forty-fifth Georgia Infantry, admitted to his wife in a letter home: "I have gone entirely wild and if I ever get back I shall have my name taken off the church book for it is a shame and disgrace to the cause of Christ for it to be there. . . . I want you all to continue to pray for me but look upon me no longer as a worthy member of the church."[1]

Army life in the early months of the Civil War was inhospitable to men of faith. Few soldiers were interested in spiritual matters, religious services were held irregularly, and the temptations in camp were fierce. Scholars writing about religion in the ranks have concluded that most soldiers succumbed to temptation during this period and only as the war wore on did they return to their religious roots. In his classic work *The Life of Johnny Reb,* Bell Irvin Wiley asserts that many Southerners "who at home took an active interest in church affairs lapsed into a state of indifference after a short time in the army. . . . They might have been good boys when they left, and they would be good boys after they returned, but in the meantime they wanted to have a fling at gambling, drinking and swearing, and they did not wish to be bothered with preachers." Other historians agree. Drew Gilpin Faust, in her influential 1987 article on Confederate revivalism, maintains that early on, camp life was not conducive to religion and suggests that many soldiers backslid because they were "removed from the restraining, 'softening' moral influences of womanhood and hearth." More recently, Steven Woodworth, in his excellent book *While God Is Marching On,* concludes that camp life "during the first year or so of the war was not having a good moral and religious effect on the soldiers." He says that for Northern and Southern soldiers alike, "the opportunity to seek imagined pleasures and practice forbidden vices in the relative anonymity of distant places, large groups, and uniform clothing was more than [they] cared to resist."[2]

The raucous atmosphere in the camps early in the Civil War provided numerous distractions and temptations, and without question, many men (like Fitzpatrick) gave in. But did they all do so, or did some remain true to their Christian convictions? Evidence suggests that some soldiers endeavored to stand fast in their religious faith despite their surroundings. Indeed, devout Christians criticized the iniquitous behavior of their comrades and persisted in their beliefs at a time when few of their fellow soldiers were interested in spiritual matters. Well before religious revivalism swept both the Union and Confederate armies beginning in the fall of 1862, pious soldiers evinced a genuine desire to continue their religious practices from the antebellum period. They did so not only because they were sincere men of God but also because their relationship with him had taken on new importance; they now faced many different trials, including the hazards of military duty. These soldiers relied on their deep faith in God to get them through these difficult times, and from that faith they drew the strength necessary to persevere. This ever-increasing reliance on their faith was manifested in their activities in camp, which they carried on with renewed fervor and dedication. They prayed fervently, read their Bibles assiduously, and attended religious services regularly when they were held; when there were no formal services, they worshipped in private or in small groups with like-minded individuals. These men maintained their religious routine not only during the early stages of the war but also throughout the four-year struggle.

The focus of this essay is on the early part of the war (1861 and 1862), before religious interest among the soldiers grew. As the fighting in 1862 drew to a close, a religious awakening began in both the Union and Confederate armies, prompting tens of thousands of battle-hardened soldiers to profess their faith in Christ. This heightened interest in religion continued more or less throughout the conflict.

The steadfastness of Christian soldiers at the commencement of the war tells us something about their religious beliefs and activities before the war. Historians contend that antebellum Christians, Southern men in particular, were often drawn to what Donald Mathews describes as the "carnal intimacies of the world" and that women were somehow "more intensely and consistently pious" than men were. Indeed, it is a historical fact that there were far more female than male church members in the decades just prior to the war. But the wartime experiences of the Christian soldiers in this study indicate that they too were intensely pious. From their first day in camp, these staunch Christians exhibited a genuine desire to worship God as they had before the war. Their own words suggest that the religious activities they engaged in were in fact a continuation of some longtime practices. "As has been my custom for years I offered my devotions to almighty God before closing my eyes to sleep," wrote a Tennessee soldier in June 1862. War-related adversity, however, soon replaced habit as the primary motivation for these activities. These men also stood fast in the face of vice in camp and sought to avoid those soldiers who partook in it, associating instead with other Christians in camp. These soldiers merit examination, for their religious convictions influenced their lives as soldiers from day one.[3]

The wartime letters and diaries of Civil War chaplains confirm that, on the whole, fighting men on both sides exhibited little interest in religion at the outset of the war. In his diary, Chaplain Nicholas A. Davis of the Fourth Texas Infantry testified to the irreligious nature of the men in his command. As he was preparing to preach his first sermon in camp, he observed that "everybody seem[ed] to be going to the city." Davis proceeded to deliver a fiery sermon from Isaiah on God's eventual judgment of the Northern aggressors but later commented that the number of men in his audience "was not great. . . . The evening I spent in reading & talking on religious subjects with those who visited my tent." Other clergyman made similar observations. Catholic chaplain Pere Louis-Hippolyte Gâche of the Tenth Louisiana Infantry corresponded regularly throughout the war with his fellow Jesuits at Spring Hill College in Mobile, Alabama. In a September 1861 letter Gâche wrote, "it is better not to talk about religious practice in this regiment. It's too discouraging. For example, at mass Sunday morning there were two or three officers and about forty men, and yet in the regiment there are at least 600 Catholics of whom probably less than thirty frequent the sacraments." Many Northern soldiers likewise manifested little interest in religion. Louis N. Beaudry, a chaplain in the Fifth New York Cavalry, described his first Sunday in camp as "a pretty cold reception for me! . . . We had no religious services during the day." Conceding that most of the men in his command had no interest in religious matters, Beaudry began holding informal meetings in his tent for those who cared to attend. After a small service the following Monday, he wrote in his diary, "This evening quite a number of singers came to our tent and we had a good time singing together. . . . We closed our services with an interesting family prayer meeting." Discouraged but undeterred, chaplains labored on in their ministries.[4]

Although most of the men expressed little interest in matters of the spirit, dedicated Christian soldiers sought to continue their prewar religious customs. Both Northerners and Southerners were certain that God sanctioned their side's cause, but they believed that it was necessary to act piously to secure the Lord's blessing and prevail over the enemy. They realized that God would not bless those he considered unrighteous, and they feared that the irreligious behavior of their comrades would provoke "the wrath of heaven." Therefore, these men endeavored to remain faithful and hoped that their fellow soldiers would humble themselves before the Lord and become genuine soldiers of the Cross, which would ensure victory.[5]

These men may have experienced hardships before they became soldiers, but those difficulties paled by comparison with the ordeals they endured during four years of civil war. The horrors of war, the prospect of their own deaths, and the separation from their families forced these soldiers to rely on their faith to persevere. Realizing that they were no longer in control of their own fate or that of their dear ones at home, Christian soldiers sought refuge in the arms of the Lord and appealed to him for protection for themselves and their loved ones. Their control over such matters was limited, but they recognized God's power over them and derived great comfort from their faith. Religion, therefore, consoled these men and helped them to endure the trials of war.[6]

John Dooley, a soldier in the First Virginia Infantry, sought solace from the Lord during his first night in camp. He wrote in his diary of being disconcerted by the "strange faces and forms, the near and distant sounds of an army of men talking, shouting, singing. . . . So, kneeling for a few moments I said some brief prayers and lay down in peace and quietness; for my Guardian Angel was watching by my side." Samuel Burney, a Georgian in the hard-fighting unit known as Cobb's Legion, acknowledged in an 1861 letter home that "prayer is the only resource left to dear friends sundered far apart. I must say that it is the greatest pleasure that I can enjoy at night before I retire to rest, to bear before the Throne of God my wife and child. Oh! What earnestness characterizes the prayers of a true Christian soldier." A few weeks before his first major engagement at Fredericksburg, Virginia, John Henry Pardington, a Union private in the renowned Iron Brigade, admitted to his wife, "Sarah I Prayed for you and Baby last night till my eyes were wet with tiers and I felt much relieved. Thank thank God." As Pardington continued to pray for God to preserve himself and his dear ones, his anxiety seemed to melt away. "Let us Put our trust in God and all will be well. Dear Sarah I Pray for you often. Yes every night," he wrote in November 1862. William R. Stilwell, a foot soldier in the Fifty-third Georgia, likewise prayed fervently for God's protection: "I always pray every night that God will guard me and you and Tommy, and I feel that he will do it so you must pray for me often and let us trust in God."[7]

Christian soldiers also manifested an earnest desire to worship early in the conflict. Congregating with other Christians in the presence of God, as well as listening to the ministers' discourses, comforted them and helped ease their fears. Mississippian William L. Lipscomb, a physician and devout Methodist from Columbus, left his lucrative medical practice in 1861 to become an assistant surgeon in the Tenth Mississippi Infantry. One Saturday evening in July 1861, he remarked in a letter to his wife that the next day he hoped to have "a comfortable quiet Sabbath—properly spent & I hope religiously enjoyed." Georgia soldier Samuel Burney echoed these sentiments in a letter to his wife from Yorktown, Virginia, in the fall of 1861: "I must close. To-morrow, Sunday, I hope we will have preaching." These men took advantage of every opportunity to attend church services. Writing from near Joliet, Illinois, one Sunday in June 1861, Private Allen Geer of the Twentieth Illinois recorded how he had spent his first day in camp: "[I was] sworn in to State Service [and] attended preaching by the Chaplain Mr. Button." Forty-three-year-old Mississippian William Cage, a lieutenant in the Twenty-first Infantry, likewise exhibited a desire to hear preaching. He wrote to his wife from Richmond in July 1861, "I went to church on last sabbath, and should have gone again to day but it is my day to be in command." Evidently he listened closely, for in the letter he provided his wife with the text and title of the sermon. Brigadier General William Pendleton, a former Episcopal minister, remained true to his promise to serve as both a minister of the Gospel and a soldier.

Pendleton preached regularly to the troops and noted, "It is good for me,—I trust it is for others,—for me thus to exercise my sacred calling while occupying this strange position." Just after his twenty-first birthday in May 1862, Ira Pettit, a farmer and devout Baptist from Wilson, New York, journeyed to nearby Lockport to enlist in the army, and while he was there he "attended the Baptist Church . . . and communed with them." The following Sunday he again attended religious services in town. A few days later, when Pettit's unit, the Eleventh New York, was sent to Canandaigua to drill, he visited a local church and attended "both morning and evening" services.[8]

The desire of these men to worship did not diminish over time. In December 1861 Samuel Burney was still attending services. "Well, Dearest," he wrote from Yorktown, "I have been to preaching and heard a good sermon. I am just from our usual prayer meeting of Sabbath evenings; we had a most precious little meeting. I love these little meetings; it appears they draw us closer to God." One Sabbath day in February 1862, he informed his wife that he "went to church to day and heard an excellent sermon from Bro. Porter. I always attend." Later that evening he attended another service, albeit an informal one: "We had preaching in Col. Cobb's cabin." Attending these services was not an act Burney performed out of habit but rather something that he looked forward to: "I went to preaching to day and listened to a sermon from our chaplain which was very solemn and impressive. Every Sabbath morning I take my hymnbook in one hand & stool in the other and go to the Colonel's house where services are held. I am sorry to say that I am usually the only attendant from this Company except Lt. Barnett." In an October 1862 letter to his sister, Isaac Jackson, an infantryman in the Eighty-third Ohio, wrote, "We have nothing today but to go to meeting and have Dress Parade this evening. We had preaching this morning by our chaplain and Sammy Keen is preach[ing] this afternoon." Michigan soldier John Henry Pardington reported to his wife one Sunday in September 1862, "We have nice Prayer meetings and class meeting and good Preaching Sunday which is a good Benefit to us [which] I am shure we ought to be thankful for."[9]

As the war continued into 1862, the frequency with which formal religious services were held diminished until the revivals began later that year. Military operations, the paucity of chaplains, and the lack of interest among the soldiers were all contributing factors. The exigencies of war often required that duties (even military operations) be carried out on the Lord's day. Their inability to hear preaching as often as they would have liked disturbed Christian soldiers, for they longed to worship. Before the war, they had regarded Sunday as a day for worship and rest—a routine that they seldom violated. But such respect could not always be shown in the military, especially during active campaigning. "Molly, this is a beautiful Sunday morning," wrote William Stilwell in 1862, "and I expect you are gone to church somewhere. You must not fail to attend church as often as you can. I have not heard a sermon in about four months. . . . I never wanted to hear preaching as bad in my life."[10]

Others likewise desired to attend religious services, but military operations prevented them from doing so. On the march near Paris, Kentucky, in October 1862, Ohio soldier Isaac Jackson penned a quick letter to his brother: "Along towards evening, we passed a very nice brick church belonging to the Christians. It put me in mind of home. I only wish I could get to stay somewhere close to where there is a church so I could go to meeting and hear some Preaching once more, but that is hardly probable. In Paris there is a large church. . . . If we stay here over Sunday I am going to try to get to town and go to meeting." Apparently, Jackson's situation improved little, for a few weeks later he again complained, "while I am writing I suppose you are enjoying yourself by hearing the word of God expounded in its true light. The bells of the village have just been ringing, I suppose for the forenoon services. But what a pity we have to stay right here in Camp and not allowed to go to church when it is right at hand. . . . I tell you, when a man goes in the army he sacrifices a great many privileges that he enjoyed at home." As an officer on the staff of Confederate general Humphrey Marshall, Edward O. Guerrant was frequently required to work on the Sabbath, a practice he detested. After one such occurrence, Guerrant expressed his displeasure at violating the Fourth Commandment: "Sweet sunny—Sabbath day. Day of rest. . . . Was called away from breakfast—to the duties of my office. Think I shall resign it or make them relieve me on the Sacred day. It is an undecided question in my mind—whether circumstances— (except of necessity) should ever force us to a violation of the Sabbath day." William Nugent, a cavalryman in the Twenty-eighth Mississippi, also exhibited an eagerness for worship. While passing through Jackson in 1862, he observed an Episcopal church and admitted, "the tears filled up my eyes as I looked upon the House of God. When shall I again be privileged to go up to the Church to worship?" In a later letter to his wife, Nugent, a longtime Methodist, lamented his predicament: "I hear no sermons, hear none of the Songs of Zion, and am verily a stranger in a strange land."[11]

The dearth of formal services led these Christians to appreciate more fully an earlier time when they had encountered few impediments to churchgoing. Indeed, attending divine worship became something of a privilege for them. Facing Union general George McClellan's massive army as it gradually advanced toward Richmond in the spring of 1862 was a Confederate force that included Georgian Samuel Burney, who admitted to his wife in a hastily penned letter, "How much I do wish that I could be with you this beautiful Sabbath day, that together we might go up to the house of God for public worship." One Sunday in June 1862, just before the Seven Days' battles began, Rufus Robbins, a private in the Seventh Massachusetts, wrote home from Virginia: "I think you are now about starting for meeting. Oh, how I should like to go with you. I think oftener of the little church and the people that assemble there. . . . I feel if I should ever take part in it again, I should work with greater zeal and strive to be more faithful." When opportunities for worship increased later in the war, Christian soldiers hastened to take advantage of them.[12]

Prevented from hearing preaching as regularly as they would have liked, pious soldiers repeatedly endured inconveniences to attend worship services. When there was no preaching in camp, Tennessee soldier Alfred Fielder often joined other like-minded soldiers in his chaplain's quarters for informal prayer meetings. Other times, he went out of his way to worship. One Sabbath in the spring of 1862, recognizing that no church service would occur in his own regiment, Fielder called on the chaplain of a nearby regiment and arranged for him to hold services later that day. Parson William Pendleton's eagerness for divine services was evident as well. In February 1862 he had the men construct a place of worship in camp in Centreville, Virginia, because the church in town was serving as a hospital. Pendleton was so anxious to hold services, however, that he did so before the structure was completed. Massachusetts private Rufus Robbins was, like Fielder, disappointed by the infrequent preaching in camp and demonstrated a determination to overcome obstacles to his attendance at services. "I went to meeting this forenoon," Robbins told his brother in 1862. "Ten of us got a pass signed by the Colonel. The church where we went is about a mile and a half from our camp."[13]

When Federal troops occupied Jackson, Tennessee, in June 1862, Allan Geer's regiment, the Twentieth Illinois, was among them. During the occupation, Geer seized the opportunity to hear preaching and attended a local Methodist church, where he "heard a good sermon." The preacher was his regiment's chaplain, because the local minister had fled. Several weeks later, before leaving Jackson, Geer was able to participate in a unique worship experience: "Attended a right out & out Ethiopean religious meeting for the first time." Later in 1862, as Union general Ulysses S. Grant's forces moved farther south during their overland campaign against Vicksburg, Geer continued to worship at the local churches he came across. At Lagrange, Tennessee, he attended the Presbyterian church but noted that "those present . . . [were] mostly ladies." Most of the men had vacated the town before the Yankees arrived. Confederate captain Giles Cooke, an assistant inspector general who served on the staffs of various generals, traveled regularly performing inspections. During his journeys he often sought out nearby churches and joined their congregations in worship. When attending formal services was infeasible, Cooke worshipped in private. Once, when sharing quarters in town with another officer, he retreated to the closet and communed privately with God. And when he traveled by train, Cooke often read the Bible and other religious books to pass the time.[14]

When attending formal services was impossible, Christian soldiers took matters into their own hands and gathered in small groups for prayer meetings. Having received a letter from his father inquiring about his church attendance while in the army, infantryman Rufus Robbins replied, "Whilst I was at Taunton [Massachusetts], I attended prayer meetings almost every evening. I was one of three or four who started them. The chaplain came in with us the second evening. I used generally to take some part in the meetings. I was often requested to read a chapter in the Bible at the commencement." In an October 1862 letter to his sister, James Gould of the 144th New York Infantry described how he and his tent mates continued to worship, despite the absence of preaching: "We are all, but one, church members, and he is trying to do what is rite. We have worship in our tent evry night. . . . To night we have another one in our tent." Responding to a letter from his sister a few weeks later, Gould again brought up the subject: "Hannah, you wanted me to tell you the news in our camp and tent. The news in our tent is that we are trying to serve the Lord. We have prayer meetings in our tent twice a week and one of us reads a chapter, and pray every night before laying down to sleep. . . . We take turns [leading]. I enjoy my[self] better here serveing the Lord then I did at home." That same month, Ohio private Isaac Jackson informed his sister from Kentucky that he and some other men met in his "captain's quarters" for "prayer meeting." Randolph McKim, a soldier from Maryland serving in the Second Virginia Cavalry, recalled that the chaplain in his regiment "was a man without much force . . . so that we felt the need of supplementing his efforts." McKim and a few other dedicated soldiers organized "social prayer-meetings" that were held "nightly, instead of weekly, or occasionally, as before. At first we met in private tents, but finally we procured a tent for the purpose, and fitted it up with rude benches so as to accommodate twenty-five or thirty men. Gradually our numbers had increased, and this would hardly give seats to as many as would come." He and his companions regularly conducted these meetings. Even duty could not deter these devoted Christians. While serving as corporal of the guard in early 1862, McKim made time to "read the xxviith chapter of St. Matthew aloud to the men."[15]

When meeting together proved impossible, Christians sought a quiet setting away from the distractions in camp and worshipped privately. Such worship often included communing with God, reading and meditating on scripture or other spiritual books, and praying. Tennessean Alfred Fielder enjoyed escaping the commotion in camp and finding a tranquil setting in which to worship. "I have just come in from a walk to the woods where I spent several hours in meditation and prayer," he wrote from Tullahoma in November 1862. "Oh! I have thought of and prayed for dear friends at home." New York private Ira Pettit, who often had guard duty on Sundays and thus missed religious services, often engaged in Bible study after his duty ended. One Sunday in August 1862 he made no mention of attending church but noted in his diary that he "read the scriptures." The following Sabbath, he again mentioned no services but recorded that he had "finished reading the book of John." Near Richmond, Virginia, in the summer of 1862, Confederate infantryman William Stilwell told his wife in a letter home, "Reckon I enjoy myself as well as any man away from those that he loves. I try to keep in good spirits all day and when evening comes I steal off in some secret place to offer my evening sacrifice to my God and can feel that it is good to be there even in a strange land." After Second Manassas in August 1862, Stilwell wrote home to his wife from near the battlefield: "Molly, we are not far from the Blue Ridge Mountains and you know what a man I am to study the works of God and here I had a great feast, something that was beautiful. One day we stopped at four o'clock in the evening on a large mountain . . . and after I got through with my work I took my little bible and got off in a lonely place and thinking of the scripture which says 'Lord, thy righteousness is like the great mountains.' I had a good time here."[16]

Christian soldiers also worshipped by reading the Bible or other religious books. "Spent the forenoon reading the scriptures," wrote Tennessee captain J. J. Womack one Sunday in early 1862, although he gave no indication that he had been able to attend religious services that day. Other days Womack engaged in Bible study to supplement the sermons he heard. One Sabbath day in mid-1862 he recorded in his diary that he had "read the book of Revelation [and] heard a sermon by a young Mr. Heiskell." Womack studied scripture faithfully throughout the war. Just days before Federal forces under General George McClellan completed their withdrawal from the Virginia peninsula in mid-August 1862, Massachusetts soldier Rufus Robbins requested that his brother secure for him "one of those little Sabbath School Question Books, if you can get it for me without too much trouble. . . . I think it was Scriptural Lessons." Nearly two weeks later, Robbins wrote to his mother, "I had time enough to read, although I had nothing with me but my Testament. But that was enough. I love to read the Psalms." He then listed the chapters he had read. In the following weeks he contracted an illness and was transported to a hospital in Philadelphia, Pennsylvania, where he died in January 1863. Knowing that he would never return home, he instructed one of his hospital caregivers to convey these words: "tell my Mother that since I went into the army, I have thought more of religious things than I ever thought before. I have read my Bible more and I feel that a new light has been given to me. I feel sure that all men are brothers and that God is the father of us all. And into his hand I am willing to consign myself."[17]

Immorality seems to have permeated every army camp during the early months of the Civil War. Soldiers commented frequently in their diaries and letters about the behavior of their comrades. Before his regiment had even departed its home state, Private Charles Gould of the Seventy-second New York Infantry had seen enough of his fellow soldiers to size them up. In a June 1861 letter to his sister he described them as "the roughest kind, gambling fighting & swearing seem to be the principal amusement, little thinking that a vast number of them will never see home again." Two months later, when his regiment was encamped near Washington, Gould observed little change in the men: "Many a mother bade her son adiou, sorry to expose him to the temptations witch he must meet in the army, but while they are praying for them, they are playing a game of cards or laying drunk on the ground." Georgian Samuel Burney reported to his wife from Yorktown in late 1861 that "there is a great deal of wickedness in this Legion, and I never see a day pass but what I see and hear things utterly revolting to the feelings of a Christian gentleman." Soldiers engaged in such licentiousness even on the Sabbath, which especially outraged more reverent soldiers. Observing one such transgression in early 1862, Iowa soldier Cyrus Boyd recorded in his diary: "The men are playing cards swearing and dancing just as on other days. This I do not enjoy. How uncomfortable it makes me to be thus surrounded on Sunday."[18]

Many men who had been moral prior to the war were led astray in the army. Twenty-three-year-old Robert Moore of the Seventeenth Mississippi Infantry had been a regular churchgoer back home in Holly Springs, but he could not resist the ever-present temptations in the army and began drinking. At winter quarters near Leesburg, Virginia, in late 1861, Moore and some of his friends occasionally sneaked away from camp and went into town, where they drank to the point of intoxication. After one such outing, Moore acknowledged whiskey's popularity among the men: "Found plenty of whiskey & brought a bottle home with us. It lasts but a short time in camp." Moore's bad behavior would not endure, however, for while his unit was in winter quarters near Fredericksburg in early 1863, he eagerly participated in revival meetings there and professed his faith in Christ. From his camp near St. Louis in the early spring of 1862, Cyrus Boyd observed, "Men [who] four months ago would not use a profane word can now outswear many others and those who would even shun a checker board now play cards for profit. The descent looks gradual from the top but how fast they seem to go as everything seems to hurry on the downward grade. . . .

How eager they seem to abandon all their early teachings and to catch up with everything which tends to debase." Although vice in the camps abated in 1863 as religious interest among the soldiers grew, it never disappeared completely.[19]

Devout Christians, however, were determined to remain untarnished despite their corrosive environment. Mississippi surgeon William Lipscomb was unyielding in his religious convictions. "I thought that it could be almost impossible to sustain myself amid the trials of a camp life," he wrote in 1861, "but knowing that there would be many lurking foes I have summoned watchfulness and stationed pickets and to my joy find that watchfulness is almost victory. It is at least assurance." Samuel Burney echoed these sentiments in a December 1861 letter to his wife: "As a professed follower of Christ I meet with many trials & temptations; but it only arouses me to be on my guard." Writing to his father from Washington in February 1862, Massachusetts private Rufus Robbins reported, "I have seen much of the workings of evil since I have been here, more than I ever dreamed of before. And more than ever do I realize the necessity of a firm belief and trust in God as I have learned of Him at home.... The burden of a soldier's life is enough without the burden which sin imposes."[20]

Their wartime writings suggest that many religious soldiers were successful in their efforts to walk the straight and narrow. Talbert Holt, a private in the Thirty-eighth Alabama garrisoned at Fort Morgan near Mobile, expressed his determination to remain unblemished and reported confidently to his wife, Carrie, in 1861 that "others . . . will return to their families as infidels having thrown off religious restraint, ought you not to be happy then that . . . is [not] the case with me! that I am well, that I still acknowledge the power & love of God." When his father-in-law and his pastor from home wrote and urged him to abide by Christ's teachings while in the army, Holt remarked, "I . . . received pa's letter in which I found advice that was good and which by the help of God I hope I have been following for some time & still expect to follow." New Yorker Charles Gould was also resolute in his faith, and evidently, his perseverance was apparent to those he served with. In early 1862, after Gould died from typhoid fever, an officer in his regiment wrote to Gould's sister that "while the life of a soldier is not calculated to improve his morals, I can with pleasure say that the vices and immoralities of camp had no influence upon Charles. He has passed through them always maintaining his rectitude of principles which were the basis of his actions, and seem to have been laid on a shure foundation."[21]

Some Christian soldiers bravely set out to correct the sinful behavior of the men in their command. "When I left home it was with the resolve that I would take good care of my moral and religious life and do all that I could to persuade others in the way which I believe is good," wrote Rufus Robbins to his father in August 1861. "There is need enough of it here." In a letter from Yorktown in November 1861, Georgian Samuel Burney revealed to his wife, "I see and hear in silence; sometimes I give a kind word of correction, but it is always to those I know will kindly receive it. I have the greater reason to guard myself lest constant companionship with such people would cause me to be like them." On Christmas Day in 1861, Alfred Fielder of the Twelfth Tennessee observed that many of his comrades had spent the sacred day drinking: "the Cause of sobriety, virtue, and piety have comparatively few advocates in the army but as for myself though it may be unpopular—I am determined by Gods grace to advocate them all and remonstrate with those who say and act differently." Apparently, Fielder found few who would listen, for a few days later he noted in his diary, "I further intend to talk less (because it anoys some) and think more as it may be more profit to myself and less annoyance to others."[22]

Christians in camp frequently sought to isolate themselves from their less righteous comrades and to fellowship instead with those who shared their views. This no doubt strengthened them in their efforts to remain faithful. In a June 1861 letter to his wife, Dr. William Lipscomb happily reported, "I thought I would be almost alone having only Mr. Sims as an ally. But to my surprise I found one night after supper, three boys singing hymns. I approached—became acquainted—found they were good pious boys, two from Mr. Stamback's church one from ours. The incident withal resulted in much encouragement to me." In the same letter he admitted, "Often in a Christian's career, those circumstances which to his view, will overwhelm him, prove the building up and strengthening of him—thus showing that all things work together for his good. This has been the case with myself." Soon after enlisting in May 1862, William Stilwell was made a guard at brigade headquarters, a position that allowed him some privacy. "I thank God that I am still permitted to read the bible and can worship God as I desire and here I am glad to say by being where I am I can get off to myself where I can read and sing and enjoy myself very well. It is not so in the regiment. You have to always be in a crowd where you are surrounded with all kinds of persons but here at headquarters I can keep company with no one but those I choose to keep company with."[23]

Some of the success that Christian soldiers had in remaining true to their convictions must be attributed to the chaplains and ministers they heard preach. Preachers regularly exhorted their listeners to resist the evils in camp. Presbyterian chaplain Nicholas Davis of the Fourth Texas Infantry reflected on a sermon he delivered one Sunday in the fall of 1861: "Read the 121 Ps.—talked about 20ms. My object was to show the importance of an upright walk & especially to the young men, that they hereafter be judged by their conduct in camp. . . . I am in the midst [of] very wicked & vulgarly profane men." The men in the audience no doubt found Psalm 121 reassuring, for it speaks of the Lord's promise to protect his children.[24]

This is not to say that the resoluteness exhibited by Christian fighting men required little effort; for some, the struggle was intense. Vice flourished in the early army camps, and these soldiers were only human, after all. Charles Gould's older brother Richard, who served in the 143rd New York Infantry, confided to his sister in a December 1862 letter, "I try to serve the Lord but it is [a] hard place I tell you, go where ever you will, you will hear some swearing or lying. You must pray for me. I will try and pray for myself." Marion Hill Fitzpatrick, as noted earlier, struggled with temptation and succumbed. Such an acknowledgment, however, is often the first step toward repentance, and as the war dragged on, Fitzpatrick's spiritual condition improved. He attended prayer meetings in camp on a regular basis and, along with a few of his companions, started a Bible class. On April 6, 1865, as the Army of Northern Virginia made its way toward Appomattox Court House, Fitzpatrick fell mortally wounded in the fighting near Sayler's Creek. As he lay dying, not only was his family on his mind, but also his Savior. He recalled the words of an old hymn and quietly sang, "Jesus can make a dying bed as soft as downy pillow are."[25]

As Fitzpatrick's last words reveal, religion sustained and consoled these men. The possibility of sudden death confronted soldiers at nearly every turn. Illness, mishap, or military action could claim their lives at any time. Recognizing the uncertainty of military life, these Christians placed their lives in the hands of their "faithful and trusty friend"; they found great comfort in the thought that a sovereign God was in control of human affairs and, as one soldier put it, had the "power to hurl by harmless the missiles of death." And, when it came to death, Christian soldiers had no fear, for they were destined for another world—an eternal one where hardship and war could not trespass. "Fear not for my safety," wrote Virginia soldier Ted Barclay to his mother. "God can protect me amidst the storm of battle as well as at home, and if I shall fall I trust that I will go to a better world and is that not gain?" In addition, the strength they drew from their faith had a positive impact on their courage. Accepting that an all-wise Heavenly Father directed events on earth, religious soldiers petitioned God for protection, and they credited him when they were spared. Likewise, they believed that if God allowed them to perish on the battlefield, then that was his will, and there was little they could do to prevent it. Such thoughts helped Christian soldiers overcome their fear of death, helped keep them going, and strengthened their will to fight. One historian even went so far as to assert that the "heightened religiosity" of the Confederates after 1862 was a major factor in prolonging the war.[26]

In the fall of 1862, religious revivals broke out in the Army of Northern Virginia, followed by others in the Army of Tennessee and in the Union armies, initiating a wave of revivalism that lasted for the remainder of the war. Chaplains, missionaries, and local ministers preached to eager audiences, and tens of thousands of fighting men experienced conversion. The role that longtime Christians played in initiating the revivals is unclear. What is clear, however, is that they helped provide fertile religious soil from which the revivals blossomed. At a time when few soldiers were interested in spiritual matters, Christian soldiers kept religious interest alive in the armies through their actions. They persisted in their religious activities openly and attended worship services regularly when they were held, thus filling the seats for the chaplains who were preaching in camp. Thus, clergymen continued to preach and win converts among those who attended out of curiosity or boredom. When formal worship was not possible, dedicated soldiers worshipped in private or in small groups, with the soldiers themselves leading the services. These informal meetings usually concluded with an invitation or appeal for those in attendance to accept Christ.[27]

Furthermore, Christian soldiers eagerly sought to advance the cause of Christ in the armies. Indeed, they may have been responsible for some of the conversions that occurred in the ranks. Virginia caval-ryman, and later Episcopal clergyman, Randolph McKim recollected after the war that he had "found many opportunities of trying to help my comrades and fellow officers in the spiritual life. . . . I have never found men so open to the frank discussion of the subject of personal religion as the officers and men of Lee's army. . . . Wide was the door of opportunity. . . . There were occasions when I was mistaken for a clergy-man." Confederate officer Giles Cooke also made clear his concern for the spiritual state of other soldiers and seized opportunities to share his faith. When he learned that a fellow officer's child had died suddenly, Cooke took advantage of the opening and talked with him "about his immortal soul." Throughout the war, devoted Christian soldiers pros-elytized when opportunities presented themselves and prayed fervently that the men would come to know Christ.[28]

Also, these Christian soldiers served as examples to those around them. Their comrades observed that these soldiers remained resolute in the face of temptation, but they also noticed that when Christians died, they were at peace, for as death approached, their thoughts were focused on the next world. As a result, less pious soldiers who witnessed their deaths were prompted to evaluate their own spiritual condition, which often led to conversion. According to one historian, "The inner peace exhibited by dying Christians never failed to impress those who saw their final moments." The actions of these longtime Christians kept religion before the troops, and even if other soldiers were not interested in religion initially, they were constantly exposed to it, as well as to the hope and contentment it offered. Indeed, the seeds of revival were being sown as early as 1861.[29]

The scene in the army camps changed considerably when the reviv-als began and religious interest among the soldiers grew. Worship ser-vices and prayer meetings took place more frequently, and vice in the camps abated, although it never disappeared completely. The longtime Christians eagerly participated in these meetings and delighted in the success of the revivals; they welcomed their newly converted brethren into Christ's fold. And, as their predecessors had been doing since 1861, these nascent Christians learned to lean on their faith in God to keep going until the bloody civil war came to an end.[30]

Regardless of their Christian denomination, age, military rank, or national loyalty, Christian soldiers endeavored to stand firm in their religious convictions and sought to continue their antebellum religious practices while in the army. They did so in part because they were faithful men of God, but more important, they did so to cope with the anxiety and adversity of military service, which was unmatched by anything they had seen in their civilian lives. These men responded to the hardships they faced by turning their worries over to their all-powerful Heavenly Father; and they found comfort and sustenance in their faith. These Christians believed that God controlled human affairs, and they trusted him to protect them and their families. They took comfort in knowing that if they fell in battle, they would take up residence in heaven, where they would reunite with loved ones who had passed on before them and live in eternal peace and happiness. Their dependence on their faith can be clearly seen in their actions in camp. Attending religious services, communing privately with God, engaging in prayer and Bible study, and even singing hymns all served to assuage the fears of men who had much to be afraid of. The experiences of the soldiers in this study demonstrate the importance that Christian fighting men placed on religion. Indeed, long before the outbreak of revivals in the fall of 1862, thousands of devout Christian soldiers were holding firm to their religious convictions and relying on their faith to get them through the first months of the Civil War.

NOTES

1. Jeffrey C. Lowe and Sam Hodges, eds., *Letters to Amanda: The Civil War Letters of Marion Hill Fitzpatrick, Army of Northern Virginia* (Macon, GA: Mercer University Press, 1998), 39. Original spelling and punctuation have been retained where possible to preserve the flow of the narrative.

2. Bell Irvin Wiley, *The Life of Johnny Reb: The Common Soldier of the Confederacy* (Baton Rouge: Louisiana State University Press, 1943), 175; Drew Gilpin Faust, "Christian Soldiers: The Meaning of Revivalism in the Confederate Army," *Journal of Southern History* 53 (February 1987): 68; Steven E. Woodworth, *While God Is Marching On: The Religious World of Civil War Soldiers* (Lawrence: University Press of Kansas, 2001), 184–85. Other Civil War historians who agree include James I. Robertson, *Soldiers Blue and Gray* (Columbia: University of South Carolina Press, 1988), and Larry J. Daniel, *Soldiering in the Army of Tennessee* (Chapel Hill: University of North Carolina Press, 1991). Robertson contends that the war "inevitably dented the faith of many Civil War participants. Leaving the restraints of home and loved ones, and then cast as soldiers in a novel environment that alternated between apa-

thy and loneliness on the one hand to excitement and danger on the other, invited a wandering from the straight and narrow" (172–73). Daniel asserts that "because of the festive atmosphere in camp," early in the war "a general religious indifference permeated the army" (115). Woodworth, admits, however, that many soldiers struggled to remain faithful followers of Christ despite the difficult conditions in camp. For more on these committed Christians, see Woodworth, *While God Is Marching On,* 175–90; Kent T. Dollar, *Soldiers of the Cross: Confederate Soldier-Christians and the Impact of War on Their Faith* (Macon, GA: Mercer University Press, 2005), 52–98. Revivalism in the ranks, the tens of thousands of conversions to Christianity, and religion's impact on morale have garnered the attention of many Civil War historians. See Wiley, *Life of Johnny Reb,* 174–75, 180–84; Faust, "Christian Soldiers," 64, 67–68, 71–72; Daniel, *Soldiering in the Army of Tennessee,* 116–17, 123; Robertson, *Soldiers Blue and Gray,* 173, 186–88; James W. Silver, *Confederate Morale and Church Propaganda* (New York: W. W. Norton, 1967), 55–63, 82–93; Richard E. Beringer, Herman Hattaway, Archer Jones, and William N. Still Jr., *Why the South Lost the Civil War* (Athens: University of Georgia Press, 1986), 268, 278; Gardiner H. Shattuck, *A Shield and Hiding Place: The Religious Life of the Civil War Armies* (Macon, GA: Mercer University Press, 1987), 9–11; Samuel J. Watson, "Religion and Combat Motivation in the Confederate Armies," *Journal of Military History* 58 (January 1994): 34–36; James McPherson, *For Cause and Comrades: Why Men Fought in the Civil War* (New York: Oxford University Press, 1997), 63–71; Earl J. Hess, *The Union Soldier in Battle: Enduring the Ordeal of Combat* (Lawrence: University Press of Kansas, 1997), 104; Woodworth, *While God Is Marching On,* 93–255.

3. Donald G. Mathews, *Religion in the Old South* (Chicago: University of Chicago Press, 1977), 101–3, 109, 111–13, 115, 120–23; John B. Boles, "Evangelical Protestantism in the Old South: From Religious Dissent to Cultural Dominance," in *Religion in the South,* ed. Charles Reagan Wilson (Jackson: University Press of Mississippi, 1985), 32–33; Orville V. Burton, *In My Father's House Are Many Mansions: Family and Community in Edgefield, South Carolina* (Chapel Hill: University of North Carolina Press, 1985), 114–15, 131–34, 138–40, 145–46. Anne Loveland agrees with Mathews and contends that backsliding was common among mid-nineteenth-century Southern Christians. "Although evangelicals denounced worldly amusements," she says, "an increasing number of Christians were indulging in them." According to Loveland, church membership and "faithful attendance on the duties it entailed" were instrumental in enabling Christians to maintain their detachment from the world. (The conscientious efforts of the soldiers in this study to continue their prewar religious practices thus contributed to their success in remaining faithful.) See Anne C. Loveland, *Southern Evangelicals and the Social Order,*

1800–1860 (Baton Rouge: Louisiana State University Press, 1980), 2, 8, 13–16, 93, 97, 103. Scholars are, however, beginning to challenge this stereotype of men in the Old South. In his latest work, Peter Carmichael contends that the "popular, but one-dimensional image of Southern youth as lazy, immoral, and hotheaded overlooks the changing nature of what it meant to be a young man in the slave South." Southern manliness was not static but evolving, asserts Carmichael, and a generation of young Virginians was reshaping what it meant to be manly. They were drawn in particular to the ideal of the Christian gentleman, a man of feeling and faith. Peter S. Carmichael, *The Last Generation: Young Virginians in Peace, War, and Reunion* (Chapel Hill: University of North Carolina Press, 2005), 6, 11, 58–88, 244n, 245n. See also Stephen W. Berry, *All That Makes a Man: Love and Ambition in the Civil War South* (New York: Oxford University Press, 2003), 9–13, 90–94, 115–16. The same Tennessee soldier made a similar comment in March 1862. See Ann York Franklin, ed., *The Civil War Diaries of Capt. Alfred Tyler Fielder, 12th Tennessee Regiment Infantry, Company B, 1861–1865* (Louisville, KY: Privately printed, 1996), 36, 56.

4. Donald E. Everett, ed., *Chaplain Davis and Hood's Texas Brigade* (San Antonio, TX: Principia Press of Trinity University, 1962; reprint, Baton Rouge: Louisiana State University Press, 1999), 2; Cornelius M. Buckley, ed. and trans., *A Frenchman, a Chaplain, a Rebel: The War Letters of Pere Louis-Hippolyte Gâche, S.J.* (Chicago: Loyola University Press, 1981), 48; Richard E. Beaudry, ed., *War Journal of Louis N. Beaudry, Fifth New York Cavalry: The Diary of a Union Chaplain, Commencing February 16, 1863* (Jefferson, NC: McFarland, 1996), 7–9.

5. After the fall of Forts Henry and Donelson in early 1862, General William Pendleton wrote home to his daughter, "there is so much sadness in the country under the danger which threatens us since the loss of [the forts]. . . . God has for us, I trust, something better in store, but we must all look up to Him & rely upon his promise to his servants. The godlessness of so many amongst us, [may be] provoking the wrath of heaven." William Pendleton to unnamed daughter, February 25, 1862, in William Nelson Pendleton Papers, Southern Historical Collection, University of North Carolina, Chapel Hill. See also Carmichael, *The Last Generation,* 184. Christian soldiers on both sides were confident of God's favor when the war began. Military setbacks, however, engendered concern, for these men believed that a sovereign God controlled all things. Although Christian soldiers maintained the belief that the Lord would act at the appropriate time, they sought an explanation for the defeats. Soon after the Union defeat at First Manassas in July 1861, New York private Charles Gould wrote home, "We are not at presant much a ahead of the rebels, but I believe that after God has duly chastised our troops for their many sins, he will give us a glorious victory." See Robert F. Harris and John Niflot, comps.,

Dear Sister: The Civil War Letters of the Brothers Gould (Westport, CT: Praeger Publishers, 1998), 4. For similar expressions by other Christian soldiers, see Franklin, *Fielder Diaries,* 22, 127–28; William M. Cash and Lucy Somerville Howorth, eds., *My Dear Nellie: The Civil War Letters of William L. Nugent to Eleanor Nugent* (Jackson: University Press of Mississippi, 1977), 63, 180, 233; Edward O. Guerrant, diary, February 20, March 8–9, 1862, Edward O. Guerrant Papers, Southern Historical Collection, University of North Carolina, Chapel Hill; Giles Buckner Cooke, diary, May 16, September 3, 6, 1862, Giles Buckner Cooke Papers, Virginia Historical Society, Richmond; and Charles W. Turner, ed., *Ted Barclay, Liberty Hall Volunteers: Letters from the Stonewall Brigade, 1861–1864* (Rockbridge, VA: Rockbridge Publishing Company, 1992), 83, 86, 90–97, 117. For more on how Northern and Southern Christians viewed military reverses and the war in general, see Woodworth, *While God Is Marching On,* 94–137. The South's surrender ended all hope of divine intervention and forced Christians in that region to reconcile their faith with the defeat of the Confederacy. Southern Christians concluded that God refused to intervene in their behalf because they were undeserving of his favor. Although tens of thousands of Confederates had become God-fearing soldiers during the war, Christians maintained that the South as a whole had turned away from the Lord. Indeed, they believed that Southerners had exhibited a lack of faith in God, placing their trust instead in Confederate military leaders. The Southern people, they insisted, were not worthy of God's blessing. Moreover, Christian soldiers believed that if God, in his infinite wisdom, allowed the defeat of the South, they must accept it as part of his plan. These men took great comfort from Hebrews 12:6: "For whom the Lord loveth he chasteneth." For more on Southern Christians' attempts to reconcile defeats (including the defeat of the South) and God's will, see Shattuck, *Shield and Hiding Place,* 40, 100, 102, 108–9, 113; Woodworth, *While God Is Marching On,* 270–86; Daniel W. Stowell, *Rebuilding Zion: The Religious Reconstruction of the South, 1863–1877* (New York: Oxford University Press, 1998), 5, 33–44; Daniel Stowell, "Stonewall Jackson and the Providence of God," in *Religion and the American Civil War,* eds. Randall M. Miller, Harry S. Stout, and Charles Reagan Wilson (New York: Oxford University Press, 1998), 197–202; Eugene D. Genovese, *A Consuming Fire: The Fall of the Confederacy in the Mind of the White Christian South* (Athens: University of Georgia Press, 1998); Dollar, *Soldiers of the Cross,* 177–222; Charles Reagan Wilson, "Introduction," in Miller, Stout, and Wilson, *Religion and the American Civil War,* 10; and Paul Harvey, "'Yankee Faith' and Southern Redemption," in ibid., 175.

6. In *The Popular Mood of Pre–Civil War America* (Westport, CT: Greenwood Press, 1980), 3–17, Lewis O. Saum maintains that the most pervasive religious theme in antebellum America was the belief in Providence.

According to McPherson, "A battlefield offers the extreme challenge to the belief that man can control his fate," and "like rain, shells and bullets fall on the just and unjust alike" (*For Cause and Comrades*, 62).

7. Joseph T. Durkin, ed., *John Dooley, Confederate Soldier: His War Journal* (Washington, DC: Georgetown University Press, 1945), 5; Nat S. Turner III, ed., *A Southern Soldier's Letters Home: The Civil War Letters of Samuel A. Burney, Cobb's Georgia Legion, Army of Northern Virginia* (Macon, GA: Mercer University Press, 2002), 19; Coralou Peel Lassen, ed., *Dear Sarah: Letters Home from a Soldier of the Iron Brigade* (Bloomington: Indiana University Press, 1999), 27, 40; Ronald H. Moseley, ed., *The Stilwell Letters: A Georgian in Longstreet's Corps, Army of Northern Virginia* (Macon, GA: Mercer University Press, 2002), 77.

8. Compiled Service Records, Tenth Mississippi Infantry, National Archives, Washington, DC; William L. Lipscomb to Talluh Lipscomb, July 6, 1861, William L. Lipscomb Papers, Mississippi Department of Archives and History, Jackson; Turner, *Southern Soldier's Letters Home*, 28; Mary Ann Andersen, ed., *The Civil War Diary of Allen Morgan Geer: Twentieth Regiment, Illinois Volunteers* (New York: Robert C. Appleman, 1977), 3; T. Harry Williams, ed., "The Civil War Letters of William C. Cage," *Louisiana Historical Quarterly* 34 (January 1956): 117; Susan P. Lee, *Memoirs of William Nelson Pendleton, D.D.* (Philadelphia: J. B. Lippincott, 1893), 171, 191; Jean P. Ray, ed., *The Diary of a Dead Man: Letters and Diary of Private Ira S. Pettit, Wilson, Niagara County, New York, Who Served Company B, 2nd Battalion, and Company F, 1st Battalion, 11th Regt 2nd Brigade, 2nd Division, 5th Corps, United States Army, during the War between the States* (New York: Acorn Press, 1979), 36, 38–39.

9. Turner, *Southern Soldier's Letters Home*, 89, 112, 118; Joseph O. Jackson, ed., *"Some of the Boys": The Civil War Letters of Isaac Jackson, 1862–1865* (Carbondale: Southern Illinois University Press, 1960), 14–15; Lassen, *Dear Sarah*, 11.

10. Moseley, *Stilwell Letters*, 69. For a list of Civil War chaplains and the regiments in which they served, see John W. Brinsfield et al., eds., *Faith in the Fight: Civil War Chaplains* (Mechanicsburg, PA: Stackpole Books, 2003), 211–56.

11. Woodworth, *While God Is Marching On*, 180–84; Jackson, *"Some of the Boys,"* 23, 26–27; Cash and Howorth, *My Dear Nellie*, 56, 113; Guerrant diary, February 23, March 9, 1862. Guerrant also expressed his disdain for violating the Sabbath in entries dated April 6, August 31, October 5, 12, and 19, and December 21 and 28, 1862.

12. Turner, *Southern Soldier's Letters Home*, 169; Ella Jane Bruen and Brian M. Fitzgibbons, eds., *Through Ordinary Eyes: The Civil War Correspondence of Rufus Robbins, Private, 7th Regiment Massachusetts Volunteers* (Westport, CT: Praeger Publishers, 2000), 145.

13. Franklin, *Fielder Diaries*, 50; Lee, *Pendleton Memoirs*, 171, 191; Bruen and Fitzgibbons, *Through Ordinary Eyes*, 121.

14. Andersen, *Geer Diary*, 37, 60, 69; Cooke diary, June 28, July 5, 17, 30, September 1, 1862.

15. Bruen and Fitzgibbons, *Through Ordinary Eyes*, 45; Harris and Niflot, *Dear Sister*, 35, 37, 56; Jackson, *"Some of the Boys,"* 14–15; Randolph H. McKim, *A Soldier's Recollections: Leaves from the Diary of a Young Confederate, with an Oration on the Motives and Aims of the South* (New York: Longmans, Green, 1910), 60–61; Lee, *Pendleton Memoirs*, 142. Robertson points out that it was common for religious soldiers to meet informally for prayer meeting (*Soldiers Blue and Gray*, 183).

16. Franklin, *Fielder Diaries*, 88; Ray, *Diary of a Dead Man*, 55–56; Moseley, *Stilwell Letters*, 29, 35.

17. J. J. Womack, *The Civil War Diary of Capt. J. J. Womack* (McMinnville, TN: Womack Printing Co., 1961), 37, 52; Bruen and Fitzgibbons, *Through Ordinary Eyes*, 160, 165, 191.

18. Harris and Niflot, *Dear Sister*, 2–3; Turner, *Southern Soldier's Letters Home*, 55; Mildred Throne, ed., *The Civil War Diary of Cyrus F. Boyd, Fifteenth Iowa Infantry, 1861–1863* (Iowa City: State Historical Society of Iowa, 1953), 24.

19. James W. Silver, ed., *A Life for the Confederacy: As Recorded in the Pocket Diaries of Pvt. Robert A. Moore* (Jackson, TN: McCowat-Mercer Press, 1959), 51, 56, 83, 96, 136; Throne, *Boyd Diary*, 24.

20. William Lipscomb to Talluh Lipscomb, June 7, 1861, Lipscomb Papers; Turner, *Southern Soldier's Letters Home*, 89; Bruen and Fitzgibbons, *Through Ordinary Eyes*, 111.

21. Talbert Holt to Carrie Holt, April 25, November 20, December 12, 1861 (typescript), Robert Partin Papers, Auburn University; Harris and Niflot, *Dear Sister*, 14.

22. Bruen and Fitzgibbons, *Through Ordinary Eyes*, 45; Turner, *Southern Soldier's Letters Home*, 55; Franklin, *Fielder Diaries*, 24–25.

23. William Lipscomb to Talluh Lipscomb, June 7, 1861, Lipscomb Papers; Moseley, *Stilwell Letters*, 16.

24. Everett, *Chaplain Davis and Hood's Texas Brigade*, 2–3.

25. Harris and Niflot, *Dear Sister*, 48; Lowe and Hodges, *Letters to Amanda*, 209.

26. In January 1865, after nearly four years of civil war and countless manifestations of God's preserving care, Captain Alfred Fielder of Tennessee recorded in his diary, "My trust is firm in God and into his hands I commit my family as into the hands of a faithful and trusty friend" (Franklin, *Fielder Diaries*, 214). Virginian Ted Barclay wrote home after a small skirmish near

the Rapidan River in February 1864: "That is the time it is to feel how sweet it is to be a Christian. When the balls are flying thick around you and dealing death all around, to commit yourself into His care, that He has power to hurl by harmless the missiles of death" (Turner, *Ted Barclay*, 86, 125). Soldiers on both sides carried into the war their antebellum beliefs about death. Saum maintains that for mid-nineteenth-century Americans, death represented "an escape from the world's sadness, an end to the pilgrimage through spiritual and bodily hostility. It meant the passage to that realm where parting is no more" (*Popular Mood of Pre–Civil War America*, 103–4). The topic of religion's impact on soldiers' combat motivation and courage has attracted the interest of several historians. In his 1994 article entitled "Religion and Combat Motivation in the Confederate Armies," Watson points out that soldiers' religious faith had a positive impact on their combat performance. According to Watson, religion provided soldiers a sense of community, helped them cope with their fear of death, and provided justification for killing and having to watch fellow soldiers die (34–36). Watson's overall contention has been seconded by Peter Carmichael in his book *The Last Generation*. "Christianity instilled a sense of duty, demanded discipline, and inspired courage," writes Carmichael, and a "saved man did not fear the dangers of battle" (182). Other scholars have also considered religion's role in helping soldiers cope with the experience of war. Hess in *The Union Soldier in Battle* argues that religion "steadied [the soldier's] emotions at a critical time and provided a rock on which he based his courage" (104). In *For Cause and Comrades*, McPherson goes even further and asserts that the "heightened religiosity helped to prevent the collapse of both armies during the terrible carnage of 1864, but was a particularly potent force in the Confederacy. It may not be an exaggeration to say that the revivals of 1863–64 enabled Confederate armies to prolong the war into 1865" (63–71, 75).

27. Woodworth, *While God Is Marching On*, 212, 232. For others who led prayer meetings, see McKim, *A Soldier's Recollections*, 60–61, 119; Harris and Niflot, *Dear Sister*, 35, 56; Bruen and Fitzgibbons, *Through Ordinary Eyes*, 45; Franklin, *Fielder Diaries*, 43; and Turner, *Ted Barclay*, 144.

28. McKim, *A Soldier's Recollections*, 137; Cooke diary, July 11, 13, 16, August 24, 27, September 14, October 5, 1862. One opportunity that McKim took advantage of was at a Confederate hospital in June 1862: "While at Charlottesville I several times went through one of the hospitals, and talked to some of the wounded, and read the Testament to them" (*A Soldier's Recollections*, 119).

29. Woodworth, *While God Is Marching On*, 194–95, 244. McPherson writes, "Bodily death held no terrors for the true believer because it meant entry of the soul into a better world where it would live in peace and happiness with loved ones for eternity" (*For Cause and Comrades*, 68).

30. Longtime Christian soldiers also assumed positions of leadership during the revivals. From Fredericksburg, Virginia, in April 1863, Confederate William Stilwell wrote to his wife, "I lead prayer meeting last Wednesday night from the 17th chapter of John and made a few remarks on the last verse. Pray that God may bless our meeting." In another letter home later that year, he wrote again about his involvement: "Last night I held meeting in Company G, we had [a] good meeting, some coming to the altar for prayer. . . . I have been invited to hold meeting in Company A tonight" (Moseley, *Stilwell Letters,* 127, 147, 208). For a description of revivals in all armies, both Union and Confederate, see Woodworth, *While God Is Marching On,* 193–255.

"A Viler Enemy in Our Rear"

Pennsylvania Soldiers Confront
the North's Antiwar Movement

Timothy J. Orr

On the afternoon of Monday, March 2, 1863, at the Union Army of the Potomac's Twelfth Corps winter encampment at Dumfries, Virginia, twenty-two-year-old Sergeant Henry Hayward, serving with the Twenty-eighth Pennsylvania Infantry, roamed the countryside in an attempt to relieve his mind from the boredom of camp life. Upon returning to his regiment's encampment, he witnessed a provocative sight. The men of the Twenty-ninth Ohio Infantry, another regiment in his brigade, had formed into a hollow square following their dress parade to discuss matters relating to politics in the state of Ohio. The rise of a strong antiwar faction inside the Democratic Party stood out as the greatest concern to the Ohio infantrymen. These antiwar advocates, known as Copperheads—from the practice of wearing Indian heads cut from copper pennies on their lapels to signify their association with elite fraternal societies—had rapidly become the most hated men in the North. Copperheads' seditious language, seemingly pro-Southern sympathies, and anger and resentment over President Abraham Lincoln's Emancipation Proclamation, Conscription Bill, and suspension of the writ of habeas corpus caused many Northerners to brand them as traitorous friends of the South. One individual of particular distaste and frequent discussion was Ohio congressman Clement Laird Vallandigham, whose anti-Lincoln tirades ranked among the most scathing.

The men of the Twenty-ninth Ohio listened intently to the words of their commanding officer, Lieutenant Colonel Thomas Clark, as he read a letter discussing the state of affairs in Ohio. Sergeant Hayward recounted, "it spoke of a set of Traitors that were Plotting against the

Government and poisening the minds of the people." After Clark finished reading the letter, he asked his men to speak on the subject freely "with out hesetation either for or against." He then asked all those in the ranks who agreed with the letter's pro-Republican interpretation to signify by saying "aye." According to Hayward, the whole regiment burst forth with one tumultuous "AYE!" Then, one of the line officers proposed three cheers for the Constitution and three more for President Lincoln. Both, said Hayward, were given "with a will." Finally, one of the privates proposed three groans for the Copperheads, which the Ohioans delivered with the same vociferousness.

Amused by these proceedings, Hayward strolled back to camp and penned a letter to his older sister, Cora. Hayward agreed with the provocative course of action he had witnessed and lamented the poor condition of public sentiment that drove the Ohioans to counter this desperate attempt by treasonous individuals to inaugurate rebellion within the Buckeye State. Hayward believed that this dissent not only plagued Ohio but also pervaded much of the North. Thus, he wrote:

> We thought we were doing much for the Great Cause, and it seemed that everywhere the work went Bravely on and that before another winter should come upon us Treason would have done its worst and this dreadfull Curse would disappear from our once Happy Country and restore us once more to our Homes and friends. But it seems that the good time has not yet come. They say the war must go on. I say let the war go on untill every traitor Copperheads and all are made to kneel before the Godess of Liberty. The army is yet true and Loyal but they feel as if there is not much chance for their lives with enemys on every side. I believe that if such men as Vallandigham should come here and talk the way he does in Congress the soldiers would kill him. We must have victory at Vicksburgh and Charlestown to give our troops confidence and silence traitors in the North. . . . These are the original times that tried mens souls. These are Americas Dark days and if I live to see her pass through them and come out whole then my fondest hopes are realized.[1]

Returning his thoughts to the Twenty-ninth Ohio, Hayward wrote, "I suppose this letter [read by Clark] will go from one Ohio Regt. to the other and will then be sent home as a warning for all the traitors at home."[2] Sergeant Hayward had just witnessed an event that occurred frequently within the ranks of the Union army during 1863. Hayward's regiment, the Twenty-eighth Pennsylvania, would participate in one later that month, denouncing the antiwar movement in the North in a set of resolutions unanimously supported by the officers and men. Fearing for the welfare of their country, Union soldiers attacked the antiwar movement with a series of public resolutions sent home to local newspapers to sway Northern citizens away from what they believed was a dangerous conspiracy designed to weaken the Union further.

The history of the Civil War has generally paid too little attention to the reverberations of partisan politics in the ranks of the Union army. The few historians who have discussed the role of the North's Democratic minority have been quick to conclude that active Democratic opposition actually helped to secure Union victory. Some argue that party competition aided the North by moderating the Republican administration's policies in ways that ultimately benefited the Union war effort. Joel Silbey and Eric McKitrick, for instance, reject the notion that Democrats disloyally obstructed Republican prosecution of the war. In Silbey's opinion, Northern Democrats remained "respectable" throughout, pledging themselves to the maintenance of the Union, the Constitution, and civil liberties. But Silbey's and McKitrick's interpretations of the Democratic Party implicitly reject the importance of the party's peace movement in 1863. Similarly, Silbey and McKitrick do not account for the violent backlash that came from the Republican Party following the advent of such ardent antiwar politics. Hardly accepting their Democratic foes as a "loyal opposition," Republican Party leaders believed that Northern Democrats could be measured only by the lines of "treason" espoused by their Copperhead leaders.[3]

This Republican reaction proved especially dangerous in the case of the North's citizen-soldiers, who directly threatened the antiwar politicians. Union army officers and enlisted men took swift action to silence "treasonous" Democrats, advocating the use of violence to ensure that Copperheads would not acquire political office. Given that Union soldiers possessed the physical means to quell dissent—with the muzzles of their rifles or the points of their bayonets—soldiers' public outcries against the antiwar movement were especially ominous. One could hardly imagine Pennsylvania's 30,000 soldiers serving in 1863 returning to Philadelphia or Pittsburgh to inaugurate martial law shortly before the beginning of the Chancellorsville Campaign, yet this is what their unit resolutions suggested. Thus, Hayward was apparently serious when he claimed that he and his fellow soldiers would kill Congressman Vallandigham if he ever came within rifle range.

Partisan strife hardly offered the North a political advantage. Early on, soldiers bitterly opposed any politician who criticized the conduct of the war. Particularly, they chastised overzealous Republicans who demanded swift military action. But by 1863, Pennsylvania soldiers had turned their sights on antiwar Democrats, berating and threatening them in the harshest of terms. They argued that partisan politics hindered the Northern war effort, dividing civilians and soldiers along party lines. By the end of the year, many soldiers had assumed the Republican vision of the war, denouncing any Democratic Northerner who criticized the war's prosecution, regardless of whether he was a soldier, a civilian, a War Democrat, or a Copperhead. Furthermore, Pennsylvania soldiers believed that they possessed the right to dictate governmental policy to the civilian population, maintaining that they wielded the authority to regulate or repress any dissent on the home front.

The political battle between pro-war soldiers and antiwar politicians became especially heated in several states, and Pennsylvania provides an excellent case study of Union soldiers' reactions to critics of the war. In this "most intensely competitive of all northern states," in Silbey's words, Union soldiers were loyal defenders of the Republican administration.[4] When antiwar Democrats, especially those in the Lower North, began criticizing the war with increasing ferocity during the winter and spring of 1863, Union soldiers responded as an organized political body, and Pennsylvania soldiers stood out as vocal supporters of the Republican Party. Although Pennsylvania units dubbed their resolutions "nonpartisan" efforts to unite the North, they supported Republican issues: acceptance of the draft, suspension of the writ of habeas corpus, limitations on free speech, support of the conduct of federal authority, and aversion to armistice. Union soldiers, especially those from Pennsylvania, saw themselves as guardians of the Republic, leading the nation down the path of wholesale support of Republican policy.

Another factor that makes Pennsylvania a good case study is its 1863 gubernatorial race. Following the military disasters in the eastern theater in 1862, Democratic candidates swept the off-year congressional elections that autumn. Their success proved so widespread that pro-war Democrats began to acknowledge the power of the antiwar faction. Eight states held gubernatorial elections in 1863, and in three of them—Ohio, Connecticut, and Pennsylvania—the Democrats chose to run antiwar candidates.

This political contest was closest in Pennsylvania. The commonwealth possessed a strong pro-war leadership headed by Republican governor Andrew Gregg Curtin, a popular Centre County native widely renowned as the "soldiers' friend." But his reelection was not assured. Pennsylvania also possessed many capable Copperhead leaders, men whose eloquence and public efforts united the Democratic populace on the prospect of immediate armistice with the South. Pennsylvania also faced an impending draft and a Confederate military invasion during the summer of 1863, two issues that did not win the Lincoln administration substantial approval. Most divisive of all, the commonwealth of Pennsylvania disfranchised its soldiers.

Soldier voting had been a contentious issue during the War of 1812, when the Pennsylvania Constitution decreed that eligible voters could cast ballots only in their home election districts. Thus, Pennsylvania militiamen serving in the field could not vote. In 1813 the state legislature passed a law enabling soldiers to vote by proxy, that is, allowing them to send their ballots back home to reliable individuals who would vote in their stead. Following revision of the commonwealth's constitution in 1838, legislators drafted a military suffrage law in 1839 that allowed soldiers to vote in the field under the direction of their officers. However, during the 1861 local elections, both Democratic and Republican candidates complained that soldiers' voting caused numerous irregularities. In Luzerne County, the Democratic candidate for district attorney, Ezra Chase, challenged the 1839 law in the courts, and in May 1862 the state supreme court, which included Copperhead justice George Washington Woodward, declared the law unconstitutional in *Chase v. Miller*. The Republicans initially approved of the decision because it allowed them to carry a few offices, including the sheriff's office in Philadelphia. However, following the disastrous elections of 1862, in which numerous Republicans lost local, state, and national seats, they vehemently accused the Democrats of subverting democracy by depriving the loyal boys in blue of the right to vote. Indeed, the issue of soldier disfranchisement worked in the Republicans' favor, because the Democratic candidate for governor in 1863 happened to be the controversial Copperhead George Woodward, the same justice who had written the majority opinion in *Chase v. Miller*. It did not take long for Pennsylvania's soldiers to deem him their enemy.[5]

Fellow Democrats attempted to defend Woodward's decision, but they only worsened their party's reputation. Democratic state senator William Wallace, for instance, argued that allowing soldiers to vote was undemocratic. Wallace asserted that the "very elements that fit a man for the proper discharge of his duties of a citizen, are those which in his position as a soldier are, and must necessarily be, denied to him." Democrats charged that soldiers lacked "self-reliance and individualism" and, consequently, could not think for themselves. Soldiers would vote according to the wills of their commanders, who, Democrats complained, were all Republicans who owed their posts to the influence of the Lincoln administration.[6]

Unable to cast their ballots in the gubernatorial election and unable to convey their condemnation of the Copperheads through the act of voting, Pennsylvania's volunteer soldiers employed a different tactic. They used unanimously approved unit resolutions not only to voice their displeasure at the recent change in the political current but also to urge all loyal Northerners to save the Union from what they considered a "viler enemy in their rear."[7] These resolutions bolstered the Republican Party, essentially placing Union soldiers and Republican politicians in the same political camp. The soldiers, the men who actually fought the Civil War and viewed governmental policy from the ground, became vital allies of the Republican Party through their wholesale acceptance of the Lincoln administration's wartime decrees and their retaliation against Copperheads' dissent.

Pennsylvania's volunteer soldiers were no strangers to political confrontation. During the war they became avid correspondents for local newspapers, frequently voicing their opinions on military and political matters. In 1861 they expressed distinct pleasure in witnessing Pennsylvanians' widespread support of the war, even though, on the whole, the commonwealth had adopted a moderate stance on the issue of Southern secession. Soldiers repeatedly thanked the populace for its continued support following the military disasters of 1861. That year, nearly every candidate in the local elections ran on a pro-war platform. Philadelphia resident Sidney George Fisher remarked that the pro-war political "current" ran so strong that every politician had to "swim" in it.[8] Soldiers graciously applauded newspapers for their continued support of Pennsylvania's soldiery. A soldier correspondent to the *Philadelphia Daily Evening Bulletin* commented in November 1861 that he and his comrades were "gratified by seeing the promotion of many deserving men to more respectable offices, thus showing that the Government is aware of and rightly appreciates the efforts of all true patriots, and rewards them accordingly."[9]

When the first murmurs of civilian discontent arose, the citizen-soldiers of Pennsylvania responded quickly to counter it. During the winter and spring of 1862, many Republican newspapers critically reviewed the performance of the Army of the Potomac's slow-moving Democratic commander, Major General George Brinton McClellan.

Although eager for battle, the men of Philadelphia and Pittsburgh's Twenty-eighth Pennsylvania, then serving at Sandy Hook, Maryland, considered such criticism unwarranted. In February 1862 the men expressed anger over the negative opinions advanced by the Republican press, and when overzealous Republican policy seemingly led to disaster, the soldiers pointed to the problems caused by interparty competition. The Twenty-eighth Pennsylvania's disaster occurred during a river crossing near Harpers Ferry on February 24, when a sudden freshet overturned a small ferryboat containing six men and a civilian boat pilot. All seven men plunged into the icy waters of the Potomac River and drowned. The crossing continued later in the day when U.S. Army engineers procured larger, supposedly safer canal boats. Unfortunately, another incident occurred when a cable guiding one of the last boats snapped, setting the vessel adrift. The helpless craft, filled to capacity with an entire company of soldiers, was swept downstream and lodged against a rocky outcropping but, luckily, did not overturn. Angered by the day's events, the men of the Twenty-eighth Pennsylvania chastised the Republican press in no uncertain terms. One soldier writing to the *Philadelphia Daily Evening Bulletin* demanded that the "'forward' shriekers of the North will cease their clamor against McClellan and his advisors and await with patience the result of the grand plan. We feel confident of his success, and will prove to the world that our former inactivity will have only fitted us for a more resolute strike at the heart of Secession."[10]

A remarkably similar accident happened to the Seventy-fifth

Pennsylvania at Castleman's Ferry, near Winchester, Virginia. On April 15, 1862, the soldiers of this Philadelphia-raised German American regiment began crossing the rain-swollen Shenandoah River. As the men were safely but slowly making their away across using small rafts, the commander, Colonel Heinrich C. Bohlen, ordered Companies I and K to use a partially burned canal boat left behind by Confederate troops to expedite the crossing. When this boat reached midstream, the current buffeted the dilapidated vessel, forcing the soldiers to release their hold on the guide cable. The canal boat capsized, pouring fifty-nine men, including two officers and an African American servant, into the river, drowning all. Sergeant Herrmann Nachtigall described the scene: "The terror of the victims was indescribable—a cry of fear, unforgettable by all who heard it, pierced the air—an instant, and the rapidly moving waves swallowed the unfortunate victims. Several packs drifting on the surface for a few moments were all that remained of the unfortunate men." Although much of the nation was still in shock from the recent bloodbath at the battle of Shiloh in western Tennessee, Pennsylvania newspapers dutifully reported the mass drowning, lamenting the fact that the accident had been caused, as they believed, by political pressures placed on the Union army. Even the ardently Republican *Philadelphia Daily Evening Bulletin* dubbed the accident an "unfortunate disaster." Some editorials claimed that military successes required time and meticulous planning, not partisan war cries for swift victory.[11]

Memories of such accidents eventually dimmed with time, but partisan politics remained constant. A year later, during the winter and spring of 1863, Pennsylvania soldiers again attacked the war's critics, but this time they targeted the antiwar Democrats. To Pennsylvania soldiers, antiwar activism was equivalent to Southern sympathy and suggested that the Democrats lacked faith in the Union army's ability to secure victory. Indeed, many soldiers considered the term *Copperhead* apt. Like the copperhead snake, antiwar Democrats gave no warning before striking their prey. Pennsylvania volunteers resented antiwar politicians so strongly that they seemed unable to fashion language expressive enough to convey their indignation and disgust at these "treasonous" antiwar arguments. One soldier correspondent to the *Philadelphia Inquirer* wrote: "We know we have a viler enemy in our rear than in our front, because [Copperheads are] more cowardly and dastardly cruel. . . . Others with whom I have conversed utter curses both loud and deep on the suicidal crew who would stab us in the back, and if they would do so, destroy us by a fire in the rear. But let them beware; the day of reckoning will come. We will save our country first by crushing the Rebellion in our front, and then turn our attention to the cowboys at home."[12]

Soldiers denounced the Copperheads in a number of ways. Sending letters to family and friends provided a simple means of influencing political sentiment on the home front. Pittsburgh artillerist James Stewart, for instance, wrote home in February 1863 when he learned that his mother planned to change her house of worship. "I heard from Lieutenant Atwell that your church in Pittsburgh has mated with the Church in Allegheny," he wrote. "If this is so, I am very glad to hear it for I dispise rebels of any kind, and I think the church in Pittsburgh is a little on the Rebel principle of the Confederate State."[13] When his brother asked him whether he would accept a surgeon's discharge on account of illness, Sergeant James Moore of the 147th Pennsylvania Infantry vowed to continue his service until victory was assured. He concluded in July 1864, "I think a man is better off in the Army than at home amongst the Damd Copperhead as I term it."[14] In their private correspondence, many soldiers pledged to enact physical violence on antiwar men once they returned from the war. Citing Clement Vallandigham, Fernando Wood, and Samuel Sullivan Cox as his primary targets, Private James Todd Miller of the 111th Pennsylvania Infantry told his parents, "I should not wonder to see the time afer this war is over that [with] our own strong arms we will take vengance on those cowardly skunks that are a disgrace to our country."[15] As a soldier with a weapon, and as one of many others in his regiment who shared his opinion, Private Miller felt certain that he could carry out his threat.

The most popular method of dealing with Copperheads proved to be open threats written to Republican newspapers. Pennsylvania's soldiers did not mince words. Lieutenant Colonel George Fisher McFarland of the 151st Pennsylvania wrote to the *Warren Mail*:

> It is hard for the soldier, when in the range of the enemy's guns, to believe that many of the very men for whom he is fighting, from whose homes and property he has kept a merciless and uncivilized foe for many long weary months, are traitors. But when the northern press comes to him, full of vile slan-

ders and vexatious criticisms upon the Administration and its
policy, upon the army and its generals, though containing not
one word of condemnation of traitors in arms against us, he can
see nothing but treason in it. . . . His soul swells with holy indignation at those of the North who would strengthen the arm of
the rebellion; openly talk and write treason, and, assassin-like,
stab those who are fighting for them! Such cowardly scoundrels
awaken his vengeance, and he vows that he will not lay down
his arms until they feel that vengeance. If these "Copperheads"
have the courage enough to inaugurate rebellion in the North,
they will find a mighty army of patriots ready to crush them to
the earth. Mark that![16]

Pennsylvania's soldiers eagerly confronted "peace men" at every
opportunity. Many were concerned about Copperheads serving in the
Union army. Lieutenant Alexander W. Acheson of the 140th Pennsylvania
Infantry admitted to his father that every regiment had a set of "grunt-
ers," men who grumbled, shirked, or bragged, sending "false reports"
home denouncing the war. Acheson, however, believed that few grunt-
ers could be found in Pennsylvania's regiments; most were New York
men. He wrote that "they [New Yorkers] are never at their posts in the
hour of danger. When the army goes into battle they stay back, and if
their side is defeated, they are the first to cry out against their leader. . . .
These men take every opportunity to run down the administration and
complain of the hardships which they have to endure."[17]

Acheson further complained that every time his Pennsylvanians
encountered New York soldiers on picket duty, the Empire Staters
boasted that they had done the hardest share of the fighting. Acheson
noted that they frequently used the phrases "Damn Nigger war," "Abe
ought to be hung," and "Wish the war was over." Acheson maintained
that if people who were not knowledgeable about current issues met
any New York troops, they would automatically conclude that the war
had "more hardships than ever." He wrote, "They . . . would go on to
talk about how hard Malvern Hill was, what a terrible time they had at
Antietam, how they fought at South Mountain; and at the same time
these men are not to be relied on except when backed and supported by
Pennsylvanians. . . . They . . . are worth nothing except for stopping bullets." Acheson concluded by describing his vision of the cardinal virtues

of an American citizen-soldier. "A good soldier," he wrote, "will say (I heard them) he is tired of the war (when he is asked) but he will not say anything in that line until asked. Moreover he does not allow any minor affair, such as a flaw in the Administration, a leader whom he does not like or a movement he does not approve of, to keep the one great object out of view. Our army is full of great soldiers and a victory will give them hope."[18]

This is not to suggest that all of Pennsylvania's citizen-soldiers were Republicans; many Pennsylvania regiments, especially those drawn from Philadelphia and Pittsburgh, contained staunch Democrats. Philadelphia's large Irish American population manifested itself in the ranks of both the Sixty-ninth and 116th Pennsylvania Infantries, two hard-fighting regiments in the Army of the Potomac's Second Corps. Both these units remained loyal to the Democratic Party, giving presidential candidate George McClellan a majority during the 1864 election.[19]

However, the rise of the Copperheads in 1863 drove many Democratic soldiers into the Republican Party's ranks. Captain Francis Adams Donaldson, a Philadelphian serving in the Seventy-first Pennsylvania Infantry and a self-described Democrat, deplored the attacks made by Republican Party newspapers against McClellan during the 1862 Peninsula Campaign. In May, after he learned of his brother's strong inclinations toward "cruel [Republican] feelings," Donaldson immediately sent a sharp reply: "Now to my mind the solution of this clamor is as plain as the nose on your face." He then added sarcastically, "McClellan is a Democrat, and as such, must be removed. Republicanism is the fashion, and all who are not of the persuasion must go, no matter how much the service suffers, no matter that the interests of the country demand support and confidence in the commander of its great army." Donaldson clearly believed that partisan propaganda— in this case, Republican propaganda—undermined the war effort and eroded army morale. He concluded his letter sternly: "I can speak with certainty of our regiment, where the situation, as you can picture it, has been discussed, and the officers, one and all, are determined to resign should rank injustice be done 'Little Mac.'"[20]

Donaldson, however, did not retain his Democratic outlook throughout the war. By October 1863, now serving with the 118th Pennsylvania Infantry, Donaldson had clearly converted to Republicanism. Unable to vote in the commonwealth's gubernatorial election while serving in northern Virginia, he agreed with his Republican brother that Pennsylvania soldiers should receive furloughs so that they could travel home to cast their ballots. He wrote to his brother Jacob from Culpeper Court House, "I do indeed most cordially join in your wish that I should be at home during the coming election. I would dearly love to cast a vote for Andrew G. Curtin." Party loyalties thus reached a state of flux among Pennsylvania's soldier population, and Copperheadism could deter even the most stalwart Democrats.[21]

Pennsylvania's pro-war soldiers and the North's antiwar citizenry often clashed over elections. The Pennsylvanians of the Twenty-eighth Infantry, for instance, expressed solidarity with the Republican citizens of Ohio, which also held a gubernatorial election in 1863. That election pitted Republican John Brough against notorious Democratic Copperhead Clement Vallandigham. In October the men of the Twenty-eighth Pennsylvania Infantry had a chance to witness this campaign firsthand when they transferred by rail to the Army of the Cumberland to reinforce the besieged Union troops in Chattanooga. During the unit's trip across Ohio, that state's Republicans bombarded the Pennsylvanians with campaign rhetoric at every train depot. "I never saw people take such an interest in Politics as the men women & Children do of Ohio," wrote Sergeant Henry Hayward.[22]

When the soldiers disembarked at a rest stop, the citizens thronged them, shouting the Republican campaign cry, "Hurrah for Brough!" The patriotic Ohioans gave the soldiers large quantities of food, refusing to accept any payment. They poured apples "by the bushell" into the railroad cars. Young women from the town of Bellaire asked the soldiers to write down their names, ranks, and companies on slips of paper so that they could write letters to them once they arrived in Chattanooga. The gratified Pennsylvanians asked these young ladies whether their town had any Vallandigham supporters, and the women replied that few Democrats ever left their homes, but they warned the soldiers that most of the railroad employees were "of that stamp." Thus, as the trip through Ohio continued, whenever the train passed railroad workers alongside the tracks, the Keystone soldiers raised the cheer, "Hurrah for Brough!" This display typically elicited a gesture of disapproval from one of the railroad workers, at which point a mischievous member of the Twenty-eighth Pennsylvania threw a hardened piece of army-issued salt pork at the offensive Democrat. This process was repeated throughout the state until every member of the 350-man regiment had thrown out his salt pork ration.[23]

Given that Pennsylvania soldiers could not cast ballots in the 1863 election, they utilized another venue to express their anti-Copperhead sentiment: the drafting of unit resolutions. During February and March 1863, many of Pennsylvania's regiments serving in the Army of the Potomac took to their drill fields in northern Virginia to challenge the antiwar Democrats.[24] No doubt, the soldiers believed that the stunning success of the Democratic Party in the 1862 elections and the anti-administration speeches delivered by arch-Copperhead Clement Vallandigham demanded an immediate response. But it is also worth noting that these resolutions surfaced during a period of prolonged inactivity by the Union armies. By January 1863, most Union forces had established winter quarters, and active campaigning had ground to a virtual halt. With little else to occupy their minds, Union soldiers must have discussed politics inside their tents and log huts, and in nearly all cases, these camp meetings led to a ringing endorsement of the Republican administration. Yet, at the same time, Union soldiers' political consciousness led to some frightening conclusions. The majority of these resolutions openly advocated violence toward the antiwar population of the North. Chillingly malevolent in their tone, they pledged to punish treason in the North, as the men of the 109th Pennsylvania claimed, as "severely as Rebellion in the South."[25]

Evidence suggests that Pennsylvania regiments constructed these resolutions with extreme care. Little is known about how they were written, but it appears that the regimental officers usually drafted them. The letters from two brothers in the 140th Pennsylvania Infantry, Captain David Acheson and Lieutenant Alexander Acheson, provide one of the few windows into the resolutions' construction. Even for a regiment almost wholly composed of Republicans, it appears that the process of drafting and accepting resolutions was no easy task. The mere act of gathering officers together inside a single tent during the middle of a busy day was frustratingly difficult. Captain Acheson noted that the 140th Pennsylvania's line officers attempted "several times to get up a meeting to pass resolutions condemning the course of Peace Men." For various reasons, including frequent drills, inspections, or intercompany feuds, the officers of the 140th Pennsylvania accomplished nothing for weeks. Acheson guessed that Colonel Richard Petit Roberts, a Republican district attorney from Beaver County, was to blame, suggesting that "while pretending to favor the movement, [he] kept it back," perhaps to curb the radical enthusiasm of the unit's Washington County officers, whom Roberts despised.[26]

Thus, despite the fact that "every soldier in the 140th hates the name Copperhead," it took three weeks for the regiment to draft a set of resolutions on which everyone could agree. Eventually, a committee that included all the field officers and three of the line officers drafted the regiment's resolutions, which then required the approval of all ten companies. According to Lieutenant Acheson, "a great majority" of the men in his company, Company C, signed them, although he admitted that a few recalcitrant soldiers "who receive their teachings from the Examiner and Review [two Democratic newspapers]" refused to add their endorsement. Acheson, however, complained that the committee had drafted a "miserable set of resolutions" because, in his opinion, they needed harsher language. Ultimately, the 140th Pennsylvania settled on only three resolutions, one of which claimed that what they felt for the Copperheads was "all the contempt that naturally springs from loyal hearts for sneaking cowards, tories, and traitors." For Acheson, this did not adequately express the hatred that he and his fellow Washington County soldiers harbored for the antiwar movement. "Oh hush!" he wrote, "is this all that the 'Hundred and fortieth'—the best regiment in the service of Uncle Sam, can say—and that too after 'three weeks' labor? . . . It wouldn't do to vote down these resolutions for fear that the Copperheads would misconstrue our actions, but they (resolutions) don't express the views of this regt. by—'a bag full.'" Lieutenant Acheson guessed that these tepid resolutions resulted from Colonel Roberts's political aspirations, making him appear softer on Copperheadism than his colleagues did. "How he tries to be as easy as he can for fear of offending the Copperheads!" Acheson lamented. The anti-Copperhead language that Roberts allowed to be printed, Acheson continued, was so benign that "the [Washington] Review and co. could adopt it with as much grace as we could."[27]

Other regiments appear to have constructed and circulated their resolutions in a similar manner. Both the 150th Pennsylvania Infantry stationed at Belle Plain, Virginia, and the 100th Pennsylvania Infantry stationed at Newport News, Virginia, organized resolution committees that consisted of the regimental field and staff officers, one or two company-grade line officers, and one or two enlisted men for good measure.[28] Typically, the officers read the resolutions to the enlisted men following their dress parade. Sometimes, as in the case of the 140th Pennsylvania, the officers copied and circulated the resolutions among the companies for the men to sign. In other cases, as in the 100th Pennsylvania, the officers elected to maintain the formal style of the dress parade and asked all those in favor of the resolutions to assume the position of shoulder arms. The enlisted men of Lawrence and Butler Counties did this unanimously on March 14, much to their officers' delight.[29]

More commonly, however, the officers and enlisted men acted informally to pass their regiments' resolutions. Despite the high degree of military formality prescribed by a dress parade, order and organization often broke down while these resolutions were being read. Dignified military ceremonies were transformed into hectic political rallies, complete with hurrahs for the Republicans and boos and hisses for the Copperheads. Philadelphia and Crawford County's 150th Pennsylvania, for instance, reported that its resolutions were "unanimously adopted amid much enthusiasm," while Philadelphia's 109th Pennsylvania adopted its resolutions "vociferously," with loud applause. The officers asked the men of the 111th Pennsylvania from Erie, Warren, and Crawford counties to cheer "no" or "aye" in favor of the resolutions; they "enthusiastically" voted "aye," followed by "three round hearty cheers." The Fifty-seventh Pennsylvania from Mercer and Bradford counties honored the passage of its resolutions with three cheers and then concluded with three more cheers for the Army of the Potomac's commander, Major General Joseph Hooker, and three more for the U.S. Army and Navy.[30] They could hardly be construed as formal ceremonies, but the raucous, politically charged demonstrations that accompanied the passage of anti-Copperhead resolutions reflected the fact that although Union volunteers saw themselves as soldiers, they were still avid political participants at heart.

Although unit resolutions contained numerous Republican Party lines, Pennsylvania's soldiers crafted them for the purpose of eliminating partisan conflict. Generally, the resolutions derided the overt partisan hostility that infused the Copperheads' rhetoric, arguing for a stronger devotion to the national government from all Northern citizens. The opening resolution of the "Bucktails" of the 149th Pennsylvania, for instance, argued that cordial support and quick obedience provided "the only doorway out of these troubled times," entreating "all citizens and soldiers to support heartily and obey with alacrity all laws and orders coming from those charged with the administration of our government."[31] Both the 111th and 150th Pennsylvania argued similarly, pledging their obedience and acquiescence to the laws of the administration, including any taxes levied for the purpose of prosecuting the war and restoring the Union. Incidentally, both regiments invoked the language of Thomas Jefferson to connect their support of the government with the notion of sacrifice, pledging to stand by the government "at all hazards" with "our lives, our fortunes, and our sacred honor."

Although many of these resolutions frequently mentioned the soldiers' "entire confidence" and "hearty support" of Republican figures, such as President Lincoln, many resolutions argued that Pennsylvania's volunteers would willingly serve under anyone brave enough to lead the Union army against the rebellion, regardless of party affiliation. The Fifty-seventh Pennsylvania's tenth resolution claimed that its soldiers would "cheerfully follow the leadership of any General whom the President, as Commander-in-chief of the Army, may, in his wisdom, see fit to appoint over us." Likewise, the men of the 150th Pennsylvania resolved that they had "no sympathy" for any man who "from real or pretended admiration of any man or general would make their earnestness in their country's cause, or perhaps their loyalty dependent or subordinate to their personal feelings." A good soldier, the resolution argued, remained eager to fight for his country, whoever his appointed commander happened to be. Given the Army of the Potomac's recent change in leadership—the replacement of Major General Ambrose Burnside with the controversial Major General Joseph Hooker—Pennsylvania's soldiers believed that they should include these lines.[32]

Pennsylvania units' resolutions also repudiated Copperhead demands for armistice. In their sixth resolution, the men of the Twenty-eighth Pennsylvania claimed that "no peace propositions could be consistently entertained by the Government of the United States, excepting those based on *unconditional* and *absolute* submission to the tenets of the Constitution *as it now exists.*" Similarly, the resolutions of the 100th Pennsylvania urged its members to "spurn with contempt every proposition of Northern Copperheads for compromise. . . . We want no peace till the emblem of the nation shall again wave over every village and hamlet in the rebellious States . . . [and] every vestige of treason and its cursed cause shall be effaced forever." In the eyes of Pennsylvania's soldiers, advocating peace remained tantamount to treason, and no respectable Northern citizen should follow the teachings of the "Peace Cowards."[33] Again, Pennsylvania soldiers believed that they could mute partisan conflict by rejecting armistice, but of course, they unintentionally advanced Republican planks.

Finally, Pennsylvania soldiers sustained a "nonpartisan" attack on the Copperheads themselves and their public addresses by demanding the sustained loyalty of the home front and the immediate silencing of all treasonous editorials written to local newspapers. The third resolution of the Twenty-eighth Pennsylvania claimed, "We would have every editor arrested who dares at this time [to] publish treasonable editorials and through the medium of their contemptible sheet endeavor to fill the ranks of the army with disaffection. . . . The country and the army should think with one mind." That unit joined the 100th Pennsylvania in applauding the formation of Union League Clubs at home and urged loyal citizens to take "decisive and summary measures" necessary to ensure the full prosecution of the current administration's acts and policies through "vigilant efforts." These lines were intended to endorse any violent acts undertaken by vigilante groups to intimidate local Copperheads, seize deserters and bounty jumpers for military prosecution, and eradicate supposedly pro-Southern secret societies such as the Knights of the Golden Circle and the Order of American Knights—organizations that some Pennsylvanians mistakenly believed had infiltrated the commonwealth.[34]

In their effort to arouse "nonpartisan" support for the war effort, these resolutions delved into a far more frightening side of politics, one that upheld the use of violence to eliminate disloyalty on the home front. Every regiment adopted at least one resolution that condemned the Copperheads with threatening language. The 149th Pennsylvania's second resolution, for instance, assured Peace Democrats of the regiment's "unmitigated hatred and contempt" for their actions, while the Twenty-eighth Pennsylvania's fifth resolution urged all loyal friends to "shun" Copperheads "as though they were pestilence." Many Pennsylvania regiments took pains to explain away Copperheads' denunciations of the army and its goals as "vile slander." They adamantly maintained that reports circulated by Copperheads about the Army of the Potomac's widespread demoralization were entirely false; the resolutions of the

111th Pennsylvania accused the Copperheads of consulting only the "burlesque upon humanity," the shirkers, cowards, and pretended patriots who had left the Union army or dishonored themselves through desertion.[35] The eighth resolution of the Twenty-eighth Pennsylvania stated:

> *Resolved,* That those *Copperheads* who denounce the further prosecution of the war and criticize the actions and conduct of the Executive powers of the country from a partisan stand point should be treated as traitors of the worst class, as they take advantage of the freedom of speech, and while scattering their own vile sentiments, give them as the views of the entire army. That in our opinion all of the army they have ever conversed with are those who have been discharged through pretended sickness, or those who have been drummed out as *Thieves, Drunkards* or *Cowards,* or those who have deserted through cowardice, as no *Soldier* will allow such traitors as [Clement] Vallandigham, [Fernando] Wood and others of that contemptible class to be his mentor, much less his mouth-piece.[36]

Yet these resolutions often went much further than mere condemnation of Copperhead slander. Frequently, they vowed vengeance in the form of the infliction of physical violence on Copperheads once the Pennsylvania soldiers returned from the war. To legitimate their beliefs, Pennsylvania soldiers took care to connect Copperheadism with secession, as the men of the 100th Pennsylvania did when they declared in their second resolution that the Copperheads were an "integral part of the Rebellion, . . . and as such, should suffer the traitor's doom." Similarly, the men of the 111th Pennsylvania claimed in their second resolution that they would "infinitely prefer that they [the Copperheads] would join their fellow-conspirators in the South" so that the Union army could meet them face-to-face on the field of battle, where justice would be served. Other resolutions were equally lax in veiling their threats of violence. The Fifty-seventh Pennsylvania's seventh resolution asserted that Copperheads deserved "unmitigated scorn" and "the hemp that is due traitors," and the 150th Pennsylvania's final resolution ominously resolved that its soldiers would save "bullets" and "head boards broad enough and heavy enough to crush the vile 'Copperheads' of the North if they persist in their insidious attempt to weaken and overthrow the

Government."[37] Clearly believing that a plot was afoot to destroy the Union from the inside, these Pennsylvania soldiers believed that their duty, in addition to suppressing the rebellion of the Southern states, was to fight traitors in the North. Armed and eager for the challenge, they required only the order to turn about and march on Pennsylvania.

The phrases that Pennsylvania soldiers employed to castigate their Copperhead enemies, such as "crush them to the earth," "unmitigated hatred and contempt," and "suffer a traitor's doom," should not be dismissed as mere campaign rhetoric. Union soldiers may well have meant what they said. They seriously feared the existence of a conspiracy organized by disloyal politicians to disrupt the Union, and they vowed to stamp it out as soon as possible. Soldiers' threats, potentially backed by their lead minié balls, conveyed a powerful message to the voting public. By drafting resolutions, Pennsylvania soldiers hoped to direct the nature of voting in the commonwealth. Unable to vote themselves, soldiers used these resolutions to express themselves politically. When taken as a whole, the resolutions from Pennsylvania regiments suggest a frightening dimension in Northern civil-military relations during the Civil War. Many hinted at legitimating violence toward a treasonous civilian population, which makes the Civil War unique in American military history. In no other case has the American military collectively voiced such an angry and malevolent response aimed at quelling antiwar dissent on the home front.[38]

Partisan politics, it seemed, frequently propelled the fears of Pennsylvania soldiers during the opening months of 1863. Consequently, despite their best efforts, their resolutions could hardly be labeled "nonpartisan." These resolutions often supported unabashedly pro-Republican issues. Some resolutions approved of the controversial Conscription Act, as did the 149th Pennsylvania's third resolution, while others supported the recent enactment of the Emancipation Proclamation as a necessary recourse in the fight against "Southern Rights," as the 150th Pennsylvania's fifth resolution argued. Others supported the enlistment of U.S. Colored Troops, as both the 57th and 111th Pennsylvania Infantries resolved, and still others focused on key state issues, as did the 109th Pennsylvania when it condemned Democratic legislators in Harrisburg for passing resolutions refusing to allow Tennessee governor Andrew Johnson and ex-governor Joseph Wright of Indiana to speak on the floor of the Hall of Representatives.[39]

However, the most partisan aspects of the Pennsylvania soldiers' resolutions proved to be their continued support for the pro-war Republican governor Andrew Curtin. Curtin was widely known for his tireless efforts to raise money for Pennsylvania soldiers and their families, his organization and support of the Pennsylvania Reserve Corps and the Soldier's Orphan Home, and his frequent visits to the Army of the Potomac. The governor received the highest encomiums from Pennsylvania soldiers, with the seventh resolution of the 100th Pennsylvania being fairly typical: "To his [Curtin's] untiring energy and patriotism the whole country is indebted, and his name cannot fail to be immortal upon the page of our national history." By March 1863, when Pennsylvania soldiers drafted the bulk of their resolutions, Curtin was in poor health, and it was rumored that he would not run for reelection that autumn. It is possible that many of Curtin's supporters inside the Union army realized this fact and drafted their resolutions in the hope of changing his mind. But it is also likely that Pennsylvania soldiers realized that their critical votes would be absent in the upcoming election. In the event that they would be unable to return to their home districts to cast their ballots—which, by the spring of 1863, seemed likely, since the prospect of a short-term war was increasingly unrealistic—Pennsylvania soldiers realized that the Republican Party might benefit from a public endorsement. These resolutions, no doubt, carried a political potency that soldiers believed might influence the October election.[40]

Pennsylvania regiments' pro-war resolutions demonstrated their commitment to restoring the Union and their unbridled confidence in the central government. They crafted angry, virulent, frequently one-sided arguments, but they also attempted to define what loyalty, patriotism, and sacrifice meant to a generation of Northerners. Their harsh, explicit words stood out as a firm challenge to the Democratic Party in 1863.[41] The twin victories at Gettysburg and Vicksburg in July finally gave soldiers the opportunity to counterattack their Copperhead detractors, proving that they were not an inept, ill-disciplined, demoralized fighting force. At Gettysburg, they showed that they could best General Robert E. Lee's Army of Northern Virginia in a fair fight, doing so on their home soil and before the eyes of their own citizens. One Beaver County native from the 140th Pennsylvania, which lost 211 of its 540 officers and men during the second day of the battle, boasted to his wife afterward, "the Rebs must not tread on the soil of my birth right State and they have paid dear for it. They are retreating and we are after them and we have taken 2000 prisoners. We have fought the good fight."[42]

The reaction to the dual victories helped take the punch out of George Woodward's gubernatorial campaign. Woodward—"every inch a Copperhead," as one newspaper described him—had wished in 1860 that Pennsylvania might secede from the Union. Yet suddenly, he was espousing a pro-war platform of "status quo antebellum," pledging to restore the Union to its former glory. But the damage had already been done. Many Pennsylvanians considered Woodward a traitor. Even though Woodward's son was serving in the army and received a slight wound at Gettysburg, many Pennsylvanians believed that he was a Southern sympathizer who hated Northern fighting men. According to a popular story circulating at the time, when Woodward was told that his son, Lieutenant Colonel George Abisha Woodward of the Second Pennsylvania Reserve Infantry, had been wounded in the leg, he curtly replied, "[He] should have been shot in the heart for fighting for such a cause." The story was widely believed, but untrue; Woodward traveled to Gettysburg to be with his son as soon as he could.[43]

Pennsylvania soldiers considered Woodward one of the rankest of the Copperheads, and many demanded that they be furloughed to their home districts so that they could cast their ballots against him in 1863. Republican politicians agreed. In Centre County, for instance, Bellefonte attorney Hugh McAllister sent Colonel James A. Beaver of the 148th Pennsylvania Infantry a letter requesting a list of voters in Centre County who could be furloughed to "render the most aid" in the coming election. Although Colonel Beaver disapproved of political interference in his unit—he opposed "soldiers mingling in politics"—his enlisted men earnestly hoped that they might be allowed to go home and vote for Curtin. Private William Williams of the 148th Pennsylvania wrote to his brother in September that he had high "hop[e]s of gitting home to vote this faul. . . . I would like to see Cirtain a lecting again. I think we can't git a better man then he is. . . . If we git home we [will] show them [Democrats] a trick or two." If Williams's prediction of the soldier vote was accurate, the Republican Party desperately needed furloughs to secure victory in Pennsylvania's central counties. Although a few of Colonel Beaver's men managed to return home in time for the election, Curtin still lost his native Centre County by 344 votes.[44]

Still, Woodward could not capitalize on the electoral advantage of having a disfranchised soldier population. In a close election, Woodward lost to Curtin by fewer than 16,000 votes. The Copperheads also lost—and lost heavily—in Ohio, due in large part to the influence of soldier voting.[45] Pennsylvania soldiers were pleased with the results, but as Private James Todd Miller of the 111th Pennsylvania lamented, if they had been given the chance to cast their ballots, "Curtin would have beaten Woodward worse than Brough has beaten Valingaham in Ohio."[46]

Indeed, the Copperheads received a severe blow in the 1863 elections. Although a variety of factors influenced the outcomes, Union soldiers' support of the Republican Party proved invaluable. Soldiers' anti-Copperhead resolutions appeared to be nonpartisan efforts to steel the populace for another year of conflict, but in many ways, they reinforced pro-Republican issues: commitment to the draft, suspension of habeas corpus, limitations on free speech, support of the federal authority and its wartime leaders, and complete aversion to armistice. Patriotism and loyalty, in the soldiers' minds, became a Republican vision, not a Copperhead one.

As the winter of 1863–1864 set in, Pennsylvania soldiers looked hopefully toward the presidential election of 1864, when they would have the opportunity to prove, once and for all, where their loyalties resided. The state constitution had finally been amended, allowing them to vote from their encampments. In April 1864, Huntingdon County native Captain Joseph Addison Moore of the 147th Pennsylvania wrote to his brother, "The expression in the army is nearly universal for Lincoln for the presidency at least in our Div. And our boys of Penna. are Exulant over the idea of having the vote in the field. The Copperheads will receive a terrible rebuke from the Army on Election day."[47] In the November 1864 election, 39,061 Pennsylvania soldiers voted in the field, with 26,712 of them (68 percent) voting for Republican candidate Abraham Lincoln.[48]

Civil War historians have yet to fully understand the complexities of the Democratic Party in the North. Clearly, the Democrats were hardly the enemies of the Union that the Republicans made them out to be, yet many Northern citizens earnestly believed and espoused Republican propaganda. Volunteer soldiers who served on the front line exemplified one group of citizens who embraced the idea that Democrats were disloyal to and opposed the Union. Soldiers from Pennsylvania believed that their state was caught in the throes of turbulent interparty competition, and they identified antiwar Democrats as the arm of the rebellion in the North. Regardless of their prewar political affiliations, Pennsylvania soldiers banded together to halt this perceived insurrection by mounting an intensive letter-writing and resolution-drafting campaign that was pledged to supporting Republican issues and inflicting violence on home-front dissenters. Antiwar Democrats, it seemed, played a dangerous game of partisan politics during the Civil War. Their oppositional rhetoric inflamed a large force of citizen-soldiers and filled them with an angry resolve. Historians can only speculate what might have happened if the Republican Party had failed to achieve electoral success in 1863 and 1864, but it seems likely that in Pennsylvania and elsewhere, the results might have been dire.

NOTES

The author would like to acknowledge his academic companions in this endeavor. Thanks to Carol Reardon, Mark E. Neely Jr., Robert Sandow, Christina Ericson-Hansen, John Quist, and Chad Chalfont.

1. Ambrose Henry Hayward to sister, March 3, 1863, quoted with special permission from Gettysburg College Special Collections Archives (hereafter GCSCA).

2. Ibid.

3. See Joel Silbey, *A Respectable Minority: The Democratic Party in the Civil War Era, 1860–1868* (New York: W. W. Norton, 1977); Eric McKitrick, "Party Politics and the Union and Confederate War Efforts," in *The American Party Systems: Stages of Political Development,* ed. William Nisbet Chambers and Walter Dean Burnham (New York: Oxford University Press, 1967).

4. Silbey, *A Respectable Minority,* 154.

5. Arnold M. Shankman, *The Pennsylvania Antiwar Movement, 1861–1865* (London: Farleigh-Dickinson University Press, 1980), 79, 171–74.

6. William A. Wallace, *Reasons of Hon. Wm. A. Wallace, of Clearfield, for His Vote on Amendments to the Constitution* (n.p., 1864), 3–8, quoted in Jonathan W. White, "Citizens and Soldiers: Party Competition and the Debate in Pennsylvania over Permitting Soldiers to Vote, 1861–64," *American Nineteenth Century History* 5, no. 2 (2004): 59.

7. *Philadelphia Inquirer,* March 23, 1863.

8. Sidney George Fisher, diary, October 13, 1861, in Nicholas B. Wainwright, ed., *A Philadelphia Perspective: The Diary of Sidney George Fisher, 1834–1871* (Philadelphia: Historical Society of Pennsylvania, 1967), 405.

9. "D. B. H.," *Philadelphia Daily Evening Bulletin,* November 26, 1861. D. B. H. was probably Commissary Sergeant David B. Hilt, Twenty-eighth Pennsylvania Infantry.

10. "H.," *Philadelphia Daily Evening Bulletin,* March 3, 1862. The soldiers who drowned were Privates Jacob Arnold, James Wood, Alexander Helverson, Abraham Spicer, John Torode, and George Ortlip, all members of Company P, Twenty-eighth Pennsylvania Infantry.

11. Herrmann Nachtigall, *History of the 75th Regiment, Pennsylvania Volunteers,* trans. Heinz D. Schwinge and Karl E. Sundstrom (Philadelphia: C. B. Kretchamn, 1886; North Riverside, IL: Willow Press, 1987), 15; *Philadelphia Daily Evening Bulletin,* April 21, 1862.

12. *Philadelphia Inquirer,* March 23, 1863.

13. James Stewart to mother, February 1, 1863, CWTI Collection, U.S. Army Military History Institute, Carlisle Barracks, Carlisle PA (hereafter USAMHI).

14. James Moore to brother, July 24, 1864, Pennsylvania Save the Flags—Moore Family Collection, USAMHI.

15. James Todd Miller to parents, March 30, 1863, in Jedediah Mannis and Galen Wilson, eds., *Bound to Be a Soldier: The Letters of Private James T. Miller, 111th Pennsylvania Infantry, 1861–1864* (Knoxville: University of Tennessee Press, 2001), 67. Fernando Wood, a former member of the Tammany Hall political machine and a noted Southern sympathizer, served as mayor of New York City from 1855 to 1858 and again from 1860 to 1862. During his second mayoral term, Wood asserted that New York City should declare independence and continue its successful cotton trade with the South. Wood subsequently won election to the House of Representatives, serving from 1863 to 1865 and again from 1867 to 1881. Copperhead Samuel Sullivan "Sunset" Cox of Zanesville, Ohio, served as a congressman from 1857 to 1865. In 1863 he published *Puritanism in Politics,* a book that condemned New England politics with the charge of abolitionism and disunionism.

16. George Fisher McFarland to *Warren Mail,* April 11, 1863, in Michael A. Dreese, *An Imperishable Fame: The Civil War Experience of George Fisher McFarland* (Mifflintown, PA: Juniata County Historical Society, 1997), 113.

17. Alexander W. Acheson to father, February 7, 1863, in Sara Gould Walters, *Inscription at Gettysburg* (Gettysburg, PA: Thomas Publications, 1991), 59.

18. Ibid.

19. U.S. War Department, *The War of the Rebellion: A Compilation of the Official Records of the Union and Confederate Armies* (Washington, DC: Government Printing Office, 1880–1901), ser. 1, vol. 42, pt. 3, pp. 561, 574 (hereafter *OR*). Both these regiments contained large numbers of Irish

Americans from Philadelphia. During the presidential election of 1864, when Pennsylvania soldiers could vote from the field, the Sixty-ninth Pennsylvania voted 119 for George McClellan and 6 for Abraham Lincoln; the 116th Pennsylvania voted 58 for McClellan and 54 for Lincoln.

20. Francis Adams Donaldson to brother, May 10, 1862, in Gregory J. Acken, ed., *Inside the Army of the Potomac: The Civil War Experience of Captain Francis Adams Donaldson* (Mechanicsburg, PA: Stackpole Books, 1998), 76.

21. Ibid., October 2, 1863, 347.

22. Ambrose Henry Hayward to father, October 12, 1863, GCSCA.

23. Ibid.

24. The resolutions drafted by Pennsylvania soldiers were not an isolated phenomenon. Regiments that hailed from states with strong antiwar movements, including Ohio, Connecticut, Indiana, Illinois, and New Jersey, also drafted anti-Copperhead resolutions.

25. *Philadelphia Inquirer,* March 16, 1863.

26. David Acheson to father, March 24, 1863, in Walters, *Inscription at Gettysburg,* 71.

27. Alexander Acheson to mother, April 4, 1863, and undated clipping, in Walters, *Inscription at Gettysburg,* 74–77.

28. Colonel Langhorne Wister, Lieutenant Colonel Henry S. Huidekoper, Major Thomas Chamberlin, Adjutant Richard L. Ashhurst, Lieutenant William P. Dougal, Quartermaster Arthur S. Voorhis, and Private Philip Hammer drafted the 150th Pennsylvania's resolutions. Lieutenant Colonel Mathew M. Dawson, Captain James H. Cline, Captain Samuel Bentley, Chaplain R. Audley Browne, Captain John P. Blair, Surgeon William C. Shurlock, Lieutenant Jefferson Justice, Corporal Horace B. Durant, and Private William Taylor drafted the 100th Pennsylvania's resolutions.

29. The 100th Pennsylvania passed its resolutions on March 14, 1863, at Newport News, Virginia, and they appeared in the *Philadelphia Daily Evening Bulletin* on March 27, 1863.

30. The 150th Pennsylvania passed its resolutions on March 11, 1863, near Belle Plain, Virginia, and they appeared in the *Philadelphia Daily Evening Bulletin* on March 27, 1863; the 109th Pennsylvania passed its resolutions on March 12, 1863, at Aquia Creek, Virginia, and they appeared in the *Philadelphia Inquirer* and the *Philadelphia Daily Evening Bulletin* on March 16, 1863; the 111th Pennsylvania passed its resolutions on March 11, 1863, at Aquia Creek, Virginia, and they appeared in the *Philadelphia Daily Evening Bulletin* on March 24, 1863; and the Fifty-seventh Pennsylvania passed its resolutions on February 25, 1863, at Falmouth, Virginia, and they appeared in the *Philadelphia Inquirer* on March 3, 1863, and in the *Philadelphia Daily Evening Bulletin* on March 14, 1863.

31. The 149th Pennsylvania passed its resolutions on March 18, 1863, near Belle Plain, Virginia, and they appeared in the *Philadelphia Daily Evening Bulletin* on March 26, 1863.

32. See the respective unit resolutions in the *Philadelphia Daily Evening Bulletin,* March 14, 24, and 27, 1863.

33. The Twenty-eighth Pennsylvania passed its resolutions on March 24, 1863, at Dumfries, Virginia, and then in an undetermined Philadelphia newspaper, date unknown; see clipping, Ambrose Henry Hayward Papers, GCSCA. See 100th Pennsylvania's resolutions, *Philadelphia Daily Evening Bulletin,* March 27, 1863.

34. *Philadelphia Daily Evening Bulletin,* March 14, 1863, and clipping, Ambrose Henry Hayward Papers, GCSCA.

35. *Philadelphia Daily Evening Bulletin,* March 24, 1863.

36. Clipping, Ambrose Henry Hayward Papers, GCSCA.

37. *Philadelphia Daily Evening Bulletin,* March 14, 24, and 27, 1863.

38. When compared with the resolutions written by soldiers from other states, the level of violence advocated by Pennsylvania soldiers is unexceptional. Resolutions from Ohio, Indiana, and Illinois regiments used a similarly brutal tone. Pennsylvania resolutions lacked the exactness of their western counterparts, however. In Illinois regiments, for instance, the threat of violence attained a certain level of urgency after Democrats captured the state legislature in 1862. Consequently, many Illinois resolutions specifically pledged to return to Springfield to disperse the legislature if the Republican governor, Richard Yates, so ordered. Although Democrats gained seats in the Pennsylvania legislature following the 1862 elections, they did not outnumber their Republican counterparts. Not having any reason to return to Harrisburg for similar reasons, Pennsylvanians drafted no such resolutions. As long as the Republican Party remained in power, politics in Pennsylvania could proceed apace without military interference. For a discussion of Illinois soldiers' resolutions, see two works by Mark E. Neely Jr.: "The Civil War and the Two Party System," in *"We Cannot Escape History": Lincoln and the Last Best Hope of Earth,* ed. James M. McPherson (Urbana: University of Illinois Press, 1995), 96–101, and *The Union Divided: Party Conflict in the Civil War North* (Cambridge, MA: Harvard University Press, 2002), 41–47.

39. *Philadelphia Daily Evening Bulletin,* March 14, 16, 24, 26, and 27, 1863.

40. Ibid., March 27, 1863.

41. Shankman, *Pennsylvania Antiwar Movement,* 171–74.

42. Unknown soldier to "My Dear Wife and Family," July 5, 1863, 140th Pennsylvania Vertical File, Gettysburg National Military Park Library, Gettysburg, PA. This soldier's name and rank cannot be determined, but it is clear that he served in Company I, 140th Pennsylvania.

43. Arnold M. Shankman, "'For the Union as It Was and the Constitution as It Is': A Copperhead Views the Civil War," in *Rank and File: Civil War Essays in Honor of Bell Irvin Wiley*, ed. James I. Robertson and Richard M. McMurry (San Rafael, CA: Presidio Press, 1976), 100–104.

44. Hugh N. McAllister to James A. Beaver, September 12, 1863; *Bellefonte Central Press*, October 2, 1863; and William Williams to brother, September 26, 1863, all quoted in Carol A. Reardon, "'We Are All in This War': The 148th Pennsylvania and Home Front Dissension in Centre County during the Civil War," in *Union Soldiers and the Northern Home Front: Wartime Experiences, Postwar Adjustments*, ed. Paul A. Cimbala and Randall M. Miller (New York: Fordham University Press, 2002), 25–26; Shankman, *Pennsylvania Antiwar Movement*, 134.

45. In Ohio's gubernatorial election, 41,467 soldiers voted for Republican candidate John Brough, and 2,288 soldiers voted for Democratic candidate Clement Vallandigham. In October 1863 the Democratic Party challenged Ohio's soldier voting act, and in December the state supreme court ruled that this act, drafted by Republicans in April 1863, was not unconstitutional. In Connecticut, where the Democratic Party ran Copperhead candidate Thomas Seymour, soldier voting was ruled unconstitutional, and soldiers were unable to vote in the field until the legislature amended the state constitution in July 1864. See Josiah Benton, *Voting in the Field: The Forgotten Chapter of the Civil War* (Boston: privately published, 1915), 73–79, 174.

46. James T. Miller to father, November 2, 1863, in Mannis and Wilson, *Bound to Be a Soldier*, 125.

47. Joseph Addison Moore to brother, April 26, 1864, Pennsylvania Save the Flags—Moore Family Collection, USAMHI.

48. Shankman, *Pennsylvania Antiwar Movement*, 201; *OR*, 560–69. Pennsylvania soldiers give Lincoln a two-thirds majority in the 1864 election, and nearly every regiment gave Lincoln at least a simple majority. In November, Major General George Gordon Meade happily reported that of fifty-four surveyed infantry regiments and artillery batteries serving in the Army of the Potomac, only six regiments gave Democratic candidate George McClellan a majority. These six regiments were the Fifty-fifth Pennsylvania (117 for McClellan, 116 for Lincoln), Sixty-ninth Pennsylvania (119 for McClellan, 6 for Lincoln), Eighty-first Pennsylvania (44 for McClellan, 23 for Lincoln), Ninetieth Pennsylvania (56 for McClellan, 34 for Lincoln), Ninety-seventh Pennsylvania (112 for McClellan, 108 for Lincoln), and 116th Pennsylvania (58 for McClellan, 54 for Lincoln). Interestingly, many regiments raised in Pennsylvania's cities, where the Democrats traditionally had their strongest support, voted Republican in large numbers. In fact, some Philadelphia-raised regiments gave Lincoln majorities of more than 50 percent, including the

Eighty-eighth Pennsylvania (135 for Lincoln, 62 for McClellan), Ninety-first Pennsylvania (144 for Lincoln, 67 for McClellan), and 121st Pennsylvania (103 for Lincoln, 14 for McClellan). Likewise, in the Pittsburgh-raised 155th Pennsylvania, 254 soldiers voted for Lincoln, and 135 voted for McClellan. In rurally based regiments, Lincoln's victory was a landslide; for instance, in the 141st Pennsylvania, raised in Bradford, Susquehanna, and Wayne counties, 195 soldiers voted for Lincoln, and only 5 voted for McClellan. It is also interesting to note the voting results in some of the regiments that had drafted pro-war resolutions in the spring of 1863. Although the resolutions had been adopted "unanimously" in 1863, by 1864 approximately one-third of the soldiers in many regiments were harboring Democratic loyalties. The voting was as follows: Fifty-seventh Pennsylvania, 95 for Lincoln and 33 for McClellan; 100th Pennsylvania, 212 for Lincoln and 41 for McClellan; 140th Pennsylvania, 147 for Lincoln and 55 for McClellan; 149th Pennsylvania, 188 for Lincoln and 102 for McClellan; and 150th Pennsylvania, 111 for Lincoln and 27 for McClellan.

Popular Sovereignty in the Confederate Army

The Case of Colonel John Marshall and the Fourth Texas Infantry Regiment

Charles E. Brooks

On October 8, 1861, the Reverend Nicholas Davis, chaplain of the Fourth Texas Infantry Regiment, wrote in his diary: "Col. Hood arrived in the camp at 3 o'cl[oc]k. Lt. Col. John Marshall brought out his camp chattles & left again in a few minutes. This is his debu[t]. And I suppose he is aware of the fact that the men receive him in the same manner that he has put himself off on the reg.—by force."[1] John Marshall, a Texas newspaper editor and Southern rights politician, had been appointed by the Confederate government to serve as lieutenant colonel of the Fourth Texas, and Chaplain Davis's observation marked the first indication that Marshall was not going to be accepted by the volunteer citizen-soldiers in the unit.[2]

These Texas soldiers became part of one of the most famous combat units in General Robert E. Lee's fabled Army of Northern Virginia. Known throughout the war as Hood's Texas Brigade, the soldiers of the First, Fourth, and Fifth regiments earned a reputation for fierce fighting that won the acclaim of every general officer who led them. Lee considered the Texans his premier shock troops when on the attack and his most dependable rear guard when in retreat. Major General Dorsey Pender proclaimed his own superb North Carolina troops second only to the "Texas boys," who were "the best material on the continent without a doubt." Historian Douglas Southall Freeman ranked the Texas Brigade as the best fighting unit in Lee's army.[3]

Successful command of volunteer troops during the Civil War required an officer with the ability to win the approval of his men. The

Texas soldiers expected and demanded a say in the selection of both their company and field-grade officers, and that is where Marshall's problems began. As Chaplain Davis's comment indicates, Marshall's commission was viewed with disdain as having been made in "the spirit of political favoritism."[4] The conflict became apparent when Marshall tried to train the green and undisciplined troops in marching and the manual of arms. On the evening of October 21, Private Thomas Selman reported that Marshall "made a perfect fool of himself" by giving the wrong orders. "When the parade was dismissed, every company left the ground whooping & yelling & repeating Marshall's commands & crying aloud Marshall's tactics." Two days later Selman noted that Marshall "carried us through the manual of arms again this evening," and the men "all laughed at him as usual."[5] Almost five months later, Marshall was still trying to drill the soldiers, and the men were still laughing and jeering at his mistakes, sometimes even walking off the field in disgust before being dismissed.[6]

The Fourth Texas's treatment of Colonel Marshall was redolent of the time-honored method of popular social control known as the charivari. Texas soldiers used spontaneous outbursts of loud noisemaking, hooting, and whooping, long associated with the charivari, whitecapping, and other forms of popular tribunal, to express local outrage against the transgression of their customary rights. The commotion that erupted whenever Marshall tried to drill the Texas volunteers was meant to shame and dishonor an unpopular officer who had been forced on these citizen-soldiers by a Confederate government with little knowledge of the men's feelings or beliefs.[7]

When Colonel John Bell Hood was promoted to command of the brigade in March 1862 and Marshall moved up to become colonel of the Fourth Texas, the discontent with the fiery secessionist leader grew to a near rebellion. Just ten days after the news spread through camp that Marshall had become their regimental commander, Private Selman observed that "most of the soldiers [were] in favor of his resigning." On March 30, several petitions were prepared asking him to resign; one petition contained 460 names, representing "over half the [regiment]." Marshall told Sergeant J. C. Roberts of Company C "that such a thing was very mortifying to him," but since he believed that he had the confidence of President Jefferson Davis and the War Department, "he wanted to hear nothing more of it."[8] Another private, Joseph Polley, explained that the "dissatisfaction of the Regiment was great," but "Marshall was too selfishly ambitious and too capable according to his own conceited estimation of his abilities to command to be induced to accede to the wish expressed in the petition and so we had to indure what we could not cure."[9]

The resentment against Marshall continued to grow, and just weeks before the bloody Seven Days' battles around Richmond, when the Texas Brigade saw its first heavy action of the war, the troops' ill will toward Marshall became unbearable. One private wrote, "The discontent against Marshall is fast reaching a climax. Our Captains and Lieutenants have determined as soon as this battle flurry is over to hand in their petition for his removal. If he is not removed they will offer to resign. If their resignations are accepted the men will stack arms and rebel sooner than serve under Marshall with new officers and if they do not accept the resignations we can stack arms all the same. We would do it now but our Country's need demands that we be a unit and no dissentions among ourselves."[10] General Hood prevented the rebellion within his old regiment by promising to lead the men into battle himself when the moment came. He kept that promise at Gaines' Mill, where he led the Fourth Texas in a desperate and furious frontal assault up a wooded hillside, against the Federal line. Colonel John Marshall was killed, shot in the neck, during the charge. The strife between Marshall and the citizen-soldiers he had tried to lead was finally over.[11]

How close had the Fourth Texas Regiment come to a rebellion against Colonel Marshall and the authority of the Confederate government and War Department? The answer begins with some advice Sam Houston offered to fellow Texans in May 1861 as they faced the prospect of war. Addressing the martial strengths and weaknesses of his countrymen, he said: "Do not be making companies to-day and unmaking them tomorrow. If you are dissatisfied with your captain, wait until the battle day comes, and he gets killed off, than you can get another. It is better to fight up to him and get rid of him in that way than to split off, and make a new company to be split up in the same way."[12] Houston's observation addressed the problematic effect that the principle of popular sovereignty was going to have on the raising of volunteers and their performance. For Houston, popular sovereignty was a deeply embedded belief at the center of the American practice of self-government. Simply put, it meant that every public official, civilian or military, was an agent of the people and, as such, had to carry out the duties and responsibilities entrusted to him in a way that gave "satisfaction" to "the sovereigns."[13]

Houston's sentiments about popular sovereignty and citizen soldiering often emphasized the importance of having officers who possessed "sympathies in common" with their enlisted men. Raising this theme in a speech to the U.S. Senate on January 22, 1847, for example, he examined how critical it was for a volunteer force to select surgeons and physicians who knew the customs and foibles of the common soldiers. "And how important would it not be," he argued, "to the health and safety of the men that such a selection should be made; because the physician taken from their own vicinity, and personally acquainted with many of the families from which they came, and with many of themselves too, would be in better circumstances to *sympathize* with them." In contrast, a physician or surgeon "perfectly ignorant of the constitutions or former habits of the soldiers, or of the region from which they came," could never win the trust and confidence of the men.[14]

Houston's understanding of popular sovereignty was rooted in the new federalism that had made adoption of the U.S. Constitution in 1788 possible. The founders' plan promised the American people, still fearful of centralized government, full representation in the new system, established on the dynamics of an eighteenth-century culture of feeling that made sympathy "a political force." The new national government would be representative of the people in exactly the same way that their state and local governments were. The accountability of the new government rested on its capacity to sympathize and empathize with the people. When applied to citizen-soldiers, this meant that militiamen and volunteers would serve under officers elected by them, commanders who possessed "fellow feeling" for their enlisted men, an ability to think as they did, and the capacity to understand the sense of injustice free men experienced when forced to give blind obedience to an officer who had little in common with them.[15]

The use of the charivari against an unpopular officer like Marshall highlighted another essential feature of popular sovereignty—its strong connection with honor. Thanks to Bertram Wyatt-Brown, historians understand how honor permeated and structured the social relations of the South before the Civil War. Honor was not, however, just a Southern cultural phenomenon. During the American Revolution, the defense of "sacred Honor" helped to inspire colonial resistance to parliamentary taxation and Thomas Jefferson's Declaration of Independence. Wyatt-Brown has argued that denying Americans the right to tax themselves violated their honor and liberty because taxes were regarded as "gifts" that could be given only by a free people to their king through their elected representatives. Coerced payment of taxes brought dishonor and disgrace; tribute and honor were incompatible.[16]

The imperatives of honor also made coercive military subordi-nation and voluntary soldiering incompatible. During the War of Independence, Philadelphia militiamen were deeply suspicious of any military system that was forced or oppressive, and they asserted their right to the "honour of command." As a concession to wartime necessity, however, they offered their subordination as a patriotic "gift." They sub-mitted voluntarily to military hierarchy and discipline and relinquished the "happy equality of rank and fortune," which made no distinction "above that of Freeman," until the fighting was over. The power of com-mand belonged to the common soldiers, whose consent was required to transfer it through a process mediated by the democratic election of officers. "The power is your gift," the militiamen told one another, and as such, it "cannot easily be abused."[17] When the citizen-soldiers of the Texas Brigade engaged in ritual actions such as the charivari to protest officers who did not meet their expectations, they too sought to recover the honor lost to a centralized military system that failed to acknowl-edge that the authority of command originated with the consent and approval of the ranks.

The volunteers of the Fourth Texas Regiment were steeped in the traditions of American citizen soldiering, and the making and unmak-ing of companies must be understood in this context.[18] The threatened rebellion against Colonel Marshall was not an exceptional event. In early November 1861 Private Robert Foster wrote home to his parents, explaining that the "Captain is not so popular with his men as he used to be. [Five] or [six] of his men Lou Wells among the number has got-ten a transfer from this company to another, on account of not being pleased with Capt Townsend."[19] Muster rolls for Company C, Fourth Texas Infantry Regiment, show that privates Rich. J. Haynes, D. H. Robertson, Frank Robertson, and Lewis Wells transferred to Company I, Fifth Texas Infantry, on October 26, 1861.[20] Private S. W. Montgomery secured a transfer to the same unit and on February 1, 1863, moved to another company in the Fifth Texas. Private Y. B. Hayne was reassigned to Company G, Fifth Texas Infantry, on November 13, 1861.[21] These transfers did not end Company C's dissatisfaction with its officers. Two months later, Private Foster reported that "quite an unusual circumstance occurred, a few days since—a petition was gotten up by the Donville crowd, for Captain Townsend and Lieut Barziza to resign— they took up an idea that Ensign Hammon would make a better captain. I do not know whom they wanted to put in Barziza's place. I can urge nothing against Capt. T. more than little seeming partiality and indifference. However, 44 members, a majority, I think, of those now encamped, signed and presented it. He called in all the officers, burnt the petition, without even looking at it, and said he would still be our captain. Another petition was gotten up."[22] Captain William Townsend's conflict with his company came to an end when he was promoted to major in July and then lost a leg at Second Bull Run in August 1862. He left the regiment and returned to Texas.[23]

The habit of joining one company and then moving to another occurred on a fairly regular basis at the level of the individual soldier. For instance, in the spring of 1862, Burnett's Thirteenth Texas Cavalry lost four soldiers to Captain John R. Woodward of Company G, First Texas Infantry, who had been detailed to recruitment in the Lone Star State. Privates Edwin (Edward) Dagg, James O. Good (Goad), and James A. Johnson were recruited by Captain Woodward at Palestine, in Anderson County, on April 8, 1862. Private John Petty was recruited there on April 11. The April 30 muster roll of the Thirteenth Texas recorded that these four men had "deserted (transf[erred] w/o permission)."[24] Musters rolls for Company G of the First Texas show that all four served honorably after the unauthorized reassignment. Dagg was promoted to the rank of second corporal and was later wounded at Chickamauga. Good was wounded the second day at Gettysburg and then, after being wounded again, had his leg amputated just two days before Lee surrendered at Appomattox. Johnson died of "lung disease" in September 1862, and Petty served in Virginia throughout the war and was paroled at Appomattox on April 12, 1865.[25] Joining more than one unit and transferring without permission could, under different circumstances, land a soldier in trouble. "There is a man in camp," Private Selman reported in September 1861, "who has one side of his head shaved because he joined several companies & refused to take the oath each time. He is a prisoner," Selman noted, "& will be held as such for some time."[26]

Meanwhile, officers regularly resigned their field commissions in Virginia and returned to Texas. Many lost their positions as a result of company reorganizations, but some left for personal or ideological reasons. For example, Lieutenant Charles L. Martin, Fourth Texas Infantry, was one of Company D's original officers, but he resigned on October 5, 1861, left Virginia, and went back to Texas. On January 7, 1862, he wrote a letter to Governor Francis R. Lubbock, explaining that for him, the war was mainly about protecting his family and his home state from Yankee invasion, so he offered the governor and the sovereign state of Texas his military service.[27]

When the volunteers of the Fourth Texas grew dissatisfied with some of their regimental and company-level officers, they attempted to reorganize under new officers who were more acceptable to a majority of the men. They used traditional shaming rituals and raised petitions demanding officers' immediate resignation. In the case of Colonel Marshall, company officers threatened to resign rather than continue serving under his command. At the same time, individual soldiers who were unhappy with a particular officer simply quit and joined another unit, sometimes with permission and sometimes without it. The volunteers of the Fourth Texas Regiment resolved some cases of dissatisfaction with their officers by following Sam Houston's advice: they waited until the colonel or captain was killed or maimed in battle and then reorganized under a new commander. What the soldiers of the Fourth Texas did in these instances was not a mutiny but the assertion of a right that had been secured by long-standing custom and usage associated with American citizen soldiering.

American volunteer soldiers serving in a national army expected to be commanded by officers who were familiar with them, and this usually meant officers from their home state. Men of the Lone Star State held a particularly strong conviction that Texans must be commanded by Texans, or at least by officers having knowledge of the region and its people.[28] During the summer of 1861, four of the companies that made up the Fourth Texas gathered at Camp Clark on the San Marcos River in Hays County and were drilled there by Colonel R. T. P. Allen of the Bastrop Military Institute. As the business of electing officers and organizing company units got under way, the men learned that a twelve-month enlistment was not possible; only companies and regiments enrolled for the duration of the war would be allowed to go to Virginia. The men were told that John Marshall, prominent politician and Southern rights advocate, had secured a place for Texas troops on the Virginia front line, where the fate of the Confederacy was going to be decided. The volunteers were to be enrolled in Texas, but "the election of company officers, and the organization of the regiments [were] to be completed after their arrival in Virginia," with President Jefferson Davis "reserving . . . the authority to appoint regimental officers." Because the volunteers were mainly plain folks who could not afford to be away from their farms and ranches for an extended tour of duty, the demand that they enlist for the war's duration, "so different from what the men had expected," provoked anger and disbelief and "disorganized the camp." In Chaplain Davis's judgment, this revelation seemed capable of breaking up the companies that were then being established.[29]

The volunteers at Camp Clark were unhappy because they now faced the prospect of serving in a national army, a long way from home, under officers appointed by a centralized government and War Department that knew very little about their habits or character. The Constitution of the Confederate States of America, just like the U.S. Constitution, gave Congress the power to raise and support armies and to call up the militia to enforce the laws, suppress insurrections, and repel invasions. In the event of a call-up, the troops would be placed under the command of the national government; however—and this was a crucial point—"the appointment of the officers" was reserved to the states.[30] At the time the U.S. Constitution was being debated, delegates at the Philadelphia convention emphasized how important it was for the states to retain a general control over the militia. Luther Martin pointed out, for instance, that each state knew best what degree of subordination and discipline its own citizen-soldiers might bear.[31] And George Mason worried that militiamen, operating as part of a national force under the direction of a centralized government, could fall victim to "severe and ignominious punishments" at the hands of military policy makers with "no fellow-feeling for the people."[32] So when the Texas volunteers grew uneasy about soldiering under officers who were strangers, they had custom and tradition, as well as the authority of both the Confederate and U.S. constitutions, behind them.

The disquiet of the volunteers at Camp Clark faded for a while,

because many were eager to fight the Yankees in Virginia. Four companies were enrolled during the week of July 4–11, 1861; three of
these units, however, were not mustered into service until they got to
Richmond, Virginia.[33] The fourth, Captain John P. Bane's Guadalupe
Rangers, was mustered into Confederate service at Camp Van Dorn,
Texas, on July 27, 1861.[34] The other companies of the Fourth Texas
were enrolled in the counties where the recruits were drawn, and the
men were deployed to Virginia probably unaware of the fact that the
Confederate government would accept their service only for the duration of the war.[35] Most of the companies constituting the Fifth Texas
were enrolled and mustered into service for the war's duration before
they arrived in Virginia.[36] In contrast, six of the original twelve companies in the First Texas were recruited and mustered into Confederate
service for only one year.[37]

When the Texas volunteers reached Richmond and set up camp
nearby, "the great topic of conversation, and the all absorbing question" for almost everyone was, "Who will be our Regimental Officers?"
"Who will command us?" For two weeks the Texas soldiers waited for
an answer. "The first attempt at giving a Colonel to the 4th Regiment,"
Chaplain Davis reported, "was the appointment of R. T. P. Allen." Even
though a Texan and known as "a man of thorough military education,"
he "was not acceptable to either men or officers."[38] On September 26 rumors
spread around camp that Allen had been appointed by President Davis
"but the Sec of War refused to sign it." Speculation was that "officers of
the companies had sent in a protest." The next day Davis observed in
his diary that the "Capts are figuring about to get the President to recall
the appointment of Allen & as I think to get some position for themselves." Meanwhile, a petition was circulated throughout the camp,
with "several hundred names to it," in support of Allen's appointment.[39]
Within a few days, however, Allen was forced out of the regiment; he
resigned on September 30, 1861, and went back to Texas. The final
push came from the men themselves. Several soldiers from Company
G of the Fourth Texas hoisted the colonel onto his horse and struck the
horse with switches, driving the humiliated rider "out of the regimental
grounds amid the hoots and jeers of the boys." According to Private
Mark Womack, "that Colonel was never seen again."[40]

Colonel Allen was a Texan, so why was he rejected? Allen was actually a native of Maryland and had arrived in Texas during the mid-1850s

after a stopover in Kentucky, where he entered the ministry before resuming a military career. He was a professional soldier, a graduate of West Point, and superintendent and president, respectively, of the Kentucky Military Institute and the Military Institute at Bastrop, Texas. Some of the Texas volunteers knew Allen from Camp Clark, where he had served as senior drill instructor. Based on the reports of soldiers who had been there, Allen had bullied the recruits, pushing them to do menial tasks.[41] In fact, there was "remarkable unanimity" among the volunteers enrolled there "that he did not suit their views of a commander."[42] When the Texas boys took matters into their own hands, the action signified the extent to which the principle of popular sovereignty had become an actual practice, hallowed by custom and usage and upheld by a constitutional norm.

The humiliating spectacle of a field officer being lifted onto his mount and whipped out of camp had another meaning, too. The Texas volunteers not only rejected Allen and the Confederate government's authority to appoint him, but they also expressed their repudiation through an action that was intended to bring public shame. And in a society like the antebellum South, where honor operated as a fundamental organizing principle, shaming a person, especially someone in authority, was a powerful rebuke.[43]

The First and Fifth Texas regiments also resisted the appointment of regimental officers in October 1861. Originally organized as an "over-strength Battalion" in June 1861, companies A through H of this unit, which were later reorganized as the First Texas Regiment, elected Louis Wigfall colonel during mid-July. Wigfall quickly became unpopular with the men, however, because he tried to enforce "rigorous discipline" by confining the soldiers to camp. Private James Hendrick explained, just a week after the election, that "a good many of the company are dissatisfied with Colonel Wigfall already because he keeps them too close. He won't allow any of us," he grumbled, "to go to town without first getting a permit from Captain Bass . . . and getting him [Wigfall] to sign it. He has sentinels stationed all around the camp night and day." Not much changed when the Texans arrived in Virginia, and during the first week of August, Hendrick lamented once again, "A great many of the battalion are dissatisfied with Colonel Wigfall."[44]

Private Joseph Polley described Wigfall as an "original secessionist," someone who sought "governmental employment" back home "or under the Confederacy, [that] would exempt [him] from military service."[45] Just as Polley predicted, Wigfall resigned his commission as brigadier general and commander of the Texas Brigade on February 21, 1862, leaving the army before any serious fighting took place to become a senator in the Confederate Congress. Calling him "Wiggletail," a nickname coined by Sam Houston, Polley explained that Wigfall's greatest shortcoming was his habit of fighting phantoms. The troops were regularly roused from their sleep by the drummer's roll, "an ear-splitting tat-tat-tat" calling the men to arms without a moment's delay.[46] Many Texas soldiers in Virginia complained loudly of forced marches to meet the enemy, frequently in the middle of the night, that often ended up being false alarms, attesting to the underlying belief among the rank and file that too many officers were incompetent as well as tyrannical.[47]

The Fifth Texas Regiment also stubbornly resisted the Richmond government's appointment of regimental officers. According to Private Val Giles, the Fifth Texas "fired colonels, lieutenant colonels and majors faster than Mr. Davis could send them out. The troops," Giles explained, "were in open rebellion against all comers."[48] For instance, when Confederate authorities appointed one Colonel Shaller to command the regiment, he lasted only about twenty-four hours. Chaplain Davis gave this account of Shaller's brief tenure: "He came out to camp in all the pomp and circumstances befitting his high position, splendidly mounted on a steed . . . glittering with the tinsel of gold, and bearing about him all the symbols of his rank." The Texans gathered around Shaller and "manifested their wonder at the liberality of the [government's] appointing power." One of the soldiers questioned whether Shaller was "a man, a fish, or a bird?" Another soldier conceded "*that thing* may be a man, but we don't call them men in Texas." At dawn the next day, as the colonel prepared for his morning horseback ride, he found that his "proud charger" had been defaced. During the night, some of the Texas soldiers had shaved the horse's tail "sleek as an opossum's" and vandalized his saddle by cutting the girth. Shaller quickly realized his predicament and left camp that morning for good.[49]

Meanwhile, Paul J. Quattlebaum, an 1857 West Point graduate from South Carolina, was selected to serve as major of the Fifth Texas. The men gave him such a hard time, however, that he resigned within a month. "Old Quattlebaum didn't stay . . . long," one Texas volunteer explained. The men "played on his name with verse and song. He said when he left them that if he had to associate with devils he would wait till he went to hell, where he could select his own company."[50]

In light of the preceding analysis, the case of Colonel John Marshall requires further examination. To be sure, he was appointed, not elected, and his commission was seen mainly as a product of his political connections. But he was a Texan, a prominent secessionist, and an ardent supporter of the Confederacy. He was a hero of the Southern rights movement and a leading defender of slavery.[51] Yet he never fulfilled the expectations of the volunteer soldiers who fought to uphold the regime he had done so much to help establish. As we have seen, Texas soldiers, like American soldiers in general, believed that a citizen-soldier had the right to choose the volunteer unit he would serve in and that he deserved to have a say in the selection of company and regimental officers, either by direct election or through some other means of popular social control. Marshall was put on the men by force and would not have been elected under any circumstances, but the crux of his inability to command stemmed from his lack of sympathies in common with the ordinary soldier. A reexamination of the complaints voiced by the enlisted men under Marshall's command highlights just how out of touch he was.

Just about the time Marshall became colonel, the Fourth Texas and the other units under Hood's command began a campaign of maneuvering, marching, and countermarching that culminated with the Seven Days' battles around Richmond in late June and early July 1862. Marshall's failure to take sides with his men during this period of physical testing and growing hardship brought the Fourth Texas to the brink of its unmaking. Marching was especially hard on the new recruits from Texas, who preferred to ride horses rather than walk on foot. As a newspaper explained, "no Texian but would ride three years with a shot-gun before he would walk a week with a musket."[52] Typical was this complaint from sixteen-year-old recruit Asa Roberts: "I had never walked much and found it very difficult." In early March 1862, Private Thomas Selman recorded in his diary: "it was nothing uncommon to see a soldier lying on the road side completely worn down from carrying his knapsack and right here I will say that no one knows how hard a soldiers life is until he marches in the night over a muddy road with a heavy knapsack on his back." The Texans' disdain for marching led to a petition requesting "President [Davis] to convert the three Texas regiments . . . in Virginia to cavalry."[53] Both state and Confederate authorities had difficulty raising Texas infantry troops, and the situation was made worse by the fact that mounted units were being recruited for periods of six or twelve months, so in addition to their natural preference for cavalry service, the volunteers favored the shorter enlistment periods that kept them closer to home.[54]

Marching was a burdensome activity for Texas soldiers under any circumstances; marching at night, however, proved particularly onerous. It often began with a call to arms, rousing soldiers from their sleep with a start and spurring frantic searches for weapons, knapsacks, and prized personal possessions that could not be left behind. Private Joseph Polley remembered that the first time he heard "the long roll . . . it awoke me from the profoundest slumber of my life so suddenly, and scared me so badly, that for two minutes I looked under my bed for my gun and out of doors for my pantaloons." Such occurrences became a routine feature of an infantryman's life. Nonetheless, every instance underscored just how uncertain a soldier's existence was and reminded him that "there may be free agency in religious matters, but . . . none in military affairs." A soldier was "an automaton, guided, directed, and controlled by wires pulled by superiors."[55]

Marshall took command of the Fourth Texas on March 12, 1862. During the weeks that followed, hard marching and skirmishes with the enemy would determine whether he was capable of winning the men's confidence. On the night of April 4, 1862, at about eleven o'clock, company officers "went around to all the tents and woke all the boys, and told them to get up & be ready to march." As the troops moved off into the night toward Stafford, Virginia, twelve miles away, Colonel Marshall fell asleep on his horse. The Fourth Texas took a wrong turn, became lost in the dark, and was not reunited with the rest of the regiment until dawn. "John Marshall lost the regt last night," one Texas private joked.[56] Four days later, Marshall again got the men up in the middle of the night to make preparations to march. "Where I did not know, nor neither do I yet," one private complained.[57] It was morning before the regiment actually got orders to march, and then it slogged along through rain, sleet, and snow. The "inimitable John Marshall" halted the column to let the men rest, but all the fence rails along the road had been stripped and burned, and it was hours before the tired and weary Texans found enough rails for their fires.[58] "Just about the time we were getting warm and dry," one Texas soldier reported, the order was given around midnight to resume the march. It was still snowing hard. Within half a mile of the railroad depot at Milford, where they were supposed to board cars to complete the maneuver, Marshall ordered the troops to an abrupt stop. According to one soldier, Marshall told the men "that there had been a collision on the RR and that we would have to return to our camp. This was really very discouraging," the soldier explained, "& many of the boys gave vent to their 'cold' feelings by cursing the world and the balance of mankind."[59] Finally, after "several days hard marching and disappointment" that had the men "worn nearly out," the Fourth Texas reached its destination at Ashland. "Every soldier was hungry, but most of them would not wait for any thing to eat, but dropped down on the wet ground & went to sleep."[60] Marshall was now held in such contempt that the men murmured and sighed at the mere sight of him, and one soldier confided to his diary that he and a fellow infantryman enjoyed a breakfast of "biscuit, coffee, bacon, and molasses stolen from the baggage of our *would be* Col. Marshall."[61]

During the same time span, Robert Gaston, Thomas Selman, and Joseph Polley took notice of an incident that occurred on Tuesday, April 8, as the Fourth Texas marched in the rain and "came to a creek about waist deep and very wide."[62] Unwilling to wade through the water, the lead troops in the column began to pile up; meanwhile, some of the boys started to inch across a single log that traversed the creek. Getting to the opposite side this way "would have taken too long for several thousand men [to] cross." At that moment, General Hood galloped up on his horse and called for the men "to pitch in," but many soldiers still refused to enter the water, waiting to see "what he would do." Hood dismounted, handed the reins over to an attendant, and asked the Texas soldiers "if they would follow him & in he went."[63] The rest of the men "went through without hesitation," and Hood's action was "greeted with loud, long and enthusiastic cheers by all who witnessed" it.[64]

Another incident occurred later that day after the regiment struck camp. It was raining hard again, and Captain Proctor P. Porter of Company H "asked Col. Marshall to let the guard off but he would not do it. He kept ten men on one post simply to wake J. H. Harrison his orderly up if any news came. So he, J. H. could tell him as he was going over to stay at a house where he could keep out of the rain."[65]

Selman's juxtaposition of the two incidents in his diary is striking, because it shows the contrast between an officer who had the confidence of the men and one who did not. General Hood understood the men's resentment of officers who would not "pitch in" and "rough it," side by side, with the common fighting man. In contrast, Colonel Marshall always made it clear that he was not one of the men. In this instance, keeping a large contingent of soldiers on guard in the pouring rain while he sought refuge in a nearby house spoke volumes about his unfitness for command. Just as he had been foisted on the regiment by force and responded to petitions calling for his removal by citing the authority of President Davis and the Confederate government, Marshall proved once more that he was tone-deaf to the feelings and sentiments of the ordinary soldier. He seemed unaware of, or perhaps he simply chose to ignore, one of the cardinal maxims of self-government in America: military officers, like other public functionaries, were agents of the people, and effective leadership required them to know and feel the burdens of the subordination they enjoined others to bear.[66] Officers had to demonstrate, in the words of Sam Houston, a "proper deference to the feelings of [their] subordinates and inferiors."[67] And the enlisted man felt his subordination keenly, as Chaplain Davis explained: "a [citizen] soldier must be patient under wrong, and . . . is remediless under injustice—that he, although the self-constituted and acknowledged champion of liberty, has, nevertheless, for the time being, parted with that boon, and that he is but the victim of all official miscreants who choose to subject him to imposition."[68]

Joseph Polley also explained Marshall's repeated failure to connect with ordinary soldiers by contrasting it with the extraordinary rapport achieved by Colonel John Bell Hood with the same men. Marshall was conceited and arrogant and looked only to the Confederate government for authority and approval. Completely indifferent to the popular dissatisfaction that pervaded the ranks, he never really understood the character of the volunteer soldiers that the Confederate armies were built on. As Houston explained: "There was one feeling common to all [volunteer soldiers], which would lead every man to yield to his own promptings, rather than to the dictates of others, and to choose under whom they would be disposed to serve. It was a proper, a natural, a becoming pride, a high-toned patriotic feeling, which made our citizens willing to come forward in the hour of danger, to serve their country, and, if needful, to die in defence of their liberties."[69] Marshall's brief tenure as colonel of the Fourth Texas rested on neither popular consent nor manly pride; instead, it depended on force and the power of political appointment. The result, as Private Polley pointed out, was that "the men lost all their *wanted pride* in drilling and general appearance and from one of the best [regiments] in the service soon became one of the worst in point of discipline and order."[70]

The relationship between the soldiers of the Fourth Texas and Colonel Hood could not have been more different. "Never did I see or know," Polley noted, "a man to rise higher and more quickly in the estimation of others than did Col. Hood. Well versed in human nature and thoroughly understanding the peculiarities of Texans character," and "knowing full well that volunteers would not submit to the same restriction that would be imposed on regulars he so tempered his conduct towards us," Polley shrewdly observed, "as to win our favor at once." Hood was also careful not to "draw the reins of true military discipline very tight at first—issuing few orders and those quite lenient for sometime but gradually increasing."[71] The language used by Texas soldiers to describe officers who knew and respected the sentiments and disposition of the common soldier emphasized the expectation that a commander behave as both friend and surrogate father to his men. A good officer had to possess an exquisite sense of timing, knowing when to exercise a firm hand and when to defer to the popular views of the ordinary enlisted man.[72] In this regard, Hood was described as "a social companion, familiar and kind" to the men, as well as a brave and fearless warrior who led by daring example.[73]

The complex soldier sentiments that gave rise to Hood's popularity came together in a single incident that merits careful examination. As the Fourth Texas assembled at dress parade on April 26, 1862, First Sergeant J. M. Bookman of Company G offered a gift to General Hood:

> Sir: In behalf of the non-commissioned officers and privates of the . . . Regiment, I present you this war-horse. He was selected and purchased by us for this purpose, not that we hoped by so doing to court your favor, but simply because we, as freemen and Texans, claim the ability to discern and the right to reward, merit wherever it may be found. In you, sir, we recognize the soldier and gentleman. In you, sir, we have found a

leader whom we are proud to follow—a commander whom it is a pleasure to obey; and this horse we tender as a slight testimonial of our admiration. Take him, and when the hour of battle comes, when mighty hosts meet in the struggle of death, we will, as did the troops of old, who rallied around the white plume of Henry, look for your commanding form and this proud steed as our guide, and gathering there we will conquer or die. In a word, General, "you stand by us and we will stand by you."[74]

Gift exchanges were an important feature of social relations among men of honor of all classes in the early American Republic and the antebellum South. "Southern men of honor loved to give gifts," and their social interactions operated inside the bounds of "a system of gift exchange" based on reciprocity between equals.[75] The Texas soldiers' gift of a warhorse, as Sergeant Bookman's words reveal, was both a customary ritual of honor and a reaffirmation of the equality of everyone present. Since "honor require[d] a sense of self-mastery and independence" on the part of the giver, only a gift exchange between equals could avoid the stigma of shame, disgrace, and dependency.[76] Bookman reminded Hood that the noncommissioned officers and privates who made this gift were "freemen and Texans," and their willingness to follow him depended on an expectation of reciprocity that marked the military relations of citizen-soldiers and their officers throughout the Confederate army. If Hood kept up his end of the bargain, they pledged as men of honor to fight and die under his command: "you stand by us and we will stand by you."

The habit of making and unmaking volunteer military units through collective political and social action and the practice of joining and then resigning from or transferring out of these units demonstrated how profoundly the idea of popular sovereignty and its implementation as a form of self-government shaped the consciousness and behavior of Texas volunteer soldiers. These citizen-warriors believed that they had a natural and a constitutional right to set the terms of their military service. Choosing to serve in a company made up of neighbors, friends, and family and electing and thinking well of a commander who knew the circumstances and temperament of his men were regarded as every recruit's due.

Many years ago, David Donald argued that the Confederate army was a blend of democracy and aristocracy. The ordinary volunteers who made up the army did not leave their populist sentiments at home when they went off to war. Ill suited to military discipline and hierarchy, they did not make good soldiers, and this contributed to the defeat of the Confederacy.[77] This essay has argued that the idea and practice of popular sovereignty shaped the experience of common soldiering in the Fourth Texas. Although recent historians have examined what the war did to the combatants on both sides, this essay picks up on Donald's perspective and looks deeper into the question of what the soldier culture did to the Confederate war effort. But my conclusion, contrary to Donald's, is that accommodation of popular sovereignty in the army strengthened rather than weakened the Confederacy's most important national institution.[78] A volunteer's rights of selection and election were an essential part of the tradition of citizen soldiering in early America, and both the state governments and the Confederate government tried hard to preserve and adapt these rights as they struggled to raise and support armies. Officials at all levels felt an urgent need to show that the war was truly a popular movement undertaken in defense of mainstream Southern values and not just a struggle to preserve the right to hold slaves as property.

It now seems clear to many historians that the Southern yeomanry had interests distinct from the slaveholding lawyers and planters who headed the drive for secession.[79] As the sectional crisis deepened, plain folks held back and did not support the slaveholders' push to dissolve the Union. In Alabama, Mississippi, and Louisiana, nonslaveholders came out for John C. Breckinridge in the presidential election of 1860 but voted for moderation, or not at all, in the secession convention elections of 1861. In the Upper South, plain folks and yeoman farmers rejected secession and supported Unionist candidates and delegates until Fort Sumter and Lincoln's response changed the meaning of the crisis. No longer a decision to leave or stay in the Union, it suddenly became a question of standing for or against the military coercion of kinfolks and fellow Southerners.[80]

In Texas, one of only three states to hold a referendum on secession, the majority of nonslaveholders stayed home and refused to participate in the vote for popular ratification.[81] In Texas and elsewhere in the South, slaveholders led the charge for secession, while nonslaveholders wondered whether this was really their fight. A representative of the latter group, for instance, gave his perspective about secession after listening to a speech on the steps of the capitol in Austin. Stepping forward, he asked: "'What the hell's it all about, anyway?' 'The nigger,' someone answered. 'The nigger! H—l. I ain't got no nigger. Give me a nigger, some of you, and I'll fight for it as long as any of you. I ain't going to fight for somebody else's nigger.'"[82] During the 1850s the price of slaves had risen sharply, and the proportion of families with slaves across the South diminished from 31 to 25 percent.[83] In Texas the proportion of slaveholding families dropped from 30 to 27 percent.[84] For Texans, the prospect of becoming a slave owner grew more remote as the sectional crisis reached a boiling point, and during the 1850s, more and more yeoman families turned their dreams of future success toward the raising of livestock on the open prairies of the Lone Star State.

Texas slaveholders achieved secession without the widespread support of plain folks, but when the war came, the task of mobilizing large armies to defend Texas and the rest of the South from Yankee invasion meant that the social dynamics that had carried the day for secession were not going to be enough to win a military conflict. Efforts to make secession and Southern independence a popular crusade had begun when the first secession convention was organized in Texas. The state's call for a convention appealed not to a legal act of secession but rather to the principle of popular sovereignty and the right of revolution.[85] The distinction was more than just a quibble. It had been a major point of contention between secessionists and Southern Unionists ever since the showdown between John C. Calhoun and Andrew Jackson during the nullification crisis of 1832–1833.

As volunteer units were raised and mobilized throughout Texas, soldiers from nonslaveholding families, still unsure about the Southern rights militants who had propelled the secessionist movement, looked to the traditions of citizen soldiering for reassurance. The spirit and practice of popular sovereignty in the Fourth Texas made this little community of volunteer soldiers a prototype of the republican society they went to war to defend and preserve. Soldiering that conformed to the norms identified in this essay—a volunteer's right to pick his unit and to serve under a commander who sympathized with the sentiments and circumstances of the ordinary soldier—served the critical purpose of reminding the common fighting man why this was more than just a fight over slavery. Examining the social and cultural dynamics of soldiering in the Fourth Texas helps illuminate the still perplexing question of why many soldiers stayed loyal to the Confederate cause and fought a slaveholders' war. And this issue brings us back to the case of John Marshall for one last observation. In the final analysis, Marshall could never settle the differences between his elitist and centralized style of command and the democratic and popular touch that ordinary Texas volunteers used to judge whether the Confederacy was truly a nation worth fighting and dying for.

NOTES

1. Nicholas A. Davis, diary, October 8, 1861, Special Archives and Collections, Coates Library, Trinity University, San Antonio, TX.

2. Larry Jay Gage, "The Texas Road to Secession and War: John Marshall and the Texas *State Gazette*, 1860–1861," *Southwestern Historical Quarterly* 62 (October 1958): 191–226; John Waller, *Colossal Hamilton of Texas: Militant Unionist and Reconstruction: A Biography of Andrew Jackson Hamilton* (El Paso: Texas Western Press, 1968), 16–17.

3. Just a few days after the battle of Antietam, Lee wrote to General Louis T. Wigfall concerning the possibility of raising some "new Texas Regiments" for the Army of Northern Virginia: "I rely upon those we have in all tight places, and I fear have to call upon them too often. . . . With a few more such regiments as Hood now has, as an example of daring and bravery, I could feel more confident of the campaign." Donald E. Everett, ed., *Chaplain Davis and Hood's Texas Brigade; Being an Expanded Edition of the Reverend Nicholas A. Davis's "The Campaign from Texas to Maryland, with the Battle of Sharpsburg"* (Richmond, 1863; reprint, San Antonio, TX: Principia Press of Trinity University, 1962), 153. See also Douglas Southall Freeman, *R. E. Lee: A Biography*, 4 vols. (New York: Charles Scribner's Sons, 1934), 2:418. Pender quoted in William W. Hassler, "Dorsey Pender, C.S.A., a Profile," *Civil War Times Illustrated* 1 (October 1962): 19; Douglas Southall Freeman, *Lee's Lieutenants: A Study in Command*, 3 vols. (New York: Charles Scribner's Sons, 1942–1944), 3:751.

4. Mary Laswell, ed., *Rags and Hope: The Recollections of Val C. Giles, Four Years with Hood's Brigade, Fourth Texas Infantry* (New York: Coward-McCann, 1961), 43–44; Harold B. Simpson, *Hood's Texas Brigade: Lee's Grenadier Guard* (Waco, TX: Hill Junior College Press, 1970), 62–63; Everett, *Chaplain Davis*, 45.

5. Thomas J. Selman, diary, October 21 and 23, 1861, typescript, Harold B. Simpson Confederate Research Center, Hill College, Hillsboro, TX (hereafter SCRC).

6. Ibid., March 21, 1862.

7. Bryan D. Palmer, "Discordant Music: Charivaris and Whitecapping in

Nineteenth-Century North America," *Labour/Le Travailler* 3 (1978): 5–62. In a Southern context, see Bertram Wyatt-Brown, *Southern Honor: Ethics and Behavior in the Old South* (New York: Oxford University Press, 1982), 435–61; and Charles L. Flynn Jr., *White Land, Black Labor: Caste and Class in Late Nineteenth-Century Georgia* (Baton Rouge: Louisiana State University Press, 1983), 44–49. For use of the charivari to express popular political and con-stitutional grievances, see Saul Cornell, *The Other Founders: Anti-Federalism and the Dissenting Tradition in America, 1788–1828* (Chapel Hill: University of North Carolina Press, 1999), 111. For an example of Texas troops using a charivari against greedy camp sutlers, see Laswell, *Rags and Hope*, 54–57.

8. Selman diary, March 21, 1862, March 30, 1862, SCRC.

9. Joseph B. Polley, diary, 51, SCRC.

10. Joseph B. Polley to mother, June 10, 1862, SCRC. See also Selman diary, March 14, 21, 25, and 30, 1862, SCRC.

11. J. B. Polley, *Hood's Texas Brigade: Its Marches, Its Battles, Its Achievements* (New York: Neale Publishing, 1910), 46. For an account of the battle of Gaines' Mill, see R. E. L. Krick, "The Men Who Carried This Position Were Soldiers Indeed," in *The Richmond Campaign of 1862: The Peninsula and the Seven Days*, ed. Gary W. Gallagher (Chapel Hill: University of North Carolina Press, 2000), 181–216.

12. Sam Houston, "Speech at Independence, May 10, 1861," in *The Writings of Sam Houston*, 8 vols., ed. Amelia W. Williams and Eugene C. Barker (Austin: University of Texas Press, 1938–1943), 8:304.

13. For the concept of popular sovereignty, see Edmund S. Morgan, *Inventing the People: The Rise of Popular Sovereignty in England and America* (New York: W. W. Norton, 1988), 271–87, and Jack N. Rakove, *Original Meanings: Politics and Ideas in the Making of the Constitution* (New York: Knopf, 1996), 203–43. My understanding of Houston's usage of popular sover-eignty is based on a close reading of his political battles in the U.S. Senate with Southern rights advocates. For example, in a speech on December 22, 1851, Houston offered this defense of the sovereignty of the people: "If I distrusted the intelligence of the American people; if I distrusted their patriotism, I might set myself up as a dictator of opinions, and instruct them in what they ought to do. But I have no pretentions to the character of a leader. I am willing to follow; and I have got the broad road before me" ("Opposing Re-Affirmation of the Compromise, December 22, 1851," in Williams and Barker, *Writings of Sam Houston*, 5:326). Typical of his use of the term *the sovereigns* was a letter to a Texas politician in which Houston wrote: "We have been to Houston, and Galveston, and our friends are very kind to us. I made two speeches on the trip & they were well received by the Sovereigns" (Houston to John R. Burke, July 19, 1851, in ibid., 303).

14. Houston, "Speech in the United States Senate, January 22, and February 1, 1847, in Favor of Volunteer Forces," in Williams and Barker, *Writings of Sam Houston*, 4:520, 512, 513.

15. For the language of sympathy and feeling and its connection with popular sovereignty, see Andrew Burstein, "The Political Character of Sympathy," *Journal of the Early Republic* 21 (winter 2001): 601–32 (quotation on 607); Andrew Burstein, *Sentimental Democracy: The Evolution of America's Romantic Self-Image* (New York: Hill and Wang, 1999); Morgan, *Inventing the People*, 239–87; Rakove, *Original Meanings*, 203–5; and Cornell, *The Other Founders*, 80. For the language of "fellow feeling," see Burstein, "Political Character of Sympathy," 612. For the use of this language in the context of military affairs, see Charles E. Brooks, "Federal Relations and Popular Sovereignty in the War of 1812" (paper presented at the twenty-seventh annual meeting of the Society for Historians of the Early American Republic, Philadelphia, July 21–24, 2005), 8–11.

16. Wyatt-Brown, *Southern Honor*. For an examination of the relation between honor and gift exchanges, see Edmund Morgan, "The Price of Honor," in *The Genuine Article: A Historian Looks at Early America* (New York: W. W. Norton, 2004), ch. 12, and Bertram Wyatt-Brown, "Honor, Dread of Enslavement, and Revolutionary Rhetoric," in *The Shaping of Southern Culture: Honor, Grace, and War, 1760's-1880's* (Chapel Hill: University of North Carolina Press, 2001), 37–39. See also Marcel Mauss, *The Gift: The Form and Reason for Exchange in Archaic Societies*, trans. W. D. Halls (New York: Routledge, 1990); Julian Pitt-Rivers, *The People of the Sierra* (New York: Criterion, 1954); and Julian Pitt-Rivers, *Honour and Shame: The Values of Mediterranean Society* (Chicago: University of Chicago Press, 1966).

17. My discussion here is based on Steven Rosswurm, *Arms, Country and Class: The Philadelphia Militia and the "Lower Sort" during the American Revolution* (New Brunswick, NJ: Rutgers University Press, 1987), 49–75 (quotations on 62, 74).

18. For the customs and traditions of citizen soldiering, see Morgan, *Inventing the People*, 153–73; David Waldstreicher, *In the Midst of Perpetual Fetes: The Making of American Nationalism, 1776-1820* (Chapel Hill: University of North Carolina Press, 1997), 156–60; Marcus Cunliffe, *Soldiers and Civilians: The Martial Spirit in America, 1775-1865* (Boston: Little, Brown, 1968); and Jeffrey Rogers Hummel, *Emancipating Slaves, Enslaving Free Men: A History of the American Civil War* (Chicago: Open Court, 1996), 156–58, 172.

19. Robert V. Foster to father and mother, November 7, 1861, Company C, Fourth Texas Infantry, file 2–13, Hood's Texas Brigade Papers, SCRC (hereafter HTBP).

20. Harold B. Simpson, *Hood's Texas Brigade: A Compendium* (Hillsboro, TX: Hill Junior College Press, 1977), 114, 116.

21. Ibid., 115, 116.

22. Robert V. Foster to sister, January 17, 1862, HTBP.

23. Simpson, *Hood's Texas Brigade: Lee's Grenadier Guard*, 149.

24. Thomas Reid, *Spartan Band: Burnett's 13th Texas Cavalry in the Civil War* (Denton: University of North Texas Press, 2005), 14–15. See also Simpson, *Hood's Texas Brigade: A Compendium*, 52–55.

25. Ibid.

26. Selman diary, September 3, 1861, SCRC.

27. As an example of a company reorganization, Company D of the First Texas held a new round of elections for officers on May 16, 1862, as permitted by the Confederate conscription law of April 1862. Captain W. M. Hewitt and lieutenants William W. Henderson, J. J. Tobin, and C. R. Cartwright were not reelected. They resigned and left the regiment. See Simpson, *Hood's Texas Brigade: A Compendium*, 32–33. For the case of Charles L. Martin, see ibid., 117, and Martin to Lubbock, January 7, 1862, Records, Texas Governor Francis Richard Lubbock, Archives and Information Services Division, Texas State Library and Archives Commission.

28. As an example of this conviction, Lieutenant Watson Williams described James J. Archer, a regular army officer and native of Maryland who was selected to replace Shaller as colonel of the Fifth Texas, as "a foreigner." See Watson D. Williams to Laura, October 7, 1861, Company F, Fifth Texas Infantry, file 3–31, HTBP. Lieutenant Tacitus Clay said this about Archer: "He is a little fellow . . . and may possibly be a very efficient man if in the Command of Regulars, but I fear he is not of the right type to control or *give satisfaction* to Texas volunteers and the dissatisfaction in and out of the ranks is very general and I think there is a movement on foot with our Captains to have him supplanted" (Tacitus Clay to Mrs. Bettie Clay, October 6, 1861, Company I, Fifth Texas Infantry, file 3–9, HTBP).

29. Everett, *Chaplain Davis*, 32, 33. For the demographics of the enlisted men in Hood's Brigade, see Charles E. Brooks, "The Social and Cultural Dynamics of Soldiering in Hood's Texas Brigade," *Journal of Southern History* 67 (August 2001): 538–41.

30. U.S. Constitution, art. 1, sec. 8; Confederate Constitution, art. 1, sec. 8.

31. "Luther Martin's Letter of the Federal Convention of 1787," in *The Debates in the Several State Conventions on the Adoption of the Federal Constitution*, 4 vols., ed. Jonathan Elliot (Washington, DC: Taylor and Maury, 1854), 1:371.

32. Speech of George Mason, June 16, 1788, in *The Documentary History of the Ratification of the Constitution*, 18 vols., ed. Merrill Jensen, John P. Kaminski, and Gaspare J. Saladino (Madison: State Historical Society of Wisconsin, 1976–), 10:1303–4, 1312–13.

33. Everett, *Chaplain Davis*, 33. The three units were companies A, B, and F. See also Simpson, *Hood's Texas Brigade: A Compendium*, 96–111, 130–37.

34. Simpson, *Hood's Texas Brigade: A Compendium*, 117.

35. Company C was raised in Robertson County, Company E in McLennan County, Company G in Grimes County, Company H in Walker County, Company I in Navarro County, and Company K in Henderson County. See Simpson, *Hood's Texas Brigade: A Compendium*, 111–17, 124–30, 137–66.

36. These included companies C, D, E, F, G, H, I, and K. See ibid., 188, 196, 203, 210, 218, 226, 234, 242.

37. They were companies A, B, C, D, E, and F. See ibid., 15, 20, 24, 32, 38, 44.

38. Everett, *Chaplain Davis*, 43, 44.

39. Davis diary, September 26, 27, and 28, 1861.

40. Simpson, *Hood's Texas Brigade: Lee's Grenadier Guard*, 61–62, n. 14. The original source is Foster B. Womack, *An Account of the Womack Family* (Waco, TX: privately printed, 1937), 11.

41. Brooks, "Social and Cultural Dynamics of Soldiering in Hood's Texas Brigade," 543.

42. Everett, *Chaplain Davis*, 44.

43. Wyatt-Brown, *Southern Honor*; Elliott J. Gorn, "'Gouge and Bite, Pull Hair and Scratch': The Social Significance of Fighting in the Southern Backcountry," *American Historical Review* 90 (February 1985): 18–43, esp. 39–41; Edward L. Ayers, *Vengeance and Justice: Crime and Punishment in the 19th-Century American South* (New York: Oxford University Press, 1984), ch. 1; Dickson D. Bruce Jr., *Violence and Culture in the Antebellum South* (Austin: University of Texas Press, 1979), chs. 1–4; Richard White, "Outlaw Gangs of the Middle Border: American Social Bandits," *Western Historical Quarterly* 12 (October 1981): 387–408.

44. Simpson, *Hood's Texas Brigade: A Compendium*, 10; Polley, *Hood's Texas Brigade*, 16; James Henry Hendrick to mother, July 20, and August 6, 1861, Company E, First Texas Infantry, file 1–10, HTBP.

45. J. B. Polley, *A Soldier's Letters to Charming Nellie* (New York: Neale Publishing, 1908), 10; Polley, *Hood's Texas Brigade*, 29–30.

46. Polley, *Soldier's Letters*, 17, 18.

47. Texas volunteers often complained about the "tyranny" imposed on them by officers. Private E. O. Perry grumbled to his father that "to take our officers as a body, I would say . . . they are nothing but a set of up starts. They are very tyrannical for a day or two, then they are entirely too lenient." Another Texan in Virginia reported that a friend of his in the Fourth Texas was muttering about the "many instances of tyranny getting so prevalent in C[onfederate] S[tates] Army." See Perry to father, December 7, 1861, Smith County Historical

Society, Tyler, TX; J. Mark Smither to mother, February 18, 1862, Company D, Fifth Texas Infantry, file 3–29, HTBP.

48. Laswell, *Rags and Hope*, 47.

49. Everett, *Chaplain Davis*, 45–46; Simpson, *Hood's Texas Brigade: Lee's Grenadier Guard*, 63–64.

50. Laswell, *Rags and Hope*, 47–48; Simpson, *Hood's Texas Brigade: Lee's Grenadier Guard*, 64, 93.

51. Gage, "Texas Road to Secession and War."

52. *Houston Tri-Weekly Telegraph*, April 7, 1862.

53. Asa Roberts, Company B, Fourth Texas Infantry, file 2–30, HTBP; Selman diary, March 8, 1862, SCRC; James Henry Hendrick to father, June 10, 1863, Company E, First Texas Infantry, file 1–10, HTBP.

54. For example, an assistant general of the Confederate army stationed in Texas wrote to Inspector General Samuel Cooper to explain the difficulty authorities faced in raising infantry troops in the Lone Star State: "I find everywhere a willingness to volunteer, but the number of persons who were authorized last summer and fall to raise regiments of mounted twelve-months' men have taken advantage of the excitement and now come in and are everywhere recruiting for mounted service, which being much more popular in Texas than foot service, and the term being shorter, makes it a preferable service to our people, and is a very serious obstacle in my way" (Samuel A. Roberts to Samuel Cooper, March 12, 1862, in *The War of the Rebellion: A Compilation of the Official Records of the Union and Confederate Armies*, ser. 4, vol. 1 [Washington, DC: Government Printing Office, 1900], 991–92).

55. Polley, *Soldier's Letters*, 18, 44.

56. Selman diary, April 4, 1862, SCRC.

57. Ibid., April 8, 1862.

58. Polley diary, 60, SCRC.

59. Selman diary, April 9, 1862, SCRC.

60. Ibid., April 10, 1862.

61. Polley diary, 63, SCRC.

62. Robert H. Gaston to father and mother, April 26, 1862, Company H, First Texas Infantry, file 1–7b, HTBP.

63. Selman diary, April 8, 1862, SCRC.

64. Gaston to father and mother, April 26, 1862, HTBP; Polley diary, 57–58, SCRC. The importance of this incident at the creek crossing is underscored by the fact that three separate accounts chronicle it.

65. Selman diary, April 8, 1862, SCRC.

66. Colonel John Salmon Ford was in charge of the Bureau of Conscription for the state of Texas, appointed in June 1862. During his tenure he "originated and wrote the system of the Sons of the South which circulated among the

soldiers of the Army of the Texas-Mississippi Department." Ford argued that popular sovereignty should act as the guiding principle of the Confederate armies. "All power is inherent in the people—they are supreme. They alone can establish and ordain constitutions, or forms of government. The processes of government are delegated by the people, and are held in trust for the people. Officers are only agents of the people, and derive the authority to exercise certain powers from the constitution and the laws made in pursuance thereof. Any officer who may transcend his authority and presume to exercise power not delegated, is, to the extent of his usurpation, a tyrant" (Ford quoted in Stephen B. Oates, ed., *Rip Ford's Texas* [Austin: University of Texas Press, 1963], 335, 334, 337). The original document was published in the *Texas Almanac–Extra* (Austin), March 17, 1863.

67. Houston, "Speech against Increasing the Regular Army, February 1, 1858," in Williams and Barker, *Writings of Sam Houston*, 6:474.

68. Everett, *Chaplain Davis*, 36.

69. Houston, "Speech in the United States Senate," in Williams and Barker, *Writings of Sam Houston*, 4:521.

70. Polley diary, 51, SCRC.

71. Ibid., 51–52, 38.

72. Brooks, "Social and Cultural Dynamics of Soldiering in Hood's Texas Brigade," 567–69.

73. Everett, *Chaplain Davis*, 150.

74. Ibid., 57.

75. Kenneth S. Greenberg, *Honor and Slavery: Lies, Duels, Noses, Masks, Dressing as a Woman, Gifts, Strangers, Humanitarianism, Death, Slave Rebellions, the Proslavery Argument, Baseball, Hunting, and Gambling in the Old South* (Princeton, NJ: Princeton University Press, 1996), as quoted in Morgan, "The Price of Honor," 128.

76. Wyatt-Brown, "Honor, Dread of Enslavement, and Revolutionary Rhetoric," 35.

77. David Donald, "The Confederate as Fighting Man," *Journal of Southern History* 25 (May 1959): 178–93, esp. 191–93.

78. Brooks, "Social and Cultural Dynamics of Soldiering in Hood's Texas Brigade," 568–69.

79. Ibid., 536–37.

80. William L. Barney, "Secession," in *Encyclopedia of the Confederacy*, 4 vols., ed. Richard N. Current (New York: Simon and Schuster, 1993), 1376; Seymour Martin Lipset, *Political Man: The Social Bases of Politics* (New York: Doubleday, 1960), 344–54; David M. Potter, *The Impending Crisis: 1848–1861* (New York: Harper and Row, 1976), 485–513, esp. 502–5; Michael P. Johnson, "A New Look at the Popular Vote for Delegates to the Georgia Secession

Convention" *Georgia Historical Quarterly* 56 (1972): 259–75; Peyton McCrary, Clark Miller, and Dale Baum, "Class and Party in the Secession Crisis: Voting Behavior in the Deep South, 1856–1861," *Journal of Southern History* 8 (winter 1978): 429–57, esp. 444–46; Paul D. Escott, *After Secession: Jefferson Davis and the Failure of Confederate Nationalism* (Baton Rouge: Louisiana State University Press, 1978), 21–33, 42–45; Daniel W. Crofts, *Reluctant Confederates: Upper South Unionists in the Secession Crisis* (Chapel Hill: University of North Carolina Press, 1989), 130–94.

81. Dale Baum, *The Shattering of Texas Unionism: Politics in the Lone Star State during the Civil War Era* (Baton Rouge: Louisiana State University Press, 1998), 47.

82. Noah Southwick, *The Evolution of a State: Recollections of Old Texas Days* (Austin, TX: Gammes Book Company, 1900), 333.

83. Barney, "Secession," 1378.

84. Randolph B. Campbell, *An Empire for Slavery: The Peculiar Institution in Texas, 1821–1865* (Baton Rouge: Louisiana State University Press, 1989), 68.

85. Ernest William Winkler, ed., *Journal of the Secession Convention of Texas 1861* (Austin, TX: Austin Printing Company, 1912), 10, 13.

"Is Not the Glory Enough to Give Us All a Share?"

An Analysis of Competing Memories of the Battle of the Crater

Kevin M. Levin

Writing in 1898 from Darlington, South Carolina, former Confederate captain John Floyd could barely contain his frustration. As a member of one of the five regiments in Stephen Elliott's South Carolina brigade, Floyd had witnessed the terrible destruction wrought by the explosion of a Federal mine and the subsequent attempt to break the growing siege around Petersburg, Virginia, during the summer of 1864. For roughly thirty years, Floyd and others had watched the Virginia veterans of Brigadier General William Mahone's division take all the credit for ultimately pushing back the Federal attackers. In a letter to the editor of Columbia's *State* newspaper, Floyd "noticed that whenever there is a reunion of the Virginia survivors of the War Between the States the orators invariably claim the victory at the Crater . . . for General Mahone and the Virginians." Floyd's concern stemmed from an address—written not by a Virginian but by a prominent South Carolinian—claiming that "Elliott's men were so demoralized that they were replaced in the lines by fresh troops brought up from the flanks by General Lee." For Floyd, this was sufficient evidence that historical revisions were needed. "It is evident that the people of our own state do not understand how that battle was fought, who conducted it, what troops were engaged, or how it was possible for Elliott's brigade to hold the lines at the Crater against such fearful odds."[1]

Over the past few years, historians such as David Blight, Fitzhugh Brundage, and David Goldfield have explained the process by which national reconciliation came to shape the way Americans understood

227

the Civil War at the turn of the twentieth century. In Blight's view, the veterans on both sides of the Potomac chose to assign the deepest meaning of the war to the heroism and valor of the soldiers on the battlefield. The shared experience of soldierhood was a theme that could bring former enemies together peacefully on old battlefields.[2] Such an analysis tells us much about the general trend toward reconciliation. Debates between one-time enemies over the meaning of the war, however, masked the extent to which former comrades in the Confederate ranks continued to wrangle over specific questions related to both defeat and victory on the battlefield. Perhaps the best example was the postwar controversy between Confederate veterans of Virginia and North Carolina over which state could claim the deepest penetration of Union lines during Pickett's charge at Gettysburg on July 3, 1863. That disagreement left lasting scars that continue to fuel heated debates among members of Confederate heritage organizations from the two states.[3]

The level of interest in the battle of the Crater easily approached that in Gettysburg, at least partly because it was the last significant Confederate victory in Virginia before the surrender at Appomattox in April 1865.[4] The victors of the contests among Confederate veterans over who would control the public memory of such battles earned the right to shake hands with their former enemies as blue and gray reunions became more popular. More importantly, veterans utilized their memories as a way to maintain pride not only in their individual units but also in the former Confederate nation. Strong feelings of nationalism could not be set aside even as the men in the ranks returned home to rebuild their lives and decide whether or when to take the loyalty oath to the Union. Recounting their heroics on the battlefield allowed some veterans to make the psychological shift that involved redefining themselves as Americans.[5] The tendency for veterans to focus on individual regiments and larger units associated with their respective states may have reflected a need for self-identification somewhere between Confederate and American. For others, concentrating on the past was simply a way to avoid thinking about defeat in the postemancipation world. Regardless of the reasons, the steps taken in the early postwar years by Virginia's veterans to celebrate and commemorate their valor and sacrifice on battlefields such as the Crater only served to isolate their former comrades from outside the Old Dominion and to diminish other veterans' service and sacrifice for the Confederacy.

Following the bloody and costly battles of the Overland Campaign between May and June 1864, General Ulysses S. Grant transferred Union operations south of the James River to the railroad hub of Petersburg, Virginia. The Union army's failure to take the city in a series of attacks in mid-June was followed quickly by the digging of complex chains of trenches and fortifications by both sides. The battle that took place on July 30, 1864, began in the final week of June as Union soldiers in General Ambrose Burnside's Ninth Corps commenced the construction of a tunnel under a Confederate salient that eventually measured 510 feet and held 8,000 pounds of explosives.

Following the massive explosion of the mine in the early-morning hours of July 30, four divisions of the Ninth Corps rushed into the resulting crater that measured 200 feet long, 60 feet wide, and 30 feet deep. The attack quickly bogged down in confusion as Union attackers converged on a narrowly defined space not much larger than the contours of the crater. Although a few Union regiments managed to push beyond the destroyed section of the Confederate line, several Confederate units situated north of the salient, including artillery and remnants of Brigadier General Stephen Elliott's South Carolina brigade and North Carolinians under the command of Brigadier General Robert Ransom, regained some organization and prevented a breakthrough. The tide turned in the Confederates' favor at around 9:00 A.M., when three brigades in Brigadier General William Mahone's division arrived just as commanders in the advance Federal units were planning a charge. The attack of Mahone's Virginia brigade—a unit he had commanded for much of the war until his promotion to division command in May 1864—was followed by attacks from both Georgia and Alabama brigades. Confederate rage over the carnage created by the explosion was surpassed only by the realization that the Union attack included a division of U.S. Colored Troops.

The fighting continued until approximately 1:00 P.M., when Federal officers ordered a retreat. The official reports put the Union dead at 504, plus another 1,881 wounded and 1,413 missing. Reports of the massacre of black soldiers following their surrender were widely documented. Confederates suffered 361 killed, 727 wounded, and 403 missing. On the morning of August 1, a truce was declared so that both sides could retrieve their wounded and bury their dead. As a result of their decisive victory, many Confederates experienced a renewed sense of purpose and commitment to the cause. Success on the battlefield reinforced their confidence that further Union advances could be stopped, and it seemed to bring the South one step closer to independence—through either a Lincoln defeat in the upcoming presidential election or an unwillingness to continue the fight on the part of Northern civilians. All these factors guaranteed that Confederate victory at the Crater would not soon be forgotten.[6]

The location of the Crater site in Petersburg made it easy to depict the battle as a Virginia victory. General Mahone himself resided in Petersburg, and his involvement in the railroad business and state politics made him a popular, though at times controversial, figure in the community. Finally, Mahone's Virginia brigade was made up of regiments formed in the Richmond-Petersburg-Norfolk area, and their involvement in reunions and reenactments helped keep the focus on Virginia. Most importantly, the reputations of Mahone and his brigade were forged at the Crater.

Early in the postwar period, few questioned that Mahone deserved praise for his role in leading the successful counterattack on July 30, 1864; however, Confederate victory at the Crater was not credited solely to Virginia units by contemporary accounts. Even local newspapers singled out individual regiments and brigades from other states for praise in the days following the battle. The coverage by the *Petersburg Express* is a case in point. Although the editorial column in the August 1 edition dedicated the most space to Mahone's Virginians, the newspaper reserved the highest praise for Mahone's Alabama brigade, which "came gallantly up to their work, and by a charge drove the enemy from the remaining portion of the works, and thus enabled us to re-establish our lines, precisely as they were before the explosion." The following day the newspaper amended its earlier account by noting that it had "omitted" any mention of "Gen. Elliott's South Carolina Brigade." Although they had "suffered heavily" owing to their location directly under the mine shaft, Elliott's men had "held their ground manfully, never yielding an inch during the day." Readers were also made aware that a number of companies had participated in Mahone's counterattack. The steps that Virginia veterans took to shape the memory of the battle in their favor eventually led to an outcry from veterans outside the commonwealth who felt betrayed by their former comrades.[7]

One of the earliest postwar accounts of the battle was written by

Edward A. Pollard, who edited the *Daily Richmond Examiner* from 1861 to 1867. In *The Lost Cause* (1866), Pollard provided a brief and narrow account of the battle, placing the Virginia brigade of Mahone's division at the center of his narrative. Pollard described the Union attack as feeble until "it was encountered by Mahone's brigade." The racial dynamic of the attack was given prominence, as Mahone's men "were ordered not to fire until they could see the whites of the negroes' eyes." The first volley left these soldiers "panic stricken and past control." Pollard's analysis thus set a solid precedent for Virginians' role in controlling how the battle would be remembered.[8]

Three years later, John Elder—who had been present in Petersburg at the time of the battle, working as an aide in the field and a mapmaker—released his dramatic oil painting, which highlighted the importance of Mahone's counterattack. Elder depicted the fighting at close range in all its gruesome detail, but the observer's eye is drawn to the advancing tide of Mahone's men in the Sixth Virginia Infantry, who are poised to sweep the area and put an end to any planned Union advance. One art critic wrote a colorful review: "The suspense in this portion of the scene is fearful; and one dreads that the reinforcements will arrive to[o] late. But they are hurrying on. With their wild, impulsive yell, so characteristic of the Southern army, regardless of rank or line, in double column, Mahone's brigade comes pouring in." The success of Elder's painting helped shape the popular belief that Confederate victory could be understood by focusing on the contributions of Virginians.[9]

This Virginia-centered account was also propagated by the veterans themselves. After ten years of what Gerald Linderman describes as "hibernation," the veterans of the Virginia brigade began to take an active interest in the Crater battlefield. Spurred by the continued bonds of esprit de corps, veterans used the battlefield to rekindle old friendships as well as to recall the role they had played in securing victory that day. Compared with casual tourists, these veterans infused the Crater battlefield with a broader meaning and a cultural significance that acknowledged their commitment to a shared cause and mirrored the growing interest in commemorating the Confederacy throughout the South.[10]

Interest in the Crater among veterans of the Army of Northern Virginia can be understood on a number of levels. First, the battle was the last decisive victory for Lee's men during the Petersburg campaign.

The use of explosives by the Federal army and the resulting destruction left an indelible impression on those present. Most importantly, the presence of a division of U.S. Colored Troops brought into sharp relief the distinction between the North and the morally bankrupt Lincoln administration, on the one hand, and the virtuous South, on the other.

Remembering the presence of African Americans at the Crater and the black soldiers' harsh treatment at the hands of Lee's men both during and after the battle may have served as a rallying point for those struggling with the postwar social and political situation in Virginia and the rest of the South. Elder's depiction of black soldiers and their "abolitionist" allies as confused, killed in action, or about to be seriously harmed highlighted the racial tensions within a white Southern population faced with the forced social changes occurring through black political action. The reviewer cited earlier understood Elder's painting of the Crater as more than an attempt to praise the fighting prowess of Mahone's men; it was intended "to rescue from oblivion one scene of our country's glory, and to lift the veil which the conqueror has attempted to cast over our nation's existence."[11] Elder's work could be interpreted as nothing less than a call to white Virginians to commit themselves to regaining control of the political field, which would be a first step toward restructuring the social and racial hierarchy in a way that more closely reflected their antebellum world.

Veterans from Mahone's Virginia brigade took an active interest in remembering their lost comrades and sanctifying their failed attempt at independence, which was still believed to be honorable. The Crater site proved to be an ideal setting for the veterans of Mahone's brigade, who met three times between 1875 and 1877. The first reunion took place in Petersburg on May 10, 1875. Veterans from every regiment traveled to the city to listen to speeches, "see each other face to face, and grasp each other's hands again." J. P. Minetree reminded his audience that those assembled were not simply part of a military organization "that ceased with the surrender at Appomattox Courthouse"; they were there to "form an organization to collect the records and preserve the history of our noble brigade, to which we are all so much attached and of which we feel justly proud." Not surprisingly, many speeches made direct reference to the Crater. For example, Thomas F. Owens urged his audience not to forget that "here are the men who hurled back the foe from within a few yards of where we now sit, who had gained posses-sion of our lines by subterranean passage." Close proximity to the old battlefield reinforced the connection between Mahone's brigade and the Crater.[12] The following day, thirty-five veterans walked the Crater site with William Mahone.

The men who took part in that first reunion created a "code of orga-nization" and voted for officers, including Mahone as president, under the name "The Memorial Association of Mahone's Old Brigade." They also agreed that future reunions should take place on the anniversary of the battle. That decision testified to the battle's importance to the identity of the association, and it guaranteed that memories of the war would be focused on the Crater.

The following July witnessed a more elaborate celebration that took place in the opera house of Norfolk, Virginia. Just over 200 veterans traveled to Norfolk for the occasion, where they were "received with the greatest enthusiasm" as they paraded up Main Street to the "beauti-fully decorated" opera house. Inside "were scrolls bearing the names of all the principal engagements in which the Brigade had participated." Foreign flags were draped on the walls, and placed prominently on the stage was a Confederate flag that had been presented to one of the regi-ments during the war. The ceremony got under way with an address by the mayor of Norfolk, John S. Tucker, who welcomed "the heroes of a lost, but glorious cause" and Mahone, "who led these hundreds through our streets" and "the thousands before whose gallant array you rode out so proudly and so worthily, and our hearts were full and our eyes were dimmed."[13]

Focusing on the Crater fight reinforced the overall goals of the reunion, one of which was to help veterans deal with the psychologi-cal scars of defeat by reminding them what the common soldier had achieved in the face of overwhelming numbers and resources. Many speeches made reference to the July 30 battle, including Mayor Tucker's, which urged the veterans to remember that "on that day you consum-mated the full measure of your fame." William Mahone also reminded his men of the "solemn sense of duty which made this day conspicu-ous in the annals of war, when, by your matchless charge and bayonet, our lines at the Crater were redeemed, and the very safety of our army for the time restored." Toward the end of the ceremony, James B. Hope offered a lengthy "metrical address" that made reference to the Crater:

Who has forgotten at the deadly Mine
How our great Captain of great Captains bade
Your General to retake the captured line?
How it was done you know, Mahone's Brigade.

Through ceremony, speech, and verse, the Crater was no longer a simple tourist attraction but a place where veterans and citizens could honor a glorious past and renew their commitment to prewar Southern values in the face of growing political and social change.[14]

The reunions inspired members of the brigade to produce written accounts that reinforced their central role in the battle. In his recollections of the battle published in 1876, William Stewart—who commanded the Sixty-first Virginia and proved to be one of the brigade's most prolific writers—concentrated on the "special acts of bravery" exhibited by his men during the unit's charge into the Crater. In emphasizing the role of the Sixty-first Virginia and the rest of Mahone's brigade, Stewart downplayed the contributions of the Alabama and Georgia brigades in retaking the salient. Whereas Stewart described the charge of the Virginia brigade in heroic terms, he wrote that the subsequent attack by Brigadier General Matthew R. Hall's Georgians was "repulsed" as they entered the Crater. Even after it "re-formed in column of regiments," according to Stewart, it "was met by such a withering fire that it again recoiled with heavy slaughter." The final attack was described as a "grand charge under a terrible fire," but Stewart failed to acknowledge how that attack contributed to the overall victory at the Crater.[15]

The consensus of these early accounts was that Virginians had played a significantly greater role in the victory than had soldiers from other Southern states. This agreement among Virginia's veterans, however, only alienated their former comrades from outside the state, who grew increasingly frustrated as their contributions were ignored. It is ironic that within a few years of the war's end, North and South Carolinians, Alabamians, and Georgians would be struggling with their Virginia neighbors to maintain their respective reputations in printed sources.

The eventual success of the Virginia-centered account is all the more impressive given the sharp split between the commonwealth's veterans during the four years of Readjuster control of state government. Following the 1876 loss of his Atlantic, Mississippi & Ohio Railroad to receivership, William Mahone entered politics as the organizer and leader of the Readjuster Party (named for its policy of downwardly readjusting Virginia's debt), which proved to be the most successful independent coalition of black and white Republicans and white Democrats. From 1879 to 1883, Readjusters governed the state; they elected a governor and two U.S. senators (Mahone being one) and represented six of Virginia's ten congressional districts. As a result of Senate patronage, African Americans played a prominent role in shaping the party's platform, which advocated their increased access to jury service, officeholding, and the polls.[16]

Readjustment of the state debt left sufficient funds for public schools, the hiring of black teachers, and additional infrastructure that benefited Virginia's African American communities. The whipping post was abolished, as was the poll tax, which had been used to disfranchise black voters. In 1882 the General Assembly passed legislation supporting the literary fund with an appropriation of $379,270, and funds were raised to establish the Normal and Collegiate Institute (later Virginia State University).[17]

Black Virginians were rewarded for their support on both the state and federal levels. The number of black employees in various federal agencies increased sharply; at the Post Office, blacks accounted for just under 40 percent of the workforce at the height of Readjuster control. In addition, African Americans served as jurors and clerks, town police officers, and guards at state penitentiaries. However, it was in the area of education where black Virginians witnessed the greatest transition. Readjuster reforms increased the number of black teachers from 415 in 1879 to 1,588 in 1884, and black enrollment went from 36,000 to 91,000 during those same years.[18]

For Virginia's more conservative white population, such changes were seen as a threat to the stability of established social hierarchies. That Mahone was the instigator of these changes was considered a serious betrayal of the Confederate goals fought for in the war. Mahone's war record proved to be a popular target, in part because he had used it to further his own business and political interests. Throughout the four years of Readjuster control, Mahone was attacked in the newspapers, where he was often compared with John Brown and Benedict Arnold.

Not surprisingly, the most common target for Mahone's political enemies, including fellow veterans, was his performance at the Crater. His detractors questioned his conduct on the battlefield, whether he had ordered the charge that led to the retaking of the salient, and whether he had actually led his old brigade in its recapture. One such challenge came from David Weisiger, who had commanded the Virginia brigade following Mahone's promotion to division command in May 1864. In addition to claiming that Mahone had shirked his duty for the safety of the "covered way" (used by the brigade for shelter before its final push into the Crater), Weisiger wrote in the pages of the *Richmond State* that he himself "gave the order to 'forward!' at the opportune moment, when it was observed that the enemy were preparing for a charge."[19]

Attacks such as Weisiger's continued unabated until the Readjusters lost control of the state legislature in November 1883. The debate surrounding Mahone's performance at the Crater reflected the political limits to which Virginia's Confederate past could be applied. It is difficult to gauge the extent of the damage to Mahone's war record. An obituary for Weisiger reprinted in the *Confederate Veteran* from the *Richmond Dispatch* described him as the "hero of the battle of the Crater," a label that had once been reserved for Mahone.[20] Although the debates among Virginians surrounding Mahone's performance at the Crater were divisive, the temporary political distractions did not make it any easier for veterans outside the commonwealth to introduce a convincing counternarrative.

Southerners outside Virginia were faced with two difficult challenges. First, they had to find a forum that could disseminate information to a wide audience. Second, and more important, they had to convince interested readers to question certain assumptions about the battle that were fast becoming deeply entrenched. Their options were few, and time was not on their side. As early as 1874, though not referring specifically to the Crater, North Carolina veteran T. B. Kingsburg noted in the pages of *Our Living and Our Dead* "that injustice was done to the character and services of North Carolina Troops—not by General Lee, or Gen'ls A. P. Hill, Hood and other distinguished officers, but by newspaper men and writers of sensational and evanescent histories." Kingsburg was not optimistic about the future, "for the time has not yet come . . . for our gallant soldiers to receive even-handed justice at the hands of the writers living beyond our State."[21]

Veterans from North and South Carolina sought to challenge the historical record on a number of points. South Carolinians who had fought at the Crater under Stephen Elliott were upset by the extent to which they were portrayed as ineffective following the initial explosion. Although they had suffered numerous casualties, veterans from both states asserted that they had regrouped in time to challenge the Union assault. More importantly, they claimed that they had pinned down the enemy up to the point of Mahone's counterattack by midmorning. Both North and South Carolinians argued that entire units or remnants of specific regiments had participated in the counterattacks that eventually resulted in the retaking of the salient. Even veterans from Mahone's division who had served in brigades from Georgia and Alabama and participated in the counterattack felt left out because of the narrow focus on the Virginia brigade. Finally, veterans from artillery units entered the debate by claiming that their close-range bombardments had sufficiently damaged attacking Union units to prevent any further advances.

Not until the publication of the *Southern Historical Society Papers* (*SHSP*) beginning in 1876 were those outside the Old Dominion able to reach an audience beyond their respective states. The first round of contributions challenged an article by Virginian Gordon McCabe that had been published in one of the first issues. McCabe's account failed to satisfy former captain Henry Flanner, commander of a North Carolina battery, who found fault "not with what is written, but what was omitted in the article referred to." What was omitted from McCabe's analysis, according to Flanner, was a balanced account of the credit that was due Mahone's division and that due other units on the field that had kept the Union advance at bay around the Crater. Although he raised what many might have considered a reasonable objection, Flanner went on to conclude that "the battery commanded by me, and composed entirely of North Carolinians, is entitled to the credit of preventing the Federal army from entering Petersburg on the morning of the springing of the mine." Flanner argued that his unit had "kept them in check alone, and without infantry support," until the arrival of Mahone's men. Such a self-serving account convinced few to alter their view of the battle, despite Flanner's concluding remarks that he remained hopeful for a "continuous narrative" that would include "contributions" that "do justice to all."[22]

Following closely on the heels of Flanner's account, Fitz McMaster—who took over command of Elliott's brigade after the latter's wounding—published an address in the *SHSP* that had originally been delivered to the veterans of the Eighteenth South Carolina in August 1879. McMaster referred to previous articles as "very imperfect" and "erroneous." Similar to Flanner's approach, McMaster singled out the Seventeenth South Carolina, along with a "small number of men" from the Twenty-sixth South Carolina plus various artillery units, and credited them with "prevent[ing] Grant from entering Petersburg that day and capturing the whole of Beauregard's army." In highlighting the role of South Carolina units, McMaster downplayed the role of Mahone's division by suggesting that it did not arrive on the scene until approximately 10:00 A.M. and was not organized sufficiently for another two hours, when a "splendid charge was made."[23]

McMaster's article was accompanied by a private letter written by former artillery officer Major James C. Coit, who confirmed many of McMaster's observations. Coit took issue with McCabe's claim that the initial explosion had left Elliott's brigade in a state of confusion and "dismay." As for the timing of Mahone's counterattack, Coit placed it "near 11 o'clock." And with regard to who was responsible for saving the army, there was little doubt: "From the time of the explosion until the charge of Mahone's Division," wrote Coit, "the men of Elliott's brigade bore the brunt of the battle, and with a portion of Ransom's, were the only infantry troops that I saw opposing the advance of the enemy to Cemetery Hill." Coit concluded that Elliott's brigade deserved "the credit of saving Petersburg on that day."[24]

This opening salvo from Flanner, McMaster, and Coit set the stage for future revisions from outside Virginia. Although all three succeeded in presenting alternative explanations to counter Virginia's growing hold on public memory, they did so at a cost. In emphasizing the fighting prowess of their own units, Flanner and McMaster came across as just as provincial and self-serving as their Virginia counterparts. Perhaps the most difficult point of contention to accept was the suggestion from McMaster and Coit that Mahone's counterattack took place much later than 9:00 A.M. Even across regional boundaries, most observers accepted the conclusion that the initial charge of the Virginia brigade under the command of Brigadier General David A. Weisiger did indeed take place close to 9:00 A.M. By convincing readers of the truth of this particular fact, Weisiger could cast doubt on competing accounts in their entirety.

The content of these challenges to Virginia's version of the battle was not the only problem. Competing accounts slowed to a trickle as the Southern Historical Society and editorial oversight of its publication fell under the control of Virginians. Editors such as Jubal Early—who exercised tight control over the content of the *SHSP*—remained focused on promoting the role of Virginians at high-profile battles such as Gettysburg and limited the publication of alternative explanations.[25] When accounts of the Crater did appear in the *SHSP*, they tended to be written by Virginians and to focus on their role in the battle. Not until the publication of the *Confederate Veteran* in 1893 would there be another concerted effort to drive a wedge between Virginians and popular memory of the Crater, although its influence on later historians would fall short of that of the *SHSP*.

The 1883 publication of *The Virginia Campaign, 1864 and 1865* by former Union Second Corps general Andrew Humphreys reflects the limited success of Flanner, McMaster, Coit, and others. Humphreys utilized the *SHSP* in his research and no doubt consulted the above-mentioned authors in his coverage of the Crater fight. In his analysis of Mahone's counterattack, Humphreys placed the lead brigade of Virginians "a short distance in the rear of the mined salient" at approximately 9:00 A.M., where "Elliott's men had aided so effectively in repelling every effort of our troops in the crater to advance." According to Humphreys, once Union soldiers showed signs of advancing out of the Crater, "Weisiger's brigade, with some of Elliott's, advanced against them, charged and drove them back in confusion."[26] Though brief, Humphreys's more nuanced account attempted to balance the contributions of Mahone's counterattack and the steadfastness of Elliott's South Carolinians to Confederate victory, without accepting the more egregious suggestion that the attack had occurred much later in the morning.

Even after twenty years, veterans from North and South Carolina remained as frustrated as ever. Challenging the tide of history and trying to loosen Virginians' hold on popular memory of the Crater proved to be a daunting task. Many were no doubt resigned to publishing accounts in local newspapers or Northern publications for audiences that did not need to be converted or had nothing at stake in the outcome.

In 1892 Virginians took a giant leap forward in solidifying their version of the Crater narrative when George Bernard, who had served in the Twelfth Virginia and fought at the Crater, published *War Talks of Confederate Veterans*. No other book published in this period had more of an influence on popular memory. The book was authorized by the A. P. Hill Camp of Confederate Veterans in Petersburg, Virginia, and a share of its profits went toward providing the necessary funds for the "collection of books and other literature relating to the late war, for the use of the camp." Bernard organized each chapter around addresses delivered before the A. P. Hill Camp on such notable battles as Sharpsburg, Chancellorsville, the Wilderness, and the Crater, followed by firsthand accounts from veterans of Mahone's Virginia brigade commissioned specifically for the volume, as well as newspaper articles and other relevant publications. Bernard ensured readers that "great care" had been taken "to eliminate all that was doubtful and to have the several statements correct before they were printed in this volume."[27]

The chapter on the Crater was easily the largest section of the book. Leading with Bernard's own address to the A. P. Hill Camp, it was followed by no fewer than fifty individual accounts, many from veterans of the Twelfth and Sixty-first Virginia regiments. Bernard hoped to set the historical record straight regarding the conduct of William Mahone, who continued to be attacked owing to his leadership of the Readjusters.[28] Such a large concentration of Virginia accounts left little room for competing interpretations, but it allowed Bernard to concentrate on confirming a number of points concerning the battle. First, he attempted to show once and for all that Mahone's counterattack did indeed take place close to 9:00 A.M. He did this by including multiple excerpts from Union commanders, including generals George Meade and Ambrose Burnside. Bernard also provided evidence that Mahone personally led his division into battle and gave the final orders that resulted in the retaking of the Crater salient.

Veterans from outside the Old Dominion with an interest in reading a balanced account of the contributions of various units to victory would have been appalled by Bernard's narrow focus on Mahone's Virginia brigade. "There may possibly have been, and I have no doubt but that there were, a few individual members of these Carolina regiments," he argued, "but, if any organized body, or bodies, of troops made the charge along with the Virginians, this important fact has hitherto wholly escaped the attention of the men of this brigade." Bernard attempted to console his fellow veterans by noting almost in passing that South Carolinians under the leadership of Colonel F. W. McMaster "did their whole duty," that the artillery "rendered most effective service," and that "the final successful charge" of the Alabama brigade "has never been questioned."[29] But in the end, according to Bernard, that "the charge of the Virginia brigade, commanded by General D. A. Weisiger and directed by Gen. Wm. Mahone made a little before nine o'clock in the morning, did the substantial work that led to the re-capturing of the Crater and the adjacent earth-works is a fact that will always stand out boldly on the pages of history." Bernard remained confident that "the fame of the brigade for its part in this brilliant action . . . will shine out in the imperishable records of the late war long after its actors shall have passed away." He was closer to the truth than he could have known.[30]

The release of *War Talks* brought about a noticeable increase in the number of accounts accusing Virginians of unfair play. The largest number of responses to appear in the wake of *War Talks* appeared in the *Confederate Veteran*. Under the editorial leadership of S. A. Cunningham, the magazine drew large numbers of subscribers by marketing itself as a forum for common soldiers and nonelitists, unlike the Southern Historical Society, which remained its chief rival. The stated goal of the publication was to "gather authentic data for an impartial history," and non-Virginia veterans may have seen it as their last opportunity to get their stories in print. Because the editor was interested primarily in accounts from the western theater, Virginians did not enjoy privileged access. This provided a unique opportunity for veterans outside the Old Dominion to correct what they perceived as inaccuracies in the historical record and reach a wider audience. These veterans remained vigilant in countering such misperceptions throughout the publication's history.

A case in point is the exchange between Colonel George T. Rogers, who had commanded the Sixth Virginia, and Captain George Clark, who had served in the Eleventh Alabama and on the staff of Brigadier General J. C. C. Saunders. Not surprisingly, Rogers focused on the conduct of Weisiger's Virginia brigade and Mahone's heroism in directing the initial assault against Union positions around the Crater. According to Rogers, "the broken line was repossessed by the Virginia Brigade of a few thin regiments," and although the Georgia brigade that followed "rendered gallant aid . . . they failed to cover the Crater proper or to oust the mixed crowd of whites and blacks now huddled there." Rogers described the final attack by Saunders's Alabamians as a "handsome walk-over for them."[31]

In the following issue, George Clark argued that the coverage of Saunders's brigade "minimizes its service" in certain "particulars." Clark prefaced his criticisms by reminding his Virginia neighbors that many Alabamians "sleep their last sleep in the soil of old Virginia, having given their lives in defense of its firesides." And in reference to the object of his rejoinder, Clark stipulated that Rogers "would not intentionally do them the slightest injustice if he knew it." As to specific points of contention, Clark argued that the final attack was not a "walk-over," as described by Rogers, but "was one of the hardest fought fields of the war, and brilliant success was wrenched by valor from serious danger." He also attempted to dispel the Virginia brigade's belief that it deserved the laurels for dislodging Union forces from the Crater. Not so, according to Clark, who denied that the Virginians had even gone "down into the crater like the Alabamians did." In closing, Clark took one final step to clarify the role of his fellow Alabamians: "With a handful of men more than triple its numbers were captured, the lines re-established, and what promised at early dawn the closing victory of the war for the enemy, was turned into disastrous defeat by a few ragged Alabamians."[32] Clark's rejoinder set the tone for the noticeable increase in the number of challenges to the Virginia version of the battle of the Crater that appeared in the pages of *Confederate Veteran* and elsewhere.

A few years later, another Alabamian who had served in the Ninth Alabama joined the growing chorus in support of Clark. B. F. Phillips also noted that after "failing to retake the breastworks," the Virginia brigade was "rushed into the left of the crater." The follow-up attack by Wright's Georgians was "driven back with heavy loss." Phillips recalled that Mahone had painted a distressing picture, saying that it was a "life-and-death struggle" and for us to "load our guns, fix bayonets . . . and go in and give them h[ell]; and we tried to obey orders."[33] Phillips's account put at least one Virginian on the defensive. In the next issue of *Confederate Veteran*, R. W. Jones contested Phillips's claim that the Virginia brigade had failed to retake the Crater. "This statement with regard to one of the most desperate battles of the war," urged Jones, "is so contrary to the facts of history that the *Veteran* should not have published it." Jones urged readers to consult Bernard's *War Talks*, Robert E. Lee's own congratulatory order to Mahone, and "one hundred and fifty survivors of that wonderful victory won by Mahone's old brigade." "You might as well publish," concluded Jones, "that Stonewall Jackson's Brigade failed to stand their ground on the First Manassas field and that Pickett's Division refused to charge at Gettysburg."[34] Implicit in this closing comment was the assumption that the mere mention of fellow Virginians could put to rest any questions about Virginians' conduct at the Crater.

Not all Virginians reacted as sharply to alternative explanations as Jones did. An account published in 1907 by Major William Etheridge, who had commanded the Forty-first Virginia, reflected a newfound willingness to extend credit to units outside Virginia for their roles in retaking the salient. In his account of the counterattacks by Mahone's three brigades, Etheridge gave equal weight to the non-Virginia units. Etheridge praised the final attack by Saunders's Alabamians, who continued to push forward toward the crest of the Crater. The men soon "started in double-quick, and before the enemy could reload the Alabamians were on them." "And, as was the case on our side of the Crater," continued Etheridge, "a hand-to-hand fight took place, and in a few minutes the gallant Alabamians had driven out the enemy, or killed those who couldn't get out, and were masters of the situation."[35]

Veterans from North Carolina also intervened in an attempt to reclaim their place in the annals of war. "I have heard disputes concerning the troops," asserted W. A. Day of the Forty-ninth North Carolina regiment, "who made that grand charge . . . known as Mahone's charge." "I believe that Tennessee, Virginia, South Carolina, and North Carolina were all represented." Another soldier from the Fifty-sixth North Carolina also attempted to correct the historical record: "I shall not attempt a description of that memorable event farther than to say Ransom's Brigade . . . held its position and helped to retake the lost ground, though none of our historians seem to be advised of that fact."[36]

Evidence that the Virginia version of the battle of the Crater had become the accepted one can be found in its 1903 reenactment at Petersburg. The location of the event and the organizational assistance of the A. P. Hill and R. E. Lee camps of the Sons of Confederate Veterans ensured that the day would celebrate Virginia's role in the war. Reinforcing this goal, organizers structured the program around Mahone's brigade, which included nothing but Virginia regiments. The address by William Stewart celebrated Virginia by placing Mahone's charge in the broader context of the war. Stewart cited three "critical occasions" during the war that required "real heroism": Stonewall Jackson's stand at First Manassas, the charge of Pickett's division at Gettysburg, and the charge of Mahone's brigade at the Crater. Not surprisingly, all three examples involved Virginians. Once again, by focusing on Mahone's brigade, Stewart ignored the contributions of other units that had been integral to Confederate success that day. "This is the great tribute to the soldiers of Virginia, which gleams out as the evening star in the shadows of night above surrounding constellations," concluded Stewart.[37]

As late as 1923, H. A. Chambers felt justified in claiming, "So far as known, no historian of the war mentions the fact that North Carolina soldiers took part in this battle." North Carolinians thus faced some of the same difficulties in trying to correct the historical record of the Crater as they did with Gettysburg. Although Mahone's charge did not rise to the mythical level of Pickett's charge, by the turn of the century, Southerners outside Virginia had to contend with the widely accepted Virginia-centered account of the Crater.[38]

Virginians never fully acknowledged the extent to which their fellow veterans from outside the commonwealth felt that they had been denied their rightful place in the collective memory of the Crater. By the turn of the century, the relationship between veterans from Virginia and other states was noticeably strained. In 1903 the History Committee of Virginia's Grand Camp of Confederate Veterans issued its official report addressing a number of disagreements with North Carolina, including the Tar Heels' belief that they had supplied 50,000 more troops than Virginia had; that the presence of North Carolinians at the battles of Gettysburg, Chancellorsville, Bethel, and Chickamauga had been integral to Confederate victories; and that the North Carolinians had been the last to surrender at Appomattox. Ironically, the authors of the report concluded that North Carolinians were working to unfairly monopolize battlefield glory and suggested that it should rightfully be shared equally: "In the Army of Northern Virginia nearly every Southern State was represented. The Confederate Secretary of War says of that army in his report of November 3, 1864, that it was one 'in which every virtue of an army and the genius of consummate generalship had been displayed.' And this again, we believe, is the world's verdict. Is not the glory enough to give us all a share? Let us then not be envious and jealous of each other where all did their part so well."[39] It is difficult to imagine that the language of reconciliation could assuage the lingering doubts and resentment of veterans outside the Old Dominion.

The decisive factor that sealed the Virginia-centered account of the battle of the Crater in popular memory took place in 1936, when the National Park Service acquired the site as part of Petersburg National Military Park. Park officers relied heavily on Bernard's *War Talks* for their interpretation, and the close relationship with the A. P. Hill Camp of Confederate Veterans guaranteed that the park would concentrate on Mahone's Virginians.

The debates between Virginia's veterans and their former Confederate colleagues from outside the state serve as a reminder that the end of the war did not signal an end to hostilities. Although commentators from both North and South eventually agreed on a national narrative that ignored the importance of slavery and emancipation, Confederate veterans battled over ownership of their past. They focused on the past as a way to ignore the drastic political and social changes brought about by defeat. Others felt a deep need to maintain contact with former comrades, which they did by commemorating and writing about their experiences. With the defeat of the Confederate nation, the remembrance of their battlefield heroics became closely identified with their respective states. And identification with their states allowed Confederate veterans to remain connected with their Lost Cause as they continued their journeys back to becoming U.S. citizens. Virginia's veterans may have had noble intentions in their attempt to preserve the memory of their battlefield exploits for posterity, but the narrow concentration on units from their own state alienated and offended their former comrades from elsewhere in the South. The intensity of the debates surrounding the Crater reflects a heightened sense of honor rooted in local and state identity. Finally, the debates serve to remind historians that the earliest interpretations of the war were written by the veterans themselves and were driven by factors rooted in unit and state pride, and not necessarily by the pursuit of historical accuracy.

Notes

1. DeWitt B. Stone, ed., *Wandering to Glory: Confederate Veterans Remember Evans' Brigade* (Columbia: University of South Carolina Press, 2002), 205.

2. David W. Blight, *Race and Reunion: The Civil War in American Memory*

(Cambridge, MA: Harvard University Press, 2001); W. Fitzhugh Brundage, *The Southern Past: A Clash of Race and Memory* (Cambridge, MA: Harvard University Press, 2005); David Goldfield, *Still Fighting the Civil War: The American South and Southern History* (Baton Rouge: Louisiana State University Press, 2002).

3. For an excellent analysis of this debate, see Carol Reardon, *Pickett's Charge in History and Memory* (Chapel Hill: University of North Carolina Press, 1997), 131–75. Other historians who have addressed the postwar debates among veterans include Timothy B. Smith, *This Great Battlefield of Shiloh: History, Memory, and the Establishment of a Civil War National Military Park* (Knoxville: University of Tennessee Press, 2004), 73–92, and Stuart McConnell, *Glorious Contentment: The Grand Army of the Republic, 1865–1900* (Chapel Hill: University of North Carolina Press, 1992), 212–20.

4. For an overview of how the Crater has been remembered, see Kevin M. Levin, "On That Day You Consummated the Full Measure of Your Fame: Confederates Remember the Crater, 1864–1937," *Southern Historian* (spring 2004): 18–39; Kevin M. Levin "The Battle of the Crater, William Mahone, and Civil War Memory, 1864–1937" (master's thesis, University of Richmond, 2005).

5. A thorough analysis of this process is provided by Anne S. Rubin, *A Shattered Nation: The Rise and Fall of the Confederacy, 1861–1868* (Chapel Hill: University of North Carolina Press, 2005), 141–208.

6. Few accounts of the Crater exist. The best overall account is Michael C. Cavanaugh and William Marvel, *The Battle of the Crater: "The Horrid Pit," June 25–August 6, 1864* (Lynchburg, VA: H. E. Howard Press, 1989). Shorter accounts can be found in Noah A. Trudeau, *The Last Citadel* (Baton Rouge: Louisiana State University Press, 1991), 98–130; J. Tracy Power, *Lee's Miserables: Life in the Army of Northern Virginia from the Wilderness to Appomattox* (Chapel Hill: University of North Carolina Press, 1998), 109–40; and William Marvel, *Burnside* (Chapel Hill: University of North Carolina Press, 1991), 390–418.

7. Passages from the *Petersburg Express* quoted in George S. Bernard, *War Talks of Confederate Veterans* (1892; reprint, Dayton, OH: Morningside Press, 1981), 317–19.

8. Edward A Pollard, *The Lost Cause* (1866; reprint, New York: Gramercy, 1994), 537.

9. "The Battle of the Crater," *Seminary Magazine* 2, no. 2 (November 1869): 93–102; Ralph Happel, "John A. Elder," *Commonwealth Magazine* (August 1937): 23–25.

10. Gerald F. Linderman, *Embattled Courage: The Experience of Combat in the American Civil War* (New York: Free Press, 1989), 266–97; it should be noted that Linderman's study focuses on Union veterans. For an interesting

analysis of the continuing ties among a Union regiment after the war, see Mark H. Dunkelman, *Brothers One and All: Esprit de Corps in a Civil War Regiment* (Baton Rouge: Louisiana State University Press, 2004), 251–77.

11. "The Battle of the Crater," *Seminary Magazine*, 98.

12. *Petersburg Daily Index-Appeal*, May 11, 1875.

13. "Second Re-Union of Mahone's Brigade," Eleanor Brockenbrough Library, Veteran's Collection, box 2, Museum of the Confederacy, Richmond, VA.

14. Ibid.; Gaines Foster, *Ghosts of the Confederacy* (New York: Oxford University Press, 1987), 40.

15. William H. Stewart, *Description of the Battle of the Crater: Recollections of the Recapture of the Lines* (Norfolk, VA: Landmark Book and Job Office, 1876), 10–11.

16. On the history of the Readjusters, see Jane Dailey, *Before Jim Crow: The Politics of Race in Postemancipation Virginia* (Chapel Hill: University of North Carolina Press, 2000); Carl N. Degler, *The Other South: Southern Dissenters in the Nineteenth Century* (New York: Harper and Row, 1974), 270–315.

17. Degler, *The Other South*, 282–85; Lawrence L. Hartzell, "The Exploration of Freedom in Black Petersburg, Virginia, 1865–1902," in *The Edge of the South: Life in Nineteenth-Century Virginia*, ed. Edward L. Ayers and John C. Willis (Charlottesville: University of Virginia Press, 1991), 140–43.

18. Statistics can be found in Dailey, *Before Jim Crow*, 67; Ann Field Alexander, *Race Man: The Rise and Fall of the "Fighting Editor" John Mitchell, Jr.* (Charlottesville: University of Virginia Press, 2003), 21.

19. For an analysis of William Mahone's postwar career, see Kevin M. Levin, "William Mahone, the Lost Cause, and Civil War History," *Virginia Magazine of History and Biography* 113, no. 4 (2005): 379–412; quote is on 403.

20. "General David A. Weisiger, of Virginia," *Confederate Veteran* 7 (August 1899): 362–64.

21. T. B. Kingsburg, "North Carolina at Gettysburg," *Our Living and Our Dead* 1, no. 3 (November 1874): 193. This was the official publication of the North Carolina branch of the Southern Historical Society.

22. Henry G. Flanner, "Flanner's North Carolina Battery at the Battle of the Crater," *Southern Historical Society Papers* 5, no. 5 (May 1878): 247–48.

23. Fitz W. McMaster, "The Battle of the Crater, July 30, 1864," *Southern Historical Society Papers* 10, no. 3 (March 1882): 119–23.

24. Letter from James C. Coit, accompanying ibid., 123–30.

25. On Virginia control of the Southern Historical Society, see Foster, *Ghosts of the Confederacy*, 50–62; on Early's role as editor of the *Southern Historical Society Papers*, see Gary W. Gallagher, *Jubal A. Early, the Lost Cause, and Civil War History: A Persistent Legacy* (Milwaukee: Marquette University Press, 1995), 22–24.

26. Andrew A. Humphreys, *The Virginia Campaign, 1864 and 1865* (1883; reprint, New York: Da Capo, 1995), 260.

27. Bernard, *War Talks,* iv.

28. On the Readjusters, see Dailey, *Before Jim Crow.*

29. Bernard, *War Talks,* 178.

30. Ibid., 177.

31. George T. Rogers, "The Crater Battle, 30th July, 1864," *Confederate Veteran* 3 (January 1895): 12–14.

32. George Clark, "Alabamians in the Crater Battle," *Confederate Veteran* 3 (February 1895): 68–69.

33. B. F. Phillips, "Wilcox's Alabamians in Virginia," *Confederate Veteran* 15 (November 1907): 490.

34. R. W. Jones, "Mahone's Men at the Crater," *Confederate Veteran* 16 (January 1908): 3.

35. William H. Etheridge, "Another Story of the Crater Battle," *Confederate Veteran* 15 (April 1907): 167.

36. W. A. Day, "Battle of the Crater," *Confederate Veteran* 2 (August 1903): 355–56.

37. Stewart's address is reprinted as "Crater Legion of Mahone's Brigade," *Confederate Veteran* 11 (December 1903): 557–58.

38. H. A. Chambers, "The Bloody Crater," *Confederate Veteran* 31 (May 1923): 174–77.

39. *Official Report of the History Committee of the Grand Camp, C.V., Department of Virginia* (Order of the Grand Camp of Virginia, 1904), 22.

Afterword

Joseph T. Glatthaar

In his final year of life, poet Walt Whitman lamented the direction of literature on the Civil War. "I know not how it may have been, or may be, to others," he recalled, but "to me the main interest I found (and still, on recollection, find) in the rank and file of the armies, both sides, and in those specimens amid the hospitals, and even the dead on the field. To me the points illustrating the latent personal character and eligibilities of these States, in the two or three millions of American young and middle-aged men, North and South, embodied in those armies—and especially the one-third or one-fourth of their number, stricken by wounds or disease at some time in the course of the contest—were of more significance even than the political interests involved."

In Whitman's time, books and articles fell into one of two categories: glorification or petty squabbles. The battlefield had shifted from one where Union and Confederate armies clashed to one where authors attempted to elevate one general or one military unit, usually at the expense of another. Participants must have wondered which battlefield was worse—the one where men were killed and maimed, or the one where men's reputations were mutilated by self-serving promoters. "The actual soldier of 1862–'65, North and South," Whitman predicted, "with all his ways, his incredible dauntlessness, habits, practices, tastes, language, his fierce friendship, his appetite, rankness, his superb strength and animality, lawless gait, and a hundred unnamed lights and shades of camp, I say, will never be written—perhaps must not and should not be."[1]

Whitman entitled his brief essay, appropriately enough, "The Real War Will Never Get in the Books." And for the next half century, his forecast held up firmly. As the generation of veterans died off, authors of various talents embraced the Civil War, with varied results. Historians

249

tended to compartmentalize their work into prewar, wartime, and postwar studies, viewing each element in isolation from the rest. But one thing was certain: no one attempted to get the real war, as Whitman defined it, into the books. The scholarship was largely devoid of any insight into the human condition.

Then, in 1938, a professionally trained scholar named Bell Irvin Wiley published a blockbuster book entitled *Southern Negroes, 1861–1865,* followed in 1943 by *The Life of Johnny Reb: The Common Soldier of the Confederacy* and, nine years later, the companion volume, *The Life of Billy Yank: The Common Soldier of the Union.* In these pathbreaking studies, Wiley explored the world of Civil War participants, black and white, civilian and soldier. The Southern-born, Northern-trained Wiley devoted scant attention to causes and consequences, unlike his many predecessors; instead, he focused on the war and what it was like for those who experienced it. He explored not just what they did but also how they thought and felt, their likes and dislikes, their joys and sorrows, their hardships and pleasantries. Based largely on soldiers' letters, diaries, and other sources, these works by Wiley seemed to answer Whitman's plea. He got the real war into the books.

Unfortunately, Wiley's books did not trigger a dramatic shift in Civil War literature. His work appeared to be so thorough, he had examined so many collections, and his approach was so nontraditional compared with that of most of his peers that no one followed his lead. For several decades, his Civil War legacy remained completely intact, as scholars refused to tread where Wiley had gone.

Not surprisingly, events outside the field of history transformed the profession and Civil War scholarship. The confluence of civil rights for African Americans, Hispanics, and women and protests over the Vietnam War demonstrated the power of individuals in American society. People did not follow in lockstep to carry out the wishes and plans of political leaders. On the contrary, they formulated independent ideas, and together they changed the social, political, economic, and cultural fabric of the nation. That era proved that the sentiments, voices, and actions of the people mattered, that they could be active agents of change. Succeeding decades have only reinforced that fact.

The Vietnam War also reminded historians just how complex wars are. Politics and protests influenced how soldiers perceived the war in Vietnam and how the nation fought it. Soldiers battled with one eye on their enemy and the other on the home front, concerned over an atmosphere of deteriorating support and the well-being of family and friends who tried to buttress them. Those at home feared for the soldiers serving in Vietnam. Both the troops and their loved ones knew that the soldiers were risking their lives for an increasingly unpopular and perhaps unwinnable cause. Nor did the impact of Vietnam on the soldiers, their families, and the nation as a whole cease after the final evacuation; it lasted for decades, as has the ever-changing meaning of the Vietnam experience. Thus, scholars gained insight into the complicated nature of war and the way battlefront and home front affect each other. All this fueled the "new" military history.

By the mid-1980s, historians had again taken up the world of the common soldier with fresh and exciting scholarship, influenced by the new social history and agency from the civil rights–Vietnam era. *The View from the Ground* draws from that legacy. The essays focus on soldiers and their attitudes and extend from the early war to the postwar years. One essay examines the changing views of Union soldiers on race and slavery, while another discusses Rebel sentiments toward Yankees in the late stages of the war. Another describes the rights that Confederate soldiers brought with them from the civilian world and how those rights played out in uniform. Two different essays draw on religion as a critical force in the lives of soldiers. A rising opposition to the war at home is the subject of two essays, one focusing on the North and the other on the South. The final essay describes the postwar battle for glory and credit and how external factors influenced these clashes. Together, they represent a worthy continuation of the scholarship that dates back to Wiley but has now found new inspiration.

Yet there are still areas that beg for greater explication through scholarship. Daniel Sutherland, Martin Crawford, George Rable, and G. Ward Hubbs introduced readers to the fascinating interplay between Confederate soldiers and their small Southern communities. All four combine to make a terrific starting point, but we have much more to learn about the relationships and influences of soldiers and their hometowns. In addition, Nicholas Salvatore traced an African American family in a Massachusetts community, and Iver Bernstein and Grace Palladino analyzed protests in New York City and Pennsylvania coal country, respectively. Still, we are lacking scholarship on the interaction of soldiers and their sending communities throughout the North.[2]

James Marten wrote a classic essay about fatherhood in the Confederacy and has launched an initial exploration into children during wartime. We need to expand on Marten's base and also explore in depth the concept of motherhood in wartime North and South. As soldiers rushed off to war, they left in their wake single mothers who had to adapt to sustaining the family in every way and to supporting the soldier emotionally and spiritually. Although some scholarship on women has addressed this theme, we have not devoted the detailed attention that the subject warrants.[3]

Most important, historians of the Civil War era have not drawn sufficiently from other academic disciplines. Historians of memory have tapped theories on remembrance, but most historians eschew sophisticated social science theories in the analysis of Civil War soldiers and their families. Nor have historians embraced quantitative analysis sufficiently. Donald Shaffer's recent study of black veterans demonstrates the value of quantitative analyses and should spawn other work on the postwar world. Scholarship on the common soldier lacks such hard data, which could be integrated beautifully with the qualitative methods historians have so readily embraced. Like people of today, Civil War soldiers' opinions ran the gamut. With the wealth of letters written and the myriad opinions espoused by these soldiers, historians can pick their evidence carefully and justify virtually any argument. By integrating statistical data into our scholarship, we can fortify our qualitative evidence and undercut arguments that misrepresent the overwhelming sentiments of soldiers and their families.[4]

Last, historians have tackled the experience of the common soldier from an ahistorical perspective. They begin with a discussion of why the soldiers joined the army, with scant attention to the previous lives that shaped those attitudes. Occasionally, some scholar injects statistics on prewar occupations or ages, but we have offered little else, with the possible exception of Edward L. Ayers's *In the Presence of Mine Enemies,* an extraordinarily detailed and skillful study of two counties, one in Virginia and the other in Pennsylvania. Before their entry into the Civil War, soldiers had pasts, which we have neglected. By the same token, scholarship on common soldiers has largely excluded postwar studies, as if we should examine the consequences of the war devoid of the war itself. A few scholars, including Larry Logue and myself, have pushed our studies beyond Appomattox, but we need more detailed studies that link wartime to postwar. Scholarship that focuses on communities before, during, and after the war, which covers the readjustment period, would also enhance our understanding of the era and the true impact of the war on those who experienced it.[5]

These suggestions are by no means the only avenues for future explorations of the common soldier. Others will doubtless propose approaches and topics that few of us can anticipate today. But their proposals will address some significant holes in our current historical literature.

Still, surveying the literature on the Civil War over the past few decades, Whitman would probably be pleased. Historians have finally gotten the "real war" into Civil War history.

NOTES

1. Walt Whitman, "The Real War Will Never Get in the Books," at http://www.bartleby.com/229/1101.html.

2. Daniel E. Sutherland, *Seasons of War: The Ordeal of a Confederate Community, 1861–1865* (New York: Free Press, 1995); Martin Crawford, *Ashe County's Civil War: Community and Society in the Appalachian South* (Charlottesville: University Press of Virginia, 2001); George C. Rable, *Fredericksburg! Fredericksburg!* (Chapel Hill: University of North Carolina Press, 2002); G. Ward Hubbs, *Guarding Greensboro: A Confederate Company in the Making of a Southern Community* (Athens: University of Georgia Press, 2003); Nicholas Salvatore, *We All Got History: The Memory Books of Amos Webber* (New York: Times Books, 1996); Iver Bernstein, *The New York City Draft Riots: Their Significance for American Society and Politics in the Age of the Civil War* (New York: Oxford University Press, 1990); Grace Palladino, *Another Civil War: Labor, Capital, and the State in the Anthracite Regions of Pennsylvania* (Urbana: University of Illinois Press, 1990). Also see Reid Mitchell, *The Vacant Chair: The Northern Soldier Leaves Home* (New York: Oxford University Press, 1993).

3. James A. Marten, "Fatherhood in the Confederacy: Southern Soldiers and Their Children," *Journal of Southern History* 63 (May 1997): 269–92; James A. Marten, *The Children's Civil War* (Chapel Hill: University of North Carolina Press, 1998).

4. Donald R. Shaffer, *After the Glory: The Struggles of Black Civil War Veterans* (Lawrence: University Press of Kansas, 2004).

5. Edward L. Ayers, *In the Presence of Mine Enemies: War in the Heart of America, 1859–1863* (New York: W. W. Norton, 2003); Larry M. Logue, *To*

Appomattox and Beyond: The Civil War Soldier in War and Peace (Chicago: Ivan R. Dee, 1996); Joseph T. Glatthaar, *Forged in Battle: The Civil War Alliance of Black Soldiers and Their White Officers* (New York: Free Press, 1989). Also see Eric T. Dean, *Shook over Hell: Post-traumatic Stress, Vietnam, and the Civil War* (Cambridge, MA: Harvard University Press, 1999).

Selected Bibliography

Books

Anderson, Paul Christopher. *Blood Image: Turner Ashby in the Civil War and the Southern Mind.* Baton Rouge: Louisiana State University Press, 2002.

Barton, Michael. *Goodmen: The Character of Civil War Soldiers.* University Park: Pennsylvania State University Press, 1981.

Berlin, Ira, Joseph P. Reidy, and Leslie S. Rowland. *Freedom's Soldiers: The Black Military Experience in the Civil War.* New York: Cambridge University Press, 1998.

Berry, Stephen W., III. *All That Makes a Man: Love and Ambition in the Civil War South.* New York: Oxford University Press, 2003.

Carmichael, Peter S. *The Last Generation: Young Virginians in Peace, War, and Reunion.* Chapel Hill: University of North Carolina Press, 2005.

Connelly, Thomas Lawrence. *Army of the Heartland: The Army of Tennessee, 1861–1862.* Baton Rouge: Louisiana State University Press, 1967.

———. *Autumn of Glory: The Army of Tennessee, 1863–1865.* Baton Rouge: Louisiana State University Press, 1971.

Cornish, Dudley Taylor. *The Sable Arm: Negro Troops in the Union Army, 1861–1865.* New York: W. W. Norton, 1966.

Current, Richard Nelson. *Lincolns' Loyalists: Union Soldiers from the Confederacy.* Boston: Northeastern University Press, 1992.

Daniel, Larry J. *Soldiering in the Army of Tennessee: A Portrait of Life in a Confederate Army.* Chapel Hill: University of North Carolina Press, 1991.

Dean, Eric T. *Shook over Hell: Post-traumatic Stress, Vietnam, and the Civil War.* Cambridge, MA: Harvard University Press, 1999.

Frank, Joseph Allan. *With Ballot and Bayonet: The Political Socialization of American Civil War Soldiers.* Athens: University of Georgia Press, 1998.

Frank, Joseph Allan, and George A. Reaves. *"Seeing the Elephant": Raw Recruits at the Battle of Shiloh.* New York: Greenwood Press, 1989.

Glatthaar, Joseph T. *Forged in Battle: The Civil War Alliance of Black Soldiers and Their White Officers.* New York: Free Press, 1989.

———. *The March to the Sea and Beyond: Sherman's Troops in the Savannah and Carolinas Campaigns.* New York: New York University Press, 1985.

Grimsley, Mark. *The Hard Hand of War: Union Military Policy toward Southern Civilians, 1861–1865.* Cambridge: Cambridge University Press, 1995.

Hess, Earl J. *Liberty, Virtue, and Progress: Northerners and Their War for the Union.* New York: New York University Press, 1988.

———. *The Union Soldier in Battle: Enduring the Ordeal of Combat.* Lawrence: University Press of Kansas, 1997.

Hubbs, G. Ward. *Guarding Greensboro: A Confederate Company in the Making of a Southern Community.* Athens: University of Georgia Press, 2003.

Jimerson, Randall C. *The Private Civil War: Popular Thought during the Sectional Conflict.* Baton Rouge: Louisiana State University Press, 1988.

Linderman, Gerald F. *Embattled Courage: The Experience of Combat in the American Civil War.* New York: Free Press, 1989.

Logue, Larry M. *To Appomattox and Beyond: The Civil War Soldier in War and Peace.* Chicago: Ivan R. Dee, 1996.

Lonn, Ella. *Desertion during the Civil War.* Gloucester, MA: American Historical Association, 1928; Lincoln: University of Nebraska Press, 1998.

Martin, Bessie. *Desertion of Alabama Troops from the Confederate Army: A Study in Sectionalism.* New York: Columbia University Press, 1966.

McConnell, Stuart. *Glorious Contentment: The Grand Army of the Republic, 1865–1900.* Chapel Hill: University of North Carolina Press, 1992.

McPherson, James. *For Cause and Comrades: Why Men Fought in the Civil War.* New York: Oxford University Press, 1997.

Mitchell, Reid. *Civil War Soldiers: Their Expectations and Their Experiences.* New York: Touchstone, 1988.

———. *The Vacant Chair: The Northern Soldier Leaves Home.* New York: Oxford University Press, 1993.

Moore, Albert Burton. *Conscription and Conflict in the Confederacy.* New York: Macmillan, 1924.

Power, J. Tracy. *Lee's Miserables: Life in the Army of Northern Virginia from the Wilderness to Appomattox.* Chapel Hill: University of North Carolina, 1998.

Prokopowicz, Gerald J. *All for the Regiment: The Army of the Ohio, 1861–62.* Chapel Hill: University of North Carolina Press, 2001.

Robertson, James I. *Soldiers Blue and Gray.* Columbia: University of South Carolina Press, 1988.

Shattuck, Gardiner H., Jr. *A Shield and Hiding Place: The Religious Life of Civil War Armies.* Macon, GA: Mercer University Press, 1987.

Smith, John David. *Black Soldiers in Blue: African American Troops in the Civil War Era.* Chapel Hill: University of North Carolina Press, 2002.

Trudeau, Noah Andre. *Like Men of War: Black Troops in the Civil War, 1862–1865.* Boston: Little Brown, 1997.

Vinovskis, Maris A., ed. *Toward a Social History of the American Civil War: Exploratory Essays.* Cambridge: Cambridge University Press, 1990.

Weitz, Mark A. *A Higher Duty: Desertion among Georgia Troops during the Civil War.* Lincoln: University of Nebraska Press, 2000.

Wiley, Bell Irvin. *The Life of Billy Yank: The Common Soldier of the Union.* Indianapolis: Bobbs-Merrill, 1952.

———. *The Life of Johnny Reb: The Common Soldier of the Confederacy.* Indianapolis: Bobbs-Merrill, 1943.

Williams, David. *Rich Man's War: Class, Caste, and Confederate Defeat in the Lower Chattahoochee Valley.* Athens: University of Georgia Press, 1998.

Williams, David, Teresa Crisp Williams, and David Carlson. *Plain Folk in a Rich Man's War: Class and Dissent in Confederate Georgia.* Gainesville: University Press of Florida, 2002.

Woodworth, Steven E. *While God Is Marching On: The Religious World of Civil War Soldiers.* Lawrence: University Press of Kansas, 2001.

Articles

Blight, David W. "No Desperate Hero: Manhood and Freedom in a Union Soldier's Experience." In *Divided Houses: Gender and the Civil War,* edited by Catherine Clinton and Nina Silber, 55–75. New York: Oxford University Press, 1992.

Brooks, Charles E. "The Social and Cultural Dynamics of Soldiering in Hood's Texas Brigade." *Journal of Southern History* 67 (August 2001): 535–72.

Carlson, David. "The 'Loanly Runagee': Draft Evaders in Confederate South Georgia." *Georgia Historical Quarterly* 84 (2000): 589–615.

Carmichael, Peter S. "So Far from God and So Close to Stonewall Jackson: The Executions of Three Shenandoah Valley Soldiers." *Virginia Magazine of History and Biography* 111, no. 1 (2003): 33–66.

Crawford, Martin. "Confederate Volunteering and Enlistment in Ashe County, North Carolina, 1861–1862." *Civil War History* 37 (March 1991): 29–50.

Cullen, Jim. "'I's a Man Now': Gender and African American Men." In *Divided Houses: Gender and the Civil War,* edited by Catherine Clinton and Nina Silber, 76–96. New York: Oxford University Press, 1992.

Donald, David. "The Confederate Man as Fighting Man." *Journal of Southern History* 25 (May 1959): 178–93.

Faust, Drew Gilpin. "Christian Soldiers: The Meaning of Revivalism in the Confederate Army." *Journal of Southern History* 53 (February 1987): 63–90.

Frank, Stephen M. "'Rendering Aid and Comfort': Images of Fatherhood in the Letters of Civil War Soldiers from Massachusetts and Michigan." *Journal of Social History* 26 (fall 1992): 5–32.

Halleck, Judith Lee. "The Role of the Community in Civil War Desertion." *Civil War History* 29 (June 1983): 123–34.

Harris, Emily J. "Sons and Soldiers: Deerfield, Massachusetts and the Civil War." *Civil War History* 30 (June 1984): 157–71.

Lee, Chulhee. "Socioeconomic Background, Disease, and Mortality among Union Amy Recruits: Implications for Economic and Demographic History." *Explorations in Economic History* 34 (1997): 27–55.

———. "Wealth Accumulation and the Health of Union Army Veterans, 1860–1870." *Journal of Economic History* 65, no. 2 (2005): 252–385.

Levine, Peter. "Draft Evasion in the North during the Civil War." *Journal of American History* 67 (1981): 816–34.

Logue, Larry M. "Who Joined the Confederate Army: Soldiers, Civilians, and Communities in Mississippi." *Journal of Social History* 26 (1993): 611–23.

Marten, James. "Fatherhood in the Confederacy: Southern Soldiers and Their Children." *Journal of Southern History* 63 (May 1997): 269–92.

Maslowski, Pete. "A Study of Morale in Civil War Soldiers." *Military Affairs* 34 (December 1970): 122–26.

Mitchell, Reid. "Christian Soldiers? Perfecting the Confederacy." In *Religion and the American Civil War,* edited by Randall M. Miller, Harry S. Stout, and Charles Reagan Wilson, 297–310. New York: Oxford University Press, 1998.

———. "The Creation of Confederate Loyalties." In *New Perspectives on Race and Slavery in America: Essays in Honor of Kenneth M. Stampp,* edited by Robert H. Abzug and Stephen E. Maizlish, 93–108. Lexington: University Press of Kentucky, 1986.

———. "The Perseverance of the Soldiers." In *Why the Confederacy Lost,* edited by Gabor S. Boritt, 109–32. New York: Oxford University Press, 1992.

Ownby, Ted. "Patriarchy in the World Where There Is No Parting? Power Relations in the Confederate Heaven." In *Southern Families at War: Loyalty and Conflict in the Civil War South,* edited by Catherine Clinton, 229–44. New York: Oxford University Press, 2000.

Reid, Richard. "A Test Case of the 'Crying Evil': Desertion among North Carolina Troops during the Civil War." *North Carolina Historical Review* 58 (1981): 234–62.

Rorabaugh, W. J. "Who Fought for the North in the Civil War? Concord, Massachusetts, Enlistments." *Journal of American History* 73 (1986): 695–701.

Ruffner, Kevin C. "Civil War Desertion from a Black Belt Regiment: An Examination of the 44th Virginia Infantry." In *The Edge of the South: Life in Nineteenth-Century Virginia,* edited by Edward L. Ayers and John C. Willis, 79–108. Charlottesville: University Press of Virginia, 1991.

Scheiber, Harry N. "The Pay of Confederate Troops and Problems of Demoralization." *Civil War History* 15 (September 1969): 226–36.

Sheehan-Dean, Aaron C. "Everyman's War: Confederate Enlistment in Civil War Virginia." *Civil War History* 50 (March 2004): 5–26.

———. "Justice Has Something to Do with It: Class Relations and the Confederate Army." *Virginia Magazine of History and Biography* 113 (December 2005): 340–77.

Smith, David P. "Conscription and Conflict on the Texas Frontier, 1863–1865." *Civil War History* 36 (September 1990): 250–61.

Talbott, John E. "Combat Trauma in the American Civil War." *History Today* 46 (March 1996): 41–47.

Watson, Samuel J. "Religion and Combat Motivation in the Confederate Armies." *Journal of Military History* 58 (January 1994): 29–55.

Historiographies

Cain, Marvin R. "A 'Face of Battle' Needed: An Assessment of Motives and Men in Civil War Historiography." *Civil War History* 28 (1982): 5–27.

Crane, Conrad C. "Mad Elephants, Slow Deer, and Baseball on the Brain: The Writings and Character of Civil War Soldiers." *Mid-America: An Historical Review* 68 (1986): 121–40.

Glatthaar, Joseph. "The Common Soldier of the Civil War." In *New Perspectives on the Civil War: Myths and Realities of the National Conflict,* edited by John Y. Simon and Michael E. Stevens, 119–44. Madison, WI: Madison House, 1998.

Mitchell, Reid. "'Not the General but the Soldier': The Study of Civil War Soldiers." In *Writing the Civil War: The Quest to Understand,* edited by James M. McPherson and William J. Cooper Jr., 81–95. Columbia: University of South Carolina Press, 1998.

Sutherland, Daniel. "Getting the 'Real War' into the Books." *Virginia Magazine of History and Biography* 98 (April 1990): 193–220.

CONTRIBUTORS

Charles E. Brooks is associate professor of history at Texas A&M University. His research interests include the political, constitutional, social, and cultural histories of rural people in antebellum America. He is currently working on two book manuscripts—one about the Civil War experience of plain white folks in Texas, and the other on the history of common soldiering in early America from the Revolution to the Civil War.

Kent T. Dollar is assistant professor of history at Tennessee Technological University in Cookeville. He is the author of *Soldiers of the Cross: Confederate Soldier-Christians and the Impact of War on Their Faith* (2005). He earned his Ph.D. from the University of Tennessee in 2001.

Joseph T. Glatthaar is the Stephenson Distinguished Professor of History at the University of North Carolina at Chapel Hill. Among his publications are *The March to the Sea and Beyond: Sherman's Troops in the Savannah and Carolinas Campaigns* (1985), *Forged in Battle: The Civil War Alliance of Black Soldiers and Their White Officers* (1989), and *Black Soldiers in the Civil War* (1996).

Lisa Laskin is lecturer on history at Harvard University and director of academic affairs for the Harvard Summer School. Her research interests are American war and society, with a particular focus on the Civil War.

Kevin M. Levin teaches American history at the St. Anne's–Belfield School in Charlottesville, Virginia. He has published articles in *Southern Historian, Virginia Magazine of History and Biography,* and *Virginia Social Science Journal* and is currently completing a manuscript on postwar commemorations and memories of the battle of the Crater.

Chandra Manning teaches nineteenth-century U.S. history at Georgetown University. She is completing a manuscript about the Civil War, soldiers, and slavery, as well as projects on Civil War soldiers' newspapers and Wisconsin's role in the Civil War. She earned her Ph.D. from Harvard University in 2002 and won the C. Vann Woodward Prize for the best dissertation in southern history in 2003.

Timothy J. Orr is a Ph.D. candidate at Pennsylvania State University. His research interests include military mobilization of the Civil War North. He has been a seasonal park ranger at Gettysburg National Military Park since 1999.

Jason Phillips, assistant professor of history at Mississippi State University, earned his Ph.D. at Rice University in 2003 under the direction of John B. Boles. He has recent or forthcoming publications on southern religion, Civil War rumors, and the Confederate origins of the New South. Phillips is currently revising his book manuscript on diehard Rebels and their influence on southern culture for the University of Georgia Press.

David W. Rolfs is an instructor of history at Maclay College Preparatory School in Tallahassee, Florida. He earned his doctorate in American history at Florida State University. He is currently revising his dissertation, *No Peace for the Wicked,* for publication.

Aaron Sheehan-Dean is assistant professor of history at the University of North Florida. He is the editor of *Struggle for a Vast Future: The American Civil War* and is completing a manuscript titled *Creating Confederates: Family and Nation in Civil War Virginia.*

INDEX